An Introduction to Indian Aesthetics

An Introduction to Indian Aesthetics

History, Theory, and Theoreticians

Mini Chandran and Sreenath V. S.

BLOOMSBURY

NEW DELHI • LONDON • OXFORD • NEW YORK • SYDNEY

BLOOMSBURY INDIA
Bloomsbury Publishing India Pvt. Ltd
Second Floor, LSC Building No. 4, DDA Complex, Pocket C – 6 & 7,
Vasant Kunj, New Delhi 110070

BLOOMSBURY, BLOOMSBURY ACADEMIC INDIA and the Diana logo are trademarks of Bloomsbury Publishing Plc

First published in India 2021
This paperback edition published 2025

Bloomsbury Academic
An imprint of Bloomsbury Publishing Plc

ISBN: PB: 978-93-69524-89-1; eBook: 978-93-89165-13-5

2 4 6 8 10 9 7 5 3 1

Typeset in Minion Pro by Manipal Technologies Limited
Printed and bound in India

Bloomsbury Publishing Plc makes every effort to ensure that the papers used in the manufacture of our books are natural, recyclable products made from wood grown in well-managed forests. Our manufacturing processes conform to the environmental regulations of the country of origin.

To find out more about our authors and books visit www.bloomsbury.com and sign up for our newsletters

Contents

Foreword by Professor Sheldon Pollock vii
Preface xi

1 Indian Aesthetics: A Historical and Conceptual Overview 1
2 Rasa 33
3 Alaṅkāra 63
4 Rīti, Guṇas, and Doṣas 81
5 Dhvani 97
6 Vakrokti 123
7 Aucitya 145
8 Conclusion 165

Appendix I: Genres of Sanskrit Literature 191
Appendix II: Categories of Drama 197
Suggested Readings 203
Index 207
About the Authors 218

Foreword

It is a fact of stunning historical irony—or historical contumely—that some of the most advanced achievements of premodern thought in the domain of the human sciences, those of classical India, are today among the least well-known, whether in the West, East Asia, or India itself. There is no doubt a range of factors that go to explain this strange state of affairs. I can think immediately of three.

One is the standard scholarly bête noire of miscognition about India that in this case truly was a bête: Orientalism, or better Macaulayism, in England—like Sinocentrism (*zhonghua minzu*) in China, Oriental studies (*toyoshi*) in Japan, and other similar early-modern and modern forms of cultural self-congratulation—sought to denigrate as nescience everyone else's science. One's own science always has "intrinsic superiority"; that of others is always nothing but "false texts and false philosophy." A second, at least in the West, and in some ways, a corollary to the first, lies in the fact that it was often missionaries who engaged, first and foremost, with classical Indian culture: Indians may have known nothing true about the world, they thought, but their spiritual achievements, however misguided, were noteworthy and a point of entry for conversion. Indian religion was, thus, foregrounded to outsiders while that very attention served at the same time to persuade insiders that the spiritual was the sum total of their intellectual achievement.

A third factor for the historical disregard or dismissal of classical Indian science stems from its having done what all sciences do, but only more so. Over the centuries, Indian science created discourses of ever greater sophistication, complexity and subtlety in expression and formulation. Forms of disciplinary knowledge—I name in the first instance language analysis (*vyākaraṇa*), hermeneutics (*mīmāṃsā*) and logic (*nyāya*), the *trivium* of classical learning, but also and especially aesthetics-and-rhetoric (*rasaśāstra*, *nāṭyaśāstra*, *alaṅkāraśāstra*), the knowledge form where those three sciences of word, sentence and reason converged—developed in unbroken succession over two or more millennia. They accordingly embodied arguments that presupposed familiarity with the whole prior history of thought, without which that thought would remain largely unintelligible. At the same time, they developed a scholarly idiom of an increasingly refined technicality that would leave critics of the abstruseness of modern jargon—Heideggerian existentialism, Derridean deconstruction, postcolonial critique—slack-jawed were they ever to encounter it.

To be sure, there have been scholars in the modern past who learned to read across the classical Indian sciences with great proficiency, but their number has substantially decreased in the present. This is true even—especially, and sadly—in India itself. There, the great authorities of the previous century—I am thinking of traditional pandits like P. N. Pattabhirama Sastry as well as quasi-modernists, such as Ganganath Jha, who were concerned with addressing non-traditional audiences—have been succeeded by ideologues who today deliver ignorant pronouncements on the Sanskrit tradition without being able to read a word of it; who turn that tradition into a political weapon of a Hindu *rashtra* even while denouncing others for supposedly having done so. While intellectual frauds take center stage, who, today in

India, is publishing editions of any of the hundreds of works that remain in manuscript form, unedited? Who is writing the kinds of intellectual histories that give the world some sense of the actual development of the classical sciences and their astonishing achievements? Who is producing the English translations—the portal through which Indian science becomes part of the global history of science—of any texts, even the core ones? (It is going on a century since the *Nyāyasūtras* or the *Mīmāmsāsūtras* have been translated; *vyākaraṇa* at least has the incomplete *Mahābhāṣya* of Joshi and Roodebergen.) As for *alaṅkāraśāstra*, the reader of Western languages has nowhere to turn for any authoritative translations, of even the leading figures—Daṇḍin, say, or Udbhaṭa, or Mammaṭa, or Hemacandra, or Jagannātha (the singular exception is the outstanding work of Ingalls, Masson and Patwardhan on the *Dhvanyāloka* and *Locana*).

As a result of all this, the true measure of the achievement of the classical Indian disciplines has rarely been taken. Nowhere is this more true, as I just implied, than in the case of aesthetics-and-rhetoric. It is thus encouraging to find two scholars in India, Dr Mini Chandran and Dr Sreenath V. S., re-engaging with the intellectual history of this discipline—which we are gradually coming to see as more sophisticated than any other in the premodern world—and trying to help others do so with such introductory surveys as the one offered in the following pages. I hope other scholars will follow their example for other *śāstras*, and that a more intensive engagement with original research on these treasures will eventually be undertaken to supplement their overviews.

Professor Sheldon Pollock

New York, May 20, 2020

Preface

The thinkers and philosophers of ancient India contemplated intensively and extensively about all aspects related to life, and art was one of the major domains they touched upon. Art, which included the performative as well as written, was not a medium of mere entertainment for them, but a path that could lead us to a transcendental state that bordered on a spiritual experience. Naturally, the vocation of the artist and the process of artistic enjoyment were subsumed under philosophic speculations on life and the different goals of life. This profound and intense analysis of the art experience in literature naturally led to the evolution of one of the most sophisticated and long-standing poetic systems in the world.

The beginnings of this systematic exploration into the realm of art and its function can be seen in the *Nāṭyaśāstra*, the text ascribed to Bharata. His concept of *rasa* was an explanation of the pleasurable aesthetic experience that is evoked by any work of art, and it started a searching analysis of the nature of beauty in art and literature down the centuries by numerous philosophers and theorists who came after him, giving rise to multiple notions of the function of art and literature. These studies were by no means confined to the realm of the Sanskrit language and occurred simultaneously in the other ancient literary Indian language of Tamil. The Tamil counterpart to the *Nāṭyaśāstra* is the *Tolkāppiyam*, which is a compendious work that covered all aspects of language and poetry. So, contrary to popular perception, the term "Indian aesthetics" refers to not just Sanskrit poetics but also the well-developed poetic system of Tamil.

Unfortunately, many of us do not have easy access to this world for a variety of reasons—irrevocable loss of texts, multiple recensions of the same text, obscurity of thought and language and a languishing interest in the field. The scholarly explanations of these concepts are often too dense for beginners to understand, and many of them assume that readers are well versed in Sanskrit. Besides this, there is the perception that Sanskrit literary systems belong to a bygone world and have no relevance in contemporary times.

This book is meant to be an introduction to the world of Sanskrit poetics, explaining its major concepts lucidly for even those who do not know Sanskrit. It offers a comprehensive historical and conceptual overview of all the major schools in Sanskrit poetics. The book, despite its primary focus on the major exponents of each school, also aims to give the reader a good idea as to how these concepts were treated before and after their major practitioners. It is hoped that such a bird's-eye view will help the reader position these theories in the vast historical expanse of Sanskrit poetics. An important part of Sanskrit poetics that often intimidates a modern reader is its seemingly difficult terminology. This book particularly addresses this issue by using a contemporary idiom for readers who have no background of Sanskrit.

However, it does not deal with Tamil poetics or the other poetic systems that developed later in the various languages of India. It is meant to be a beginner's guide to the awe-inspiring immensity of Sanskrit literature and literary thought, the first step in a journey that should ideally lead to the profundities of ancient thought. This book should be seen as a mere grain of sand that attempts to hold the infinity of a world.

1

Indian Aesthetics: A Historical and Conceptual Overview

Aesthetics is the broad generic term for a systematic exploration of beauty and the nature of beauty, and by extension, the philosophy of art. Poetics, which falls under the purview of aesthetics, is the theory of literary forms and devices, and the term is familiar to us mainly through the Greek philosopher Aristotle's work of the same name. Aristotle's *Poetics* is believed to be an incomplete treatise and the work that we have with us today is a systematic attempt to define only one genre, namely the art of tragedy. The treatise explores the various aspects of the genre, providing answers to what goes into the making of a tragedy and how it evokes the right kind of aesthetic response in a spectator. This attempt to systematize the study of poetry or all forms of literary composition is not specific to Greek or Western literature but can be found in all kinds of literature worthy of the name.

In Sanskritic cultural history, the term "poetics" in its broadest sense was concerned with two domains of art, namely *nāṭya* (a play which blended drama, music and dance) and *kāvya* (poetry and other forms of literary composition). The factors that distinguished *nāṭya* from *kāvya* in terms of form as well as content were so discernible that Sanskrit poetics virtually got bifurcated into two streams, namely *nāṭyaśāstra* and *kāvyaśāstra*. The *nāṭyaśāstra* tradition of poetics, as the term denotes, focused primarily on *nāṭya* or performance of plays on stage with the accompaniment of dance and music; these aspects were technically termed in Sanskrit as *āṅgika* (pertaining to gestures), *vācika* (verbal elements), *āhārya* (make-up and dress), and *sāttvika abhinaya* (representation of emotions). *Kāvyaśāstra*, on the other hand, was exclusively concerned with the ontology of *kāvya* (poetry and literary prose). However, Bharata's *Nāṭyaśāstra*, which is a text based on the performance arts, should be seen as a seminal work in both the *nāṭya* and *kāvya* traditions, primarily for its conceptualization of *rasa*. It cannot be said with certainty whether Bharata was the first person to propound the concept of *rasa*—that *rasa* or aesthetic enjoyment is the ultimate purpose of art—but this theory was to monopolize all discussions of the nature of art and literature for centuries to come. Later theoreticians in the *nāṭya* and *kāvya* traditions did not contest this basic notion; all they did was think of the various paths through which one could arrive at the final destination of *rasa*.

Sanskrit in which *kāvya* was later profusely written was originally a Vedic language, used mainly for liturgical and ritualistic purposes. It was not the language used every day by the people or the language used in administration. The presence of Sanskrit in the public realm was felt prominently only by 200 CE. According to available historical evidence, the first major non-Vedic employment of standard Sanskrit was found in the Junāgaṛh inscription (150 CE) from present-day Gujarat. It was composed by the Western Kṣatrapa ruler Rudradāman to mark the reconstruction of a great water reservoir, Sudarśana, which was heavily damaged in a storm.

Close on the heels of Sanskrit's emergence outside the closet of the Vedic realm is the beginning of the *kāvya* tradition in the language. At the earliest, the beginning of the *kāvya* tradition can be traced back to the last centuries before the advent of the common era (CE). Creative writers and literary critics of Sanskrit literary culture consider Vālmīki's *Rāmāyaṇa* as the first *kāvya* (*ādikāvya*) in Sanskrit. The earliest testimony regarding this is given by Aśvaghoṣa who in his *Buddhacarita* (200 CE) says, "Vālmīki created the first poem" (*vālmīkir ādau ca sasarja padyam*; I.43).

Whatever may be the theory of historians about the genesis of the *ādikāvya*, the *Rāmāyaṇa* self-reflexively proposes an altogether different story about its origin. According to the omniscient narrator of the text, the events which lead to the composition of the *Rāmāyaṇa* begin with Vālmīki asking the celestial sage Nārada about the worthiest of all human beings then living on earth. In response to this query, Nārada narrates to Vālmīki the legendary story of Rāma, the king of Ayodhyā. Thereafter, Nārada leaves, and Vālmīki, along with his disciple Bharadvāja, goes to the riverside for his prayers. At the riverside, Vālmīki chances upon an act of violence—a hunter shooting one of a mating pair of birds. The sage overcome with pity for the mourning mate curses the hunter, which surprisingly comes out in the form of a *śloka*. Astounded by his own accidental invention, the sage returns to his hermitage and finds Brahmā, the lord of creation, patiently awaiting him. Brahmā tells Vālmīki that what he has just accidentally invented is a *śloka* and commands him to compose the whole story of Rāma using that format. He also assures the sage that whatever he says in his poem will be absolutely true. Thus, at the behest of

Brahmā, Vālmīki reproduces the story of Rāma in a unique way that is quite distinct from the ordinary form of speech.

Though *kāvya* is often flaunted as a unique product created by Vālmīki, it is greatly possible to draw a parallel between *kāvya* and the Vedic tradition that antedated it. First of all, the use of defamiliarized language in versified form, later conceptualized as the hallmark of literary language, had already been used to its optimum by many Vedic scriptures such as *Ṛgvedasaṃhitā*. The function of the Vedas and *kāvya* (according to literary theoreticians) was the same, in the sense that both these traditions ultimately aimed to transform their readers into ideal subjects. While the Vedas performed this deontic function explicitly, *kāvya* served this purpose implicitly by consistently showing the eventual victory of the righteous (*dhārmika*) hero and the decay of the degenerate (*adhārmika*) villain. In his commentary on Ānandavardhana's *Dhvanyāloka* (9th century), Abhinavagupta talks about the different ways in which the Vedas and *kāvya* carry out their deontic functions. According to Abhinavagupta, while *kāvya* implicitly "instructs after the fashion of a wife," the Vedas explicitly "instruct after the fashion of a master" (1.1 e *L*).

Origin and Evolution of *Kāvyaśāstra*

As is and should be the case, the theorization of *kāvya* evolved and gained a definite shape only after its writing had been prevalent for some time. Although *kāvya* originated as early as the beginning of the common era and flourished through the works of writers like Aśvaghoṣa (2nd century), and Kālidāsa (4th century), there was no attempt to develop a *śāstric* tradition for *kāvya* until the 7th century. According to available historical evidence, Bhāmaha's *Kāvyālaṅkāra* (7th century) is the earliest available text in the *kāvyaśāstra* tradition. This does not mean that prior to Bhāmaha there was a total absence of discussions about *kāvya*. The reason for the lack of texts could be that the deliberations about the art of composing poems were conducted orally by poets and lay connoisseurs of verbal art without collating their ideas into a systematic body of knowledge; Bhāmaha must have been the first to produce a written text. But his influence upon later writers and theoreticians was so great that they often treated him as the founding father of Sanskrit poetics.

So, it is safe to consider Bhāmaha's *Kāvyālaṅkāra* as the beginning of a systematic discussion of poetics in the Sanskrit literary tradition, which lasted till the 17th century. Mastering *kāvyaśāstra* (the formal study of literature as well as what makes good literature) was considered an essential prerequisite for an aspiring poet. This is attested by all major theoreticians and practitioners of the art of poesy. According to Bhāmaha, an aspiring poet should venture into composing *kāvyas* only after achieving mastery over all the *śāstras* related to it (I.10). Daṇḍin's (7th century) observation regarding the importance of education in poetic composition stresses the value of acquired skill besides inherent poetic genius. According to Daṇḍin, just as a blind person cannot distinguish between different colors so also a poet untrained in poetics cannot differentiate between poetic merits and faults (I.8). He went on to say that a poet, irrespective of whether he is naturally endowed with poetic genius or not, can master the art of poetry simply by learning and practising *kāvyaśāstra* (I.104). Vāmana in his *Kāvyālankārasūtravṛtti* (8th century) held that a poet should understand the *guṇas* or poetic qualities, and *doṣas* or blemishes of *kāvya* by being educated in *kāvyaśāstra*, and even if a person was endowed with poetic talent by birth, s/he should definitely undergo training in poetics (I.1.4–5). In his *Kāvyamīmāṃsā* (10th century) Rājaśekhara emphasized the importance of education in *kāvyaśāstra* by saying that the prior knowledge of *śāstra* was essential for an appreciation of *kāvya*. According to him, just as nothing is visible in the dark without the aid of light, so also a poet cannot create without the knowledge of *śāstra* (20). All these observations attest to the fact that mastery over *kāvyaśāstra* was as important as *pratibhā* (inborn genius) for a person to become a *kavi* or poet.

Centers of Learning

As in the case of Sanskrit *kāvya*, the royal court was often one of the major locations for the production of treatises on literary science. Daṇḍin, for example, was associated with the court of Śivaskandavarman of the Pallava dynasty in Kāñcīpuram; Vāmana and Udbhaṭa (8th–9th century) were associated with the court of King Jayāpīḍa of Kashmir; Ānandavardhana and Mukula (9th century) with King Avantivarman in Kashmir; Dhanañjaya (11th century) with the court of the Paramāra King Vākpati Muñja, the uncle of King Bhoja; Vidyādhara and Viśvanātha (14th century) with an unknown king in Kaliṅga; Jagannātha (17th century) with the court of Shah Jahan and Viśveśvara (18th century) with the royal court of Almora. Bhoja (11th century), the author of the voluminous *Śṛṅgāraprakāśa* and

Sarasvatīkaṇṭhābharaṇa, himself was a king who ruled the city of Dhara (today's Madhya Pradesh). Arjunavarmadeva, who is the author of *Rasikasaṃjīvanī* (13th century) was a king in the lineage of Bhoja of Dhara. Śiṅgabhūpāla (14th century), the author of *Rasārṇavasudhākara*, was the king of a small country in today's Andhra Pradesh.

Among the various centers of Sanskrit scholarship, what rose to fame as the prime locus of the production of Sanskrit literary theories was undoubtedly the place which we now call Kashmir. A few names that mark the prominence of Kashmir in the intellectual history of Sanskrit *kāvyaśāstra* include Bhāmaha (7th century), Vāmana (9th century), Udbhaṭa (9th century), Ānandavardhana (9th century), Rudraṭa (9th century), Pratihārendurāja (10th century), Mukula Bhaṭṭa (9th century), Kuntaka (10th century), Bhaṭṭa Tauta (10th century), Mammaṭa Bhaṭṭa (11th century), Mahimabhaṭṭa (11th century), Abhinavagupta (11th century), Ruyyaka (12th century), and so on. Even though Kashmir's tradition of literary science began with Bhāmaha's *Kāvyālaṅkāra* in the 7th century, what gave it a real impetus was the reign of King Jayāpīḍa (8th to early 9th century). King Jayāpīḍa was the grandson of King Lalitāditya, a celebrated patron of art and science. Lalitāditya's reign was followed by an age of political turmoil and a consequent stagnation in intellectual and creative works. Jayāpīḍa who wished to restore his grandfather's era of glory generously funded intellectuals and creative writers and this led to an output unparalleled in range and breadth. One can undoubtedly say that it was under King Jayāpīḍa that the school of literary criticism in Kashmir properly came into being. As far as *kāvyaśāstra* is concerned, this crucial movement was led by two major intellectuals namely Udbhaṭa and Vāmana.

Udbhaṭa and Vāmana's texts were undoubtedly the forerunners of systematization of Sanskrit poetics in terms of their size, style, and approach. First of all, the critical corpus of Vāmana and Udbhaṭa alone is as large as all the earlier works on poetics put together. Udbhaṭa authored three books on *kāvyaśāstra* namely *Kāvyālaṅkāra-sāra-saṃgraha*, *Bhāmahavivaraṇa* and a commentary on Bharata's *Nāṭyaśāstra*. These works set an example for his followers in the composition of manuals on poetry. While Udbhaṭa's predecessors like Bhāmaha and Daṇḍin, for the most part, spontaneously composed stand-alone verses in order to explicate the literary tropes and figures of speech, Udbhaṭa used verses from his own full-fledged poem *Kumārasambhava* to serve this purpose. This was the first time when *kāvyaśāstra* borrowed verses from an independent literary work to explicate various critical concepts. Vāmana, Udbhaṭa's successor, even went a step further by incorporating poems from other writers of his period. Through his *Kāvyālaṅkāra-sāra-saṃgraha*, Udbhaṭa also set a new model for the composition of literary treatises, which was the method of adding critical commentary to an already existing text. So *Kāvyālaṅkāra-sāra-saṃgraha* was essentially Bhāmaha's text along with the commentary of Udbhaṭa. This method proved useful in the preservation of texts; many of the critical works would have been lost in oblivion if they had not been cited by critics like this.

After Jayāpīḍa's reign, the second crucial landmark in the history of *kāvyaśāstra* in Kashmir occurred during the rule of King Avantivarman of Utpala dynasty in the 9th century.

During the reign of kings before Avantivarman, the critics and practitioners of *kāvya* did not get much support and patronage from the royal court probably because of the political instability during this period. It was in Avantivarman's court that the great literary theorist Ānandavardhana produced his famous *Dhvanyāloka* which revolutionized Sanskrit literary science through the concept of *dhvani*. After the death of king Avantivarman (883 CE), courtly patronage for literature and literary criticism again faced a setback.

During the reign of Śaṅkaravarman in the late 9th century and that of Queen Diddā in the mid-10th century, Sanskrit literary production declined again because of political turmoil. Diddā's reign was particularly a period of rebellion and violence. Following her husband's death, she placed her son Abhimanyu on the throne and ruled on his behalf for some time. To secure her own safety, she fomented rivalry between the military and political factions of the country. Not long after his coming of age, Diddā's son Abhimanyu passed away. After Abhimanyu, Diddā, by turn, placed three of her grandsons on the throne, but they were all murdered after enjoying brief stints of sovereignty. Finally, from 980 CE to 1003 CE, she assumed power in her own right and finally left the kingdom to her nephew whom she had chosen after careful examination (Ingalls 9).

The withdrawal of royal patronage during the time of Śaṅkaravarman and Diddā eventuated in a near dearth of literary production in Kashmir. We have no Sanskrit lyric or play from Kashmir during this period. The only *mahākāvya* that is available from this period is Abhinanda's *Kādambarī-kathā-sāra*. However, the tradition of Sanskrit scholarship, especially Śaiva philosophy and *kāvyaśāstra*, continued to flourish chiefly because of the Brahmins living in the capital or on their tax-free grants of land. They made sure that their sons were trained in grammar and other scholarly disciplines in Sanskrit (Ingalls 28–29). So, we have a lot of texts on literary theory from both the 10th and 11th centuries, such as Bhaṭṭa Nāyaka's *Hṛdayadarpaṇa* (10th century), Bhaṭṭa Tauta's *Kāvyakautuka* (10th century), Kuntaka's *Vakroktijīvita* (10th century), Abhinavagupta's *Abhinavabhāratī* (11th century), Mahimabhaṭṭa's *Vyaktiviveka* (11th century), and Mammaṭa's *Kāvyaprakāśa* (11th century).

Of all these texts, Mammaṭa's *Kāvyaprakāśa* deserves special mention because of the large number of commentaries it invited from both his contemporaries and successors. These numerous commentaries bear testimony to the popularity that *Kāvyaprakāśa* enjoyed in Sanskrit literary circles. Indicating the large number of commentaries on *Kāvyaprakāśa*, Bhāskara (15th century) bragged that there were almost a thousand commentaries on *Kāvyaprakāśa* and among them his was the best one (Jhalakikar 30). In his commentary on *Kāvyaprakāśa*, Bhīmasena Dikṣita (17th century) expressed his belief that although several commentaries on *Kāvyaprakāśa* were available, none of them was as good as his (Jhalakikar 34). Maheśvara (17th century), the author of *Kāvyaprakāśādarśana*, said that although a commentary of *Kāvyaprakāśa* was prepared in almost all the houses, most intellectuals were unable to comprehend it because it was such a pathbreaking study (Jhalakikar 39). Among the numerous commentaries on *Kāvyaprakāśa*, some of the important ones include *Kāvyaprakāśasaṅketa*-s of Ruyyaka (11th century), Māṇikyacandra (12th century),

Someśvara (12th century), and Śrīdhara Thakkura (13th century); *Bālacittānurañjanī* of Narahari (13th century) and Sarasvatītīrtha (13th century); *Kāvyaprakāśadīpikā* of Jayanta Bhaṭṭa (13th century); *Sāhityadīpikā* of Caṇḍidāsa (14th century), *Kāvyaprakāśādarśana*-s of Viśvanātha (14th century), and Maheśvara (17th century); and *Kāvyaprakāśaṭīkka* of Kamalākara Bhaṭṭa (17th century).

Kāvyaprakāśa was mostly a reformulation of the ideas already discussed in detail by other literary theoreticians, so it is still a matter of wonder as to what element in *Kāvyaprakāśa* endeared it so much to scholars. Two possible reasons could be its text-bookish nature and the comprehensive collation of almost all the ideas from preceding scholars; this could have helped both the preceptors and disciples of Sanskrit literary science to have a comprehensive overview of all the major lessons of *kāvyaśāstra.* Under King Harṣa's reign in the 12th century (not to be confused with King Harṣa of 7th-century Kanauj), Sanskrit learning in Kashmir again faced a serious crisis from which it could never revive. After the 12th century, no new literary theory was produced in Kashmir and the last major *kāvyaśāstra* text to be circulated outside of Kashmir was *Alaṅkāraratnākara* of Śobhākaramitra from the end of the 12th century (Pollock, "Death of Sanskrit," 396).

Major Theoreticians

However, the field of Sanskrit aesthetics, before its gradual decline, was dominated by towering personalities. Most of them left very little evidence of their personal lives, and this fact coupled with the loss of significant texts like Bhaṭṭa Nāyaka's *Hṛdayadarpaṇa* makes it very difficult for us to trace the intellectual history of ancient India. Nevertheless, there are a few fragments that we have to pick up and piece together to form a picture.

The first among the ancients is Bharata, the author of *Nāṭyaśāstra* and the proponent of the *rasa* theory. Although the *rasa* theory is still discussed and recognized today, Bharata remains an enigmatic figure. There has been much debate about whether he is an individual or the acronym formed out of the first syllables of the Sanskrit words *Bhāva*, *Rāga* and *Tāla* (Vatsyayan 6). He is usually referred to as Bharatamuni, indicating that he was a mendicant. Scholars differ about the timeline of the composition of the *Nāṭyaśāstra*; Kapila Vatsyayan's view is that "...the *Nāṭyaśāstra* is a post-Upaniṣadic text. It also precedes the composition of the earliest *Purāṇa*s, possibly most of Sanskrit drama, and certainly the schools of philosophy" (24). Scholars like her have located the *Nāṭyaśāstra* as a text from sometime between 2nd century BCE and 2nd century CE. Despite these speculations about his personal life, there has never been any doubt about the significant contribution he made to the field of Sanskrit poetics; he is the foundation on which the entire edifice of Sanskrit *kāvyaśāstra* was built.

Another pioneer is Bhāmaha, who is believed to have initiated the rigorous analysis of literature through his work *Kāvyālaṅkāra*. He was renowned as an *ālaṅkārika* who focused on the nature of poetic language, especially figures of speech. The fact that later theoreticians like Ānandavardhana and Abhinavagupta quote him with respect is evidence enough of his stature in the field. He is believed to have lived in Kashmir around the 7th century. Nothing much is known about his life other than that he could have been a Buddhist, and supposedly a contemporary of another theoretician, Daṇḍin. He is supposed to have written *Prākritmanorama*, a commentary on Vararuci's Prākrit work.

Daṇḍin's *Kāvyādarśa* contains aspects that appear to refute some of Bhāmaha's views. Scholars believe he was from South India and was a court poet of the Pallava kings. *Daśakumāracarita* and *Avantisundarīkathā* are other works that are attributed to Daṇḍin; both are incomplete prose texts. Although Daṇḍin is associated closely with the way in which he identified certain qualities that were essential to a literary work, he also had insightful observations on the use of figurative language.

Udbhaṭa is another major figure in the line of critics who devoted their attention to figurative language in poetry. He was the chief poet in the court of King Jayāpīḍa of Kashmir. Pollock describes him as "a very independent-minded grammarian, even a contrarian, as well as a materialist (*cārvāka*), and a renegade materialist (*dhūrta*) at that" (*A Rasa Reader*, 65). His major contribution was the *Kāvyālaṅkārasārasaṃgraha* (*A Compendium of the Most Important Figures of Speech in Poetry*). It is believed that he wrote a commentary to Bharata's *Nātyaśāstra*, and also a commentary to Bhāmaha's work titled *Bhāmahavivaraṇa*, both of which were unfortunately lost. Scholars like Jacobi think that he was the first to elevate the concept of *rasa* to the soul of poetry.

Ānandavardhana, the author of *Dhvanyāloka,* was the next important person to have forged a new path in Sanskrit poetics. His concept of *dhvani* became the most important theoretical concept since *rasa*. He too was a native of Kashmir and was fortunate to have lived during the best of days of literature, which was the rule of King Avantivarman in the 9th century. Kalhaṇa's *Rājataraṅgiṇī*, which is considered to be a chronicle of Kashmir, mentions four stalwarts of the court of Avantivarman, one of whom is Ānandavardhana. Nothing much is known about his personal life except that he was the son of Noṇa who perhaps was the recipient of a stipend from the King. Ānandavardhana's other works include the *Viṣamabāṇalīlā* and *Arjunacarita*. The *Viṣamabāṇalīlā* was in the form of a play written in Mahārāshtri Prākrit, and *Arjunacarita* was a *mahākāvya* in Sanskrit. According to the author himself, the play was written to instruct writers on poetry (this must have been an accepted practice in those days because we also have Bhaṭṭi in the 7th century composing the *Bhaṭṭikāvya* like an instruction manual for aspiring writers). Ānanda used verses from his own compositions to exemplify varieties of *dhvani* in *Dhvanyāloka*. He was also a philosopher and is believed to have written the verbally intricate *Devīśataka*.

Abhinavagupta was a multifaceted genius who lived during the second wave of intellectual glory that Kashmir saw in the latter half of the 10th century. He was a Śaivite philosopher, poet, and literary critic; he has written on a wide range of subjects and has numerous works to his credit. His major works are *Tantrāloka* and *Tantrasāra* besides devotional hymns and the critical commentaries he wrote for two important aesthetic works—the *Abhinavabhāratī* on the *Nāṭyaśāstra* and the *Locana* on *Dhvanyāloka*. His greatest contribution was that he was able to merge the concepts of *rasa* and *dhvani* in a manner that had not been attempted until then. Abhinavagupta's major area of interest was philosophy and we can see how his philosophical principles impacted his perception of literature and literary appreciation. Pollock points out that "...Abhinavagupta's theory of aesthetic consciousness shares many traits with, though it is not necessarily conceptually dependent on, his theory of liberated consciousness;..." (*A Rasa Reader* 36). He was undoubtedly a multifaceted genius, an embodiment of the qualities that would much later occasion the term "Renaissance man." Unfortunately, this philosopher-aesthete remains somewhat obscure, compared to other figures like Ādi Śaṅkara.

Kuntaka who lived in Kashmir in the 10th century is the author of *Vakroktijīvita*. According to Pollock, "The only work in the Sanskrit tradition that can be likened to what today we would regard as literary criticism is Kuntaka's *Vakroktijīvita*" (*A Rasa Reader* 98). In his introduction to Kuntaka's *Vakroktijīvita*, Krishnamoorthy also makes a similar observation. According to him, "In the whole range of Sanskrit poetical theory, we do not have anyone who can be termed a practical literary critic in the modern sense of the term except Kuntaka" (XXXV). Kuntaka's *Vakroktijīvita* was thought to have been lost forever for a long time. A glance at the various stages through which Kuntaka's *Vakroktijīvita* was reconstructed bears witness to the amount of energy and meticulous research that went into this process. Kuntaka's *Vakroktijīvita*, which was long thought to be lost and known only through the citations in the later texts of *kāvyaśāstra* is now available to us primarily through the efforts of S. K. De and Krishnamoorthy.

Kṣemendra was born in the latter half of the 11th century in a noble family in Kashmir. His father Prakāśendra was a wealthy man who was very keen on giving his son training in all streams of knowledge. Prominent among the literary output of Kṣemendra are his abridged versions of the *Rāmāyaṇa*, *Mahābhārata*, and *Bṛhadkathā*, which are respectively titled *Rāmāyaṇamañjarī*, *Bhāratamañjarī*, and *Bṛhadkathāmañjarī*. Kṣemendra is also the author of various satires such as *Kalāvilasā*, *Samayamātṛkā*, *Narmamālā*, and *Daśopadeśa*. These satires that were sharp critiques of the sociopolitical condition of those times belie the general impression that classical Sanskrit literature did not have any social or political objectives.

His works on Sanskrit poetics include *Aucityavicāracarcā*, *Kavikaṇṭhābharaṇa*, and *Suvṛttatilaka*. In *Kavikaṇṭhābharaṇa*, Kṣemendra discusses at great length a wide variety of topics such as the training one necessarily needs to go through to become a poet; the factors a poet should take into account while adopting stories from the works of great masters, etc. In this work, he also gives budding poets a hundred-point advice. Kṣemendra's *Aucityavicāracarcā*, as the title suggests, primarily deals with the importance of propriety in the composition of literary works. Other major works by Kṣemendra include *Nītikalpataru*, *Darpadalana*, *Caturvargasaṅgraha*, *Cārucaryā*, *Sevyasevakopadeśa*, *Lokaprakāśa*, and *Stūpavādana*.

In the 11th century, we have two important figures, Mahimabhaṭṭa and Bhoja. Mahimabhaṭṭa was also known as Rājānaka Mahimabhaṭṭa and belonged to Kashmir. He is reputed primarily for his *Vyaktiviveka* which discusses the *rasa* concept in detail. He is the best-known proponent of the concept of *anumāna* and maintained that *rasa* is not produced, but inferred by the reader. By elaborating on this concept, the text also refuted the idea of his eminent predecessors like Ānandavardhana and Abhinavagupta that *dhvani* is the primary component of good poetry. His defiance of his formidable predecessors by coming up with an intellectually sound theory like *anumāna* is an index of the scholarship of Mahimabhaṭṭa.

Bhoja is an exception in this line of scholars and critics because he was a king who had the administrative responsibility of a kingdom. Bhoja belonged to the Paramāra dynasty and ruled over the Malwa region with Dhara as the capital city, from 1010 to 1055 CE. His court was somewhat similar to that of the legendary Vikramāditya, as it attracted poets and scholars from around India. His significant contribution to Sanskrit poetics is his *Śṛṅgāraprakāśa.* Another work is *Sarasvatīkaṇṭhābharaṇa. Śṛṅgāraprakāśa* is significant because this work reduces all *rasas* to just one, which is that of *śṛṅgāra.* Bhoja's theory was that this was the basic emotion that motivated all other emotions; all the human emotions were derivatives of *śṛṅgāra.* This was a radical departure from the catalogue of eight *rasas* that was drawn up by the pioneer Bharata. It is no wonder that the work was controversial and not readily accepted by later scholars like Mallinātha in the 15th century.

Mammaṭa was a Kashmiri pandit who lived in the 12th century. He is said to have traveled from Kashmir to Benares for studies. Next to nothing is available about the personal life of Mammaṭa. Bhīmasena Dīkṣita provides us with some pieces of information regarding the life of Mammaṭa in the introductory verses of his celebrated *Sudhāsāgara* (his commentary on Mammaṭa's *Kāvyaprakāśa*). According to Dīkṣita, Mammaṭa was the son of Jaiyaṭa. His younger brothers Kaiyaṭa and Uvaṭa were also great scholars. *Kāvyaprakāśa,* the magnum opus of Mammaṭa, is divided into ten chapters called *ullāsas*. *Kāvyaprakāśa* opens with a definition of literature and then discusses the linguistic modalities underpinning a *kāvya*, the ontology of aesthetic emotion, different powers of a *śabda* including the idea of *dhvani*, poetic merits and flaws, and figures of sound and sense.

It is important to note that thousands of manuscript copies of *Kāvyaprakāśa* were available all over India. It also attracted many commentaries from scholars from different parts of the country—a trend which began in the mid-12th century and went on till the 18th century. Considering the impact that Mammaṭa's *Kāvyaprakāśa* exercised upon people in the education of Sanskrit poetics, Bhīmasena Dīkṣita in his commentary on *Kāvyaprakāśa* with all sincerity calls Mammaṭa an "incarnation of Sarasvatī, goddess of language" (1).

Jagannātha was a scholar from what we now call Telangana. His father Peru Bhaṭṭa was also his teacher and mentor. A member of the court of Emperor Shāhjahān, Jagannātha was known in literary circles as "the Emperor of Poets." He is believed to have received the title "King of Scholars" (*paṇḍitarāja*) from the emperor himself. Along with the strong patronage of the emperor, he was also supported by many other princely houses for whom he often wrote *praśastis* or eulogies. He could also be viewed as an example of the cultural syncretism of the times, having married a Muslim woman and becoming an integral part of the Mughal courts. His most famous literary work is *Bhāminīvilāsa* (*The Games of Beautiful Women*). In many of his treatises on poetics, Jagannātha quotes from this work to illustrate the literary concepts that he was discussing. *Rasagaṅgādhara*, his magnum opus in the field of literary theory, is often considered a "curious mixture of modernity, and tradition" (Pollock, *A Rasa Reader*, 315). In *Rasagaṅgādhara*, Jagannātha effectively employed the framework of Vedanta to understand literary categories. Unlike many of his contemporaries, such as Jīva Gosvamin, who invented a new *rasa* called *bhakti*, Jagannātha was a thorough traditionalist. He holds an important position in Sanskrit poetics as the last literary theoretician in the Sanskrit cosmopolis. As Pollock rightly observes,

> Jagannātha marks a historical endpoint in a number of important ways. If it can be said that his ontogeny recapitulated the phylogeny of Sanskrit literary culture, this was probably the last such case; we know of no later poet who circumambulated the quarters of Sanskrit's cosmopolitan space. (Pollock, *Sanskrit Literary Culture*, 96)

What Is a *Kāvya*?

Before discussing the science of poetry, it is important to understand what our ancestors meant by the term "poetry" or *kāvya*. Other than the drama, which was termed *nāṭya*, poetry was the most prevalent and popular form of literary composition; consequently, *kāvya* as we understand it today, is rather loosely defined as poetry. But we can use the term in a broader sense, where it encompasses all forms of literature like the *mahākāvya* (long poem), the *kathā* (prose story), and other shorter verse forms. So *kāvyaśāstra* would mean the science of literary composition.

What is the hallmark of *kāvya*? Language rather than theme or content was considered to be the distinctive trait that separated it from other cultural discourses. *Kāvyaśāstra* always considered *kāvya* as a "specialized" mode of language marked by the ingenious use of certain distinctive linguistic devices. We should keep in mind that Sanskrit was the language used by the Vedas and the *śāstras*. This is why *kāvyaśāstra* very carefully attempted to delimit the language of *kāvya* from other uses of language such as *śāstra*, the Vedas, and the language used in daily life. We have a host of literary theoreticians in Sanskrit poetics who typify this exclusionist view of literature; they observed that the language of literature was not ordinary but was embellished with certain qualities and figures of speech. Hemacandra in *Kāvyānuśāsana* observed that it is the presence of four components such as *śabda* (word), *artha* (meaning), *guṇa* (poetic quality), and *alaṅkāra* (figures of speech) that constitutes a *kāvya* (I.22). Vāgbhaṭa II delimited the ambit of *kāvya* by defining it as a composition of *śabda* (word) and *artha* (meaning) marked by the absence of *doṣa*s and the presence of *guṇa*s and *alaṅkāra*s (14). Mammaṭa observed that *kāvya* is composed of flawless words and sense adorned with merits and excellences of style (I.4). In *Candrāloka*, Jayadeva also set the limit of poetic expression by defining *kāvya* as a verbal icon characterized by the absence of *doṣa*s and the presence of *lakṣaṇā* (deviant utterance), *rīti* (diction or style; literally means "path"), *guṇa*, *alaṅkāra*, *rasa* (aesthetic emotion), and *vṛtti* (linguistic modality) (I.7).

Vidyānātha in *Pratāparudrīya* saw *kāvya* as a special composition of both *gadya* (prose) and *padya* (poetry) bereft of *doṣa*s and adorned by *guṇa*, *alaṅkāra*, *śabda*, and *artha* (II.1). Bhaṭṭa Nāyaka talked about three crucial components that were conspicuously absent in other uses of language and present only in *kāvya*. According to him, these three elements were *abhidhāyakatva* (denotative function), *bhāvakatva* (ability to evoke aesthetic experience), and *bhogakṛttva* (the experience of aesthetic emotion). In his commentary on *Dhvanyāloka*, Abhinavagupta reproduced this view of Bhaṭṭa Nāyaka (*Locana* 2.4 *L*). Kuntaka opined that the figurative deviation of speech (*vakrokti*) makes *kāvya* different from ordinary expression and the use of language in *śāstras* (291). According to Bhoja, although poetry is called the combination of word and meaning, not all compositions of word and meaning could claim the status of a *kāvya*. In *Śṛṅgāraprakāśa*, Bhoja made a clear distinction between *kāvya* and other linguistic genres based on the nature of language employed in them. According to Bhoja, workaday language is the explicit language of science and daily life. On the other hand, *kāvya* was the deviant language found in texts teeming with aesthetic pleasure (I; 221). We can see this view of *kāvya* as a special linguistic category with complex literary conventions and elaborate metrical schemes, unchangingly going down the line till the end of the active phase in Sanskrit literary culture in the 17th century, with Jagannātha observing that *kāvya* is a special combination of word and meaning, with beautiful words denoting noble significations (*ramaṇīyārthapradipādakaḥ śabdaḥ kāvyaṃ*; 4).

Another major distinctive feature was identified as *rasa*. Although the idea of *rasa* was an important point of discussion in *nāṭyaśāstra* and was well known to literary critics from Bhāmaha onwards, none of the literary theoreticians until Udbhaṭa considered it to be a criterion of literariness or an independent category. One reason could have been that *rasa* was also a quality closely associated with *nāṭya*; then how could it be termed an exclusive aspect of literature? As far as the earlier *kāvyaśāstra* exponents were concerned, *rasa* was not the primary factor that separated *kāvya* from other uses of language; it was but one of the many qualities of poetic language, a quality that was usually subsumed under the larger category of figures of speech. Bhāmaha incorporated the idea of *rasa* under three verbal expressions of emotions such as *rasavat* or *rasa*-laden expression, *preyaḥ* or "affectionate utterance" and *ūrjasvin* or "haughty declaration" (53–55). Like Bhāmaha, Daṇḍin also reserved no special category for *rasa* other than that of a figure of speech. In *Kāvyādarśa*, he used the idea of *rasa* in two different senses—first as a general term for any deviant linguistic expression and second as a technical term for various instances of affective expressions such as *rasavat*, *preyaḥ*, and *ūrjasvin* (I.51–52, I.62–63).

In Udbhaṭa's critical corpus also the idea of *rasa* is largely a figure of speech. By adding "quiescent" or *samāhita* to the already existing categories of *preyaḥ* (the affectionate), *rasavat* (the *rasa*-laden), and *ūrjasvin* (the haughty speech), Udbhaṭa increased the number of *rasa*-related figures from three to four (*Kāvyālaṅkāra-sāra-saṃgraha* IV.1). He also mentioned the components conducive to the production of *rasa* namely *vibhāva* (foundational factor), *anubhāva* (stimulant factor), *vyabhicāribhāva* (transitory emotion), *sthāyibhāva* (stable emotion), and *svaśabda* (proper name) (IV.2). It is with Ānandavardhana's *Dhvanyāloka* that the idea of *rasa* made its way to literary criticism as a prominent constituent of literariness. According to Ānandavardhana, among all the three varieties of *dhvani, rasadhvani* was the soul of poetry (I.5 K).

All these observations point out that *kāvyaśāstra* was incessantly preoccupied with the task of pinpointing factors that were responsible for the specificity of poetic language. This can be considered natural enough in a literary culture that was finding its feet in the early centuries of the first millennium. It was important to understand the nature of literature as well as the workings of the literary mind. Although there were differences of opinion among literary theoreticians as to which element had to be treated as the most important element of *kāvya*, they all had a consensus on the idea that *kāvya* is a unique use of language, and hence their efforts were unidirectionally oriented toward unraveling the various formal factors that attribute an aura of uniqueness to literature. The term *alaṅkāraśāstra*, which was often used synonymously with Sanskrit poetics, readily functions as a pointer to the teleology of Sanskrit *kāvyaśāstra*. Because of *kāvyaśāstra*'s unwavering interest in the ornaments (*alaṅkāra*) of *kāvya* that made literature a higher-order linguistic composition, the term *alaṅkāraśāstra* was often used synonymously with *kāvyaśāstra*.

Six Schools of Poetic Thought

Sanskrit *kāvyaśāstra* is believed to consist mainly of six schools of thought, based on the poetic qualities they emphasize. They are *alaṅkāra*, *rīti*, *guṇa*, *vakrokti*, *dhvani*, and *aucitya*. All the theoreticians discussed above fall into one or more of these schools of thought.

Bhāmaha, the earliest known exponent of *kāvyaśāstra*, considered *alaṅkāra*s or figures of speech to be the primary factors that transform a piece of writing into *kāvya*. Therefore, in his *Kāvyālaṅkāra*, Bhāmaha was chiefly concerned with the identification and analysis of *alaṅkāra*s that beautify a work of literature. He listed and analyzed about thirty-eight *alaṅkāra*s in his attempt to identify the unique nature of *kāvyaśarīra* or the body of poetry. According to Bhāmaha, what made an *alaṅkāra* different from other uses of language was its extraordinary usage or figurative deviation (*vakratā*) from ordinary language. Therefore, he employed the term *alaṅkāra* to encompass all the deviant linguistic expressions (I.36). Bhāmaha was of the view that a poet should always be diligent in developing this art of figurative deviation, which functions as the vital force of all *alaṅkāra*s (II.85). In the second chapter of *Kāvyālaṅkāra*, Bhāmaha pointed out that a composition devoid of figurative deviation of sense—such as "the sun has set," "the moon shines," or "the birds fly back to their nest"—is a mere "report" or *vartā* and not *kāvya* (II.87). What Bhāmaha's theory of *alaṅkāra* shows is that *kāvya* is distinct from other uses of language due to the presence of *alaṅkāras*. The *kāvya* arouses *rasa* through the skilful use of *alaṅkāra*s, and so *rasa* is seen as a subset of these figures of speech.

Daṇḍin in his *Kāvyādarśa* declared that the aim of his work was to identify the elements that make up the body of *kāvya* (I.2). In *Kāvyādarśa*, Daṇḍin broadened the scope of his scrutiny of *kāvyaśarīra* by increasing the number of figures of speech to thirty-five and that of poetic merits (*guṇa*s) to ten. Considering the amount of attention he paid to the analysis of *alaṅkāra* and *guṇa*, we can assume that in Daṇḍin's conception *guṇa*s and *alaṅkāra*s primarily constitute the *kāvyaśarīra*. Vāmana's

Kāvyālaṅkārasūtravṛtti opens with a chapter titled *kāvya-śarīra-nirṇaya* or the "understanding of the anatomy of *kāvya*." Such a self-explanatory title immediately informs us that the purpose of his work is to identify and analyze the formal factors that go into the making of the body of *kāvya*. Vāmana sees *guṇa*s or poetic merit as the vital force of literature. According to him, a verbal expression without ten *guṇa*s cannot become a *kāvya*; just as a group of words without syntax cannot make coherent meaning (*guṇāṇāṃ daśatā tyakto yasyārthastadapārthakaṃ* | *dāḍimāni daśetyādi na vicārakṣamaṃ vacaḥ*||; see *kārika* on III.2.14). He was of the view that a literary style (*rīti*) where all the *guṇa*s are properly knit together serves as the soul of *kāvya* (I.2.3). Though Vāmana opined that the body of *kāvya* is characterized by sound and sense adorned by *guṇa*s and *alaṅkāra*s, he valued *guṇa*s more than *alaṅkāra*s as the source of beauty in a poem (III.1.1). According to him, it is *guṇa*s such as *ojas* and *prasāda* that are responsible for the unique nature of *kāvya*; a style or *rīti* that has these *guṇa*s transform a piece of writing into a literary work. The function of *alaṅkāra*, on the other hand, is only to enhance the beauty of *kāvya* which is already beautified by the presence of *guṇa*s (*ye khalu śabārthayodharmāḥ kāvya śobhāṃ kurvanti te guṇāḥ; te caujaḥ prasādādayaḥ, na yamakopamādayaḥ, kaivalye teṣāṃkāvya śobhākaratvāt;* III.1.1). Though in Vāmana's theory, there is a shift of focus from *alaṅkāra* to *guṇa* and *rīti*, like his predecessors and successors, he remains steadfast on the idea that *kāvya* is a supra-normal entity.

Ānandavardhana (9th century) who is the successor of Vāmana is such a formidable figure in Sanskrit literary criticism that he was able to strongly establish his viewpoint and remained uncontested for many centuries to come. He criticized Vāmana's view that *rīti* is the soul of *kāvya*. According to Ānanda, it was people unable to identify the true nature of poetry who propounded the doctrine of "styles" (3.46 *K*). For Ānanda, *dhvani* or poetic suggestion is the soul of *kāvya* (*kāvyasayātmādhvaniriti*; 1.1 *K*). Therefore, in his *Dhvanyāloka*, Ānandavardhana examined the nature of *dhvani* in detail. According to Ānandavardhana, *dhvani* is the linguistic device by which a word or a set of words expresses something more than what it signifies. According to Ānandavardhana's theory, what primarily distinguishes *kāvya* from other uses of language is the presence of *dhvani*. This does not mean that he turned a blind eye to the other linguistic devices such as *alaṅkāra*, *guṇa*, and so on, the textual elements that his predecessors had identified as the distinguishing mark of *kāvya*. According to Ānandavardhana, *alaṅkāra*s function like ornaments on a person's body, while *guṇa*s are qualities like courage (2.5 g *K*). However, he subordinated all these elements to *dhvani* which is the soul of *kāvya*.

Kuntaka, a 10th century Sanskrit literary critic, considered *vakrokti* (figurative deviation of speech) as the chief source of literariness. It is to explicate this point that Kuntaka wrote his *Vakroktijīvita* which means the "vital force of deviant utterance." According to Kuntaka, *kāvya* is that combination of *śabda* (word) and *artha* (meaning) which shines with *vakratā* (figurative deviation of speech) or unusual usage, so that it would impart pleasure to readers (I.7). He categorized *vakratā* under six important heads, such as *varṇa-vinyāsa-vakratā* (figurative deviation of phonemes, consonants, and syllables); *pada-pūrvārtha-vakratā* (figurative deviation of speech to transcend the literal meaning of a word); *pada-parārtha-vakratā* (figurative deviation of the terminal part of a word); *vākya-vakratā* (figurative deviation of a sentence); *prakaraṇa-vakratā* (figurative deviation of episodes); and *prabandha-vakratā* (figurative deviation of the plot). To Kuntaka, *vakrokti* was the supreme governing principle of *kāvya*. He considered it important enough to make a thorough analysis of the various forms of *vakrokti* in the four chapters of his *Vakroktijīvita*.

Kṣemendra held that *aucitya* or propriety is an essential part of *kāvyaśarīra*. Unlike the literary theoreticians we have seen before, Kṣemendra did not introduce any new formal feature as the source of literariness; on the other hand, he emphasized the proper organization of the linguistic devices which were already considered the hallmark of literature. He was of the view that the proper organization of these distinct linguistic devices was as important as their presence in *kāvya* (I.23). According to him, neither figures of speech nor poetic merits would look charming without propriety. Kṣemendra's concept of *aucitya* became an all-encompassing precept that is applied to almost all aspects of *kāvya*.

Conclusion

It is clear that classical Sanskrit theoreticians spent a great amount of time and effort in thinking about the origin and purpose of art and literature. It is also obvious that these literary discussions are not radically different from similar discussions we have come across in the West. Many people have pointed out the similarities between Bharata's

Nāṭyaśāstra and Aristotle's *Poetics*. The concept of *rasa* is somewhat akin to Longinus's concept of the sublime. Sir Philip Sidney's *Apology for Poetry*, Dryden's *Of Dramatic Poesy*, and Matthew Arnold's *Essays in Criticism* are all explorations of the nature of literature which are similar to Ānandavardhana's or Rājaśekhara's treatises. But what makes these Indian works different is their deep indebtedness to Indian philosophical schools; Sanskrit poetics also has a spiritual dimension that is difficult to ignore. It has to be emphasized that here spiritual should not be read synonymously with religious, but with intellectual explorations of human existence and the nature of existence.

It is not surprising, then, that most of the Indian theoreticians of literature were also philosophers. For instance, Ānandavardhana who is considered by Sanskritists today as the most influential thinker in Sanskrit criticism, was a *Śaivite* philosopher and his views of poetry and poesy were influenced by his philosophical beliefs. Abhinavagupta who wrote the all-important interpretation for Ānandavardhana's *Dhvanyāloka* was primarily a *Śaivite* philosopher who belonged to the *pratyabhijñā* school of philosophy, and his observations about poesy were those of a *yogi* rather than a litterateur. This is not to say that we have to be well-versed in Indian philosophy to comprehend Sanskrit literary criticism, but just to point out that we have to perhaps develop a different mental approach to what we usually think of as completely "secular" and non-spiritual entities. According to classical Sanskrit belief, a poet was considered to be a *ṛṣi–nanṛṣi kavi* or a person who is not a rishi cannot be a poet (Hemacandra 369). Vālmīki, who is hailed as the *Ādikāvi* or

First Poet, was a sage revered for his wisdom and spiritual eminence. The poet was a seer who could penetrate the outer layers of mundane existence and decipher the hidden spiritual dimensions of life; according to the *Rāmāyaṇa*, "*Tataḥ paśyati dharmātmā tatsarvam yogamāsthitaḥ / purā yattat nirvṛttam pāṇāvāmalakam yatha*" [With the power of yoga, the righteous (Vālmīki) saw clearly, like an *āmalaka* fruit in the palm the entire course of events that happened in the past relating to Rāma]; I.3.6). The calling of a poet and critic was then of the highest order, which had to be thought of at the same level and of the same nature as that of the ascetic who was willing to forego the pleasures of the world through spiritual contemplation and attain a transcendent state.

The six schools of poetic thought that are outlined above should, therefore, be seen as the literary streams that ran parallel to philosophical thought. However, this does not mean that all writers and critics of Sanskrit wrote only literature of a very serious nature on topics of spiritual nature. Literary works came in all sorts and varied in extent as these dos today; writers wrote about life in all its best and worst aspects. However, it is the vocation of a writer or litterateur that has to be differently understood when we approach Sanskrit poetics. The philosophical dimension has to be kept in mind to comprehend and imbibe the theoretical concepts of art/literature that these philosopher-critics believed in.

The next chapters will undertake a systematic and more analytical journey through each of the six schools of poetics which have been only briefly mentioned in this chapter.

Works Cited

Abhinavagupta. *Locana*. In *The Dhvanyāloka of Ānandavardhana with the Locana of Abhinavagupta*, translated and edited by Daniel Ingalls, Jeffrey Masson, and M. V. Patwardhan, Harvard University Press, 1990.

Ānandavardhana. *The Dhvanyāloka of Ānandavardhana with the Locana of Abhinavagupta*. Translated and edited by Daniel Ingalls, Jeffrey Masson, and M. V. Patwardhan, Harvard University Press, 1990.

Aśvaghoṣa. *Life of Buddha*. Translated by Patrick Olivelle, New York University Press, 2008.

Bharata. *Nāṭyaśāstram*. Translated (Malayalam) and edited by K. P. Narayana Pisharody, Kerala Sahitya Akademi, 2004.

Bhāmaha. *Kāvyālaṅkāra*. Edited by B. N. Sarma and Baldeva Upadhyay, Chowkhamba Sanskrit Series Office, 1998.

Bhoja. *Śṛṅgāraprakāśa*. Vols 1 and 2, Edited by G. S. Josyer, 1955 and 1963.

Daṇḍin. *Kāvyādarśa of Daṇḍin*. Edited by P. Tarkabagisa, Royal Asiatic Society, 1962.

Dīkṣita, Bhimasena. *Sudhāsāgara*. Chowkamba Sanskrit Series, 1927.

Hemacandra. *Kāvyānuśāsana*. Edited by Rasiklal C. Parikh, Mahavira Jaina Vidyalaya, 1938.

Ingalls, Daniel H. H. "Introduction." In *The Dhvanyāloka*, by Ānandavardhana, Harvard University Press, 1990, pp. 1–39.

Jagannātha. *The Rasagaṅgādhara of Jagannātha Paṇḍita with the Commentary of Nāgeśa Bhaṭṭa*. Edited by D. Prasad and K. P. Parab, The Nirnaya Sagara Press, 1888.

Jayadeva. *Candrāloka of Jayadeva*. Edited by A. S. Vetal, Chowkamba Sanskrit Series Office, 1932.

Jhalakikar. Vāmanācarya. *Balabodhini Commentary on Kavyaprakasa*. Bhandarkar Oriental Research Institute, 1950.

Krishnamoorthy, K. "Introduction." In *Vakroktijīvita* by Kuntaka, Karnatak University, 1977.

Kuntaka. *Vakroktijīvita*. Translated by Krishnamoorthy, Karnatak University, 1977.

Kṣemendra. *Aucityavicāracarcā*. In *Kṣemendra Studies: Together with an English Translation of his Kavikanṭhābharaṇa, Aucityavicāracarcā and Suvṛttatilaka*, Oriental Book Agency, 1954, pp. 118–172.

Mammaṭa. *Kāvyaprakāśa of Mammaṭa*. Edited by G. Jha, Bharathiya Vidya Prakashan, 1966.

Pollock, Sheldon. *A Rasa Reader: Classical Indian Aesthetics*. Columbia University Press, 2016.

———. "Sanskrit Literary Culture from the Inside Out." In *Literary Cultures in History: Reconstructions from South Asia*, University of California Press, 2003.

———. "The Death of Sanskrit." *Comparative Studies in Society and History*, vol. 43, no. 2, 2001: 392–426.

Rājaśekhara. *Kāvyamīmāṃsā*. Edited by Sadhana Parashar, D. K. Print World, 2000.

Udbhaṭa. *Kāvyālaṅkārasārasaṃgraha with the commentary, the Laghuvṛtti of Indurāja*. Edited by Narayana Daso Banhatti, Bhandarkar Oriental Research Institute, 1982.

Vatsyayan, Kapila. *Bharata: The Nāṭyaśāstra*. Sahitya Akademi, 2003.

Vāgbhaṭa II. *Kāvyānuśāsana*. Nirnaya Sagar Press, 1915.

Vālmīki. valmiki.iitk.ac.in. 2000. Accessed December 18, 2017.

Vāmana. *Kāvyālaṅkārasūtravṛtti*. Translated (Malayalam) and edited by E. Easwaran Nambootiri, Kerala Bhasha Institute, 2000.

Vidyānātha. *Pratāparudrīya*. Edited by K. Ramamurti and S. R. Matha, Oriental Research Institute, 1933.

2

Rasa

Rasa theory is *the* theory in classical Sanskrit literary studies. It would not be an exaggeration to say that all the literary theories in Sanskrit revolve around this single concept. Originally meaning "juice" or "sap," the word *rasa* is used in dramaturgy and literary theory to mean the idea of "aesthetic emotion," which a spectator or a reader derives from watching/reading a work of art. The experience of "aesthetic emotions" or *rasa* is distinct from the experience of normal emotions in real life; the experience of aesthetic emotion gives rise solely to pleasure, while real-life emotions can arouse actual emotions such as pain, pleasure, anger, or revulsion in us. Had the aesthetic emotions also possessed the same characteristics of real emotions, a spectator would not have wished to watch *Romeo and Juliet* where the star-crossed lovers die through no fault of their own. Death of loved ones in real life causes acute pain and trauma while death on the stage or screen or white page, even as it causes pain, also evokes pleasure. This pleasure that we feel is confined to the aesthetic realm and can be described as *rasa*.

According to the available historical evidence, Bharata's *Nāṭyaśāstra* is the first work to systematically reflect upon the concept of *rasa*. Bharata summed up the *rasa* experience in an aphorism: "*Vibhāvānubhāva vyabhicāri saṃyogād rasa niṣpattiḥ*" or "Rasa arises from the conjunction of factors, reactions, and transitory emotions" (*Nāṭyaśāstra* VI.31).

This *rasasūtra* or the "formula" for *rasa* seems simple, but its very simplicity and cryptic nature led to the diversity of interpretations that we see down the centuries.

What are the elements of this *rasasūtra*? There is a crucial element which Bharata has not mentioned here, which is the *sthāyibhāva* or the emotion that we experience in real life. K. C. Pandey describes the *sthāyibhāva* as "… a basic state of mind which binds together in an organic whole," the other aesthetic stimulants and responses (22). Bharata emphasized the importance of the *sthāyibhāva,* describing it as the king who is the center of attention amidst official paraphernalia (VII.13). This state of mind or stable emotion is responsible for engendering what are called *rasa*s or aesthetic emotions. Bharata listed eight *sthāyibhāva*s and eight corresponding *rasa*s. These eight *sthāyibhāva*s are desire (*rati*), amusement (*hāsa*), grief (*śoka*), anger (*krodha*), determination (*utsāh*), fear (*bhaya*), revulsion (*jugupsā*), and amazement (*vismaya*). The eight aesthetic emotions that arise out of these *sthāyibhāva*s respectively are the erotic (*śṛṅgāra*), comic (*hāsya*), tragic (*karuṇa*), violent (*raudra*), heroic (*vīra*), fearful (*bhayānaka*), macabre (*bībhatsā*), and wonder (*adbhuta*) (VI.16). The ninth *rasa* of *śānta* was added later and its *sthāyibhāva* is *nirveda.*

The common explanation for Bharata's *rasasūtra* is the following: a *sthāyibhāva,* in conjunction with *vibhāva, anubhāva,* and *vyabhicāribhāva* that are present in a work of art produces *rasa* or an aesthetic emotion. *Vibhāva* is the stimulant of *rasa.* In other words, it is the determinant factor stimulating a particular emotion in a reader or spectator. *Vibhāvas* are divided into two, namely *ālambana vibhāva* and *uddīpana vibhāva. Ālambana vibhāva* is the object or person that stimulates a particular emotion. For instance, the *ālambana vibhāva* for the character of Rāma would be his wife Sītā. For Daśaratha who is destined to exile his son Rāma, *ālambana vibhāva* is Rāma.

Uddīpana vibhāvas are the external factors or ambience that strengthens the emotion. For *śṛṅgāra rasa*, the stimulative determinants or *uddīpana vibhāvas* are factors such as springtime, the gardens teeming with flowers, the bridal chamber, and so on. An example would be the *śṛṅgāra rasa* evoked in the balcony scene of *Romeo and Juliet*—here, Juliet is Romeo's *ālambana vibhāva* while the moonlit garden provides the *uddīpana vibhāva*. In *karuṇa rasa* or the aesthetic emotion of the tragic, the stimulative determinants are separation from dear ones, death or fear.

Vyabhicāribhāvas or transient emotions are the temporary feelings that come and go when you are under the grip of a larger emotional state (VII.34). Longing, jealousy or despair can be felt when someone is experiencing sexual desire; so these can be the *vyabhicāribhāvas* of *śṛṅgāra rasa*. According to Bharata, *vyabhicāribhāvas* are thirty-three in number (VII.34). *Anubhāva* is the physical manifestation of the various *vyabhicāribhāvas* resulting from the experience of a particular emotion. For example, *viṣāda* or depression is one of the *vyabhicāribhāvas* of *karuṇa rasa*. An actor experiencing *karuṇa rasa* should enact *viṣāda* through appropriate *anubhāvas*, that is through expressing lack of energy, remaining pensive, heaving sighs, etc. For *raudra rasa* or the aesthetic emotion of anger, *garva* or haughtiness is a *vyabhicāribhāva*, and the actors can present the psycho-physical changes by showing disrespect toward elders, not answering questions or by butting in while others are speaking. It should be remembered that Bharata's *rasasūtra* was advocated for staged performances. So, the *anubhāvas* and *vyabhicāribhāvas* were primarily meant to be enacted for the benefit of spectators. These terms are understood differently in the context of literature that is primarily meant to be read.

A *bhāva* is called so because it brings (*bhāvayanti*) *rasas* into being (VII.1). Bharata mentioned the ideas of *vibhāva*, *anubhāva*, and *vyabhicāribhāva* in relation to the actor, not the reader or spectator. In other words, *vibhāva* is the cause of aesthetic emotion in the actor, not the reader, and *anubhāva* exercises emotional impact only upon the actor.

Though Bharata's celebrated *sūtra* on *rasa* is the founding statement on aesthetics, it referred to only the basic aesthetic elements that constitute *rasa*, without delving into the depth of the process through which these aesthetic elements generate *rasa* in a work of art. It is to be noted that Bharata does not specify where or in whom the *rasa* is aroused. Moreover, the word "*niṣpatti*" was hotly discussed and debated—does it mean "produced," "is manifested," or "felt"? Bharata's *rasasūtra* is not a solution but a riddle, which none of his descendants could quite satisfactorily resolve; it cannot be claimed that it has been resolved even today. He merely formulated the *sūtra* without explaining the ""why" of it, leaving hair-splitting definitions of the process to later generations.

Bhaṭṭa Lollaṭa and *Rasa* in Character

There were numerous commentaries on the *Nāṭyaśāstra* of Bharata, but most of them are irrevocably lost. The major commentators are Bhaṭṭa Lollaṭa, Sri Śaṅkuka, and Bhaṭṭa Nāyaka, besides Abhinavagupta. Bhaṭṭa Lollaṭa in the 9th century was the first of these commentators. According to Bhaṭṭa Lollaṭa, *rasa* is nothing but stable emotions or *sthāyibhāvas* strengthened by aesthetic elements namely *vibhāva*, *anubhāva*, and *vyabhicāribhāva*. If not properly strengthened by aesthetic elements, stable emotions cannot be transformed into aesthetic emotions. For Lollaṭa, the locus of *rasa* is the character although we can figuratively say that the actor also experiences *rasa* by the power of his or her identification with the characters they enact. The spectator figures nowhere in Lollaṭa's theory of *rasa*. According to him, *vibhāvas* are the immediate sources of stimulus to a particular mental state or stable emotion (*sthāyibhāva*). Once the *sthāyibhāva* in the character is aroused by the *vibhāvas*, the *vyabhicāribhāvas* or transitory emotions further accentuate it. After the *sthāyibhāvas* have been properly strengthened with the help of *vyabhicāribhāvas*, the actor, with the help of *anubhāvas*, expresses it as *rasa*. According to Lollaṭa, the *sthāyibhāva*, and *vibhāva* are connected by a product–producer relationship (*utpādya-utpādaka-bhāva-bandha*)—the *vibhāva* produces the *sthāyibhāva*; the *sthāyibhāva* and *anubhāva* by a relation of indicated-indicator (*gamya-gamaka-bhāva-bandha*)—the *anubhāva* shows the mental state or the *sthāyibhāva*; and the *sthāyibhāva* and *vyabhicāribhāva* by a relation of nourishing-nourisher (*poṣya-poṣaka-bhāva-bandha*)—the *vyabhicāribhāva* helps in engendering the *sthāyibhāva* (for a detailed reading of these views, see *Locana* 2.4 *L*; *Abhinavabhāratī* I.266). Lollaṭa believed that *rasa* inheres originally in the character as a readily available product for the spectator to relish. So, his theory is known as *utpatti vāda*, and is more or less consonant with that of Bharata's. Its focus was on the intensified state of the *sthāyibhāva* in the character or the actor, but it could not explain how this was transferred to the spectator who experienced *rasa*. For example, what made the spectator feel the agony of Othello who is forced to kill Desdemona? Bhaṭṭa Lollaṭa's theory failed to explain this.

Śaṅkuka and *Rasa* through Inference

The major counter-argument to Lollaṭa came from Śaṅkuka who argued that *rasa* can only be *inferred* from what is depicted on stage. This approach which depends on *anumāna* or inference is described as the *anumiti vāda*. To him, *rasa* was an experience to be inferred by the spectator rather than an aesthetic object that was presented on stage. He, unlike Lollaṭa, was interested in the manner in which the aesthetic experience evolved from the performance or literary text. Lollaṭa stated that *rasa* is the *sthāyibhāva* that has been intensified with the help of *vibhāva*s. Śaṅkuka opposed this. According to him, the *sthāyibhāva* and *rasa* were two distinct entities; the *rasa* was but an imitation of a *sthāyibhāva*. He pointed out that the *vibhāva*s are the signs through which we infer the presence of *sthāyibhāva*. Sometimes there are no *vibhāva*s, and we become aware of the *sthāyibhāva* only through words; then the problem is that such a *sthāyibhāva* cannot be presented on stage.

Śaṅkuka also refuted Lollaṭa's theorization of the relation between the *vibhāva*s and *sthāyibhāva*s as that of cause and effect. He was of the view that *vibhāva*s are not the causes of *sthāyibhāva* but are symbols that indicate the presence of the *sthāyibhāva*. According to him, *vibhāva* is but an inferential sign and *sthāyibhāva* is what is inferred.

Śaṅkuka had further objections to Lollaṭa's view that *rasa* is stable emotion intensified by *vibhāva*s, etc.—even if it is said that the term *rasa* is reserved exclusively for that single point where a stable emotion intensifies, there are numerous other problems. In *Nāṭyaśāstra* Bharata mentions six varieties for the *sthāyibhāva* of *hāsya*. If *rasa*s were stable emotions at the maximal level, then we would have had six types of comic *rasa*s from six kinds of stable emotion of *hāsya*. But Bharata mentions only one comic *rasa*.

Moreover, according to Bhaṭṭa Lollaṭa, emotions always progressively intensify to the highest level at which point it becomes *rasa*. But what happens in reality, said Śaṅkuka, is the opposite. Grief, for example, is powerful at first, and then it gradually weakens, as opposed to getting strengthened. The intensity of emotions tends to decrease once it has reached the pinnacle; to say that *rasa* arises out of strengthened emotions then, is a fallacy.

According to Śaṅkuka, nobody can perceive stable emotions with their eyes. We can only infer the presence of stable emotions through *vibhāva*, *anubhāva*, and *vyabhicāribhāva*. During a dramatic performance, the actor imitates the stable emotions residing in the characters through his skilful representation of *vyabhicāribhāvas*. It is on this basis that the spectators infer the stable emotion of the character. Therefore, *rasa* is a stable emotion in the characters, imitated by actors through their skilful enactment of *vyabhicāribhāva* and later inferred by the spectators through these aesthetic elements. This inferential theory of Śaṅkuka is known as *anumiti vāda.*

Śaṅkuka's theory does not allow the spectator to doubt the world of illusion created by the performance. He is famous for his "*citra-turaga-nyāya*" or the theory of the painting of a horse. The viewer who sees the picture of a horse does not mistake it for the real horse. But s/he cannot derive the full enjoyment from the picture unless s/he thinks of the horse as real. During the process of aesthetic enjoyment, the viewer/reader will be in a peculiar position where s/he neither takes the horse for real nor doubts its actuality. The reality of the horse is inferred from the artistic depiction of the horse, and this gives rise to aesthetic pleasure or *rasa* (*Locana* 2.4 *L* and *Abhinavabhāratī* 1.266–267). Similarly, in the context of a play or film, the spectator is watching an actor playing a character; not for a moment does she identify the actor with the character. A viewer who watches Amjad Khan act as the villain Gabbar Singh in *Sholay* will hate Gabbar Singh, but not the real-life actor called Amjad Khan. The *rasa* of *bībhatsā* that the spectator feels by watching Gabbar Singh is real in the world of art but s/he does not extend it to the real world by hating Amjad Khan. According to Śaṅkuka, the spectator experiences *rasa* by inferring the emotional aspects of the character through the depiction by the actor. This inference of aesthetic enjoyment, as Śaṅkuka sees it, transcends all doubts about the real existence of the characters, and the spectators accept the world that the characters inhabit. It is important to keep in mind that Śaṅkuka was primarily thinking of *rasa* in the context of the drama, or "rasa seen, in the play" (Pollock, *A Rasa Reader,* 6), and so his idea of *rasa* was that which occurred in audio-visual performance.

Rasa as a Figure of Speech

With the development of *kāvya* or literature that was read as opposed to *nāṭya* that was staged, the concept of *rasa* also underwent a change. *Rasa* came to be understood as part of the literary language or as a figure of speech. This happened from Bhāmaha, the earliest authority on poetics, onwards up to Udbhaṭa. Bhāmaha in his *Kāvyālaṅkāra* maintained that the soul of poetry is figurative language, and *rasa* was one of the many *alaṅkāras* or ornaments that helped to enhance the poetic effect. *Rasa* is evoked with the help of three categories of verbal expressions of emotions: *rasavat* or statements where *rasas* like *śṛṅgāra* are manifested, *preyaḥ* or "affectionate utterance," and *ūrjasvin* or "haughty declaration" (*Kāvyālaṅkāra* III.5–7). Likewise, Daṇḍin also reserved no special category for *rasa* other than that of a figure of speech. In Daṇḍin's *Kāvyādarśa*, the idea of *rasa* was used in two different senses—first as a general term for any ornate expression and second as a technical term for various instances of affective expressions such as *rasavat*, *preyaḥ*, and *ūrjasvin* (*Kāvyādarśa* II.275–284). To him, the *guṇas* or poetic qualities were more important in the making of poetry, and *rasa* was a by-product when these qualities were present in the right proportion. Vāmana, who emphasized the importance of style or *rīti*, also placed *rasa* in a subservient position. In Udbhaṭa's critical corpus too the idea of *rasa* largely remained as a figure of speech. By adding "quiescent" or *samāhita* to the already exiting category of *preyaḥ* (the affectionate), *rasavat* (the *rasa*-laden), and *ūrjasvin* (the haughty speech), Udbhaṭa increased the number of *rasa*-related figures from three to four. He also mentioned the components conducive for the production of aesthetic emotion namely *vibhāva* (foundational factor), *anubhāva* (expression of emotion), *vyabhicāribhāva* (transitory emotion), *sthāyibhāva* (stable emotion), and *svaśabda* (the proper name of *rasas*) (*Kāvyālaṅkāra-sāra-saṃgraha* IV.2). Udbhaṭa's view that the utterance of proper names of *rasas* such as *śṛṅgāra*, *karuṇa*, etc. can bring *rasa* into being was later criticized by Ānandavardhana in his *Dhvanyāloka* (I.4 g *A*).

Rudraṭa was the first literary theoretician in Sanskrit poetics to treat *rasa* as an independent category (Pollock, *A Rasa Reader*, 11). His theoretical corpus is particularly important in the sense that he challenged Bharata's category of eight *rasas* and maintained that since any emotion can be relished, the number of *rasas* in principle is virtually limitless (*Kāvyālankāra* XII.4). He is also the first literary theoretician in the world of classical Sanskrit literary theory to assign a didactic function to *rasa*, a view which was later reinforced by writers like Bhaṭṭa Nāyaka, Abhinavagupta, Kuntaka, and Bhoja.

Ānandavardhana and *Rasa* through Suggestion

Ānandavardhana's theory of *rasa* called into question Udbhaṭa's view that *rasa* can be brought into being by merely uttering the names of *rasas*, such as *śṛṅgāra* or *hāsya*. Ānandavardhana negated this view definitively. He observed that *rasa* can only be suggested with the help of aesthetic elements like *vibhāva*, *anubhāva*, and *vyabhicāribhāva*. If we were able to experience *rasa* simply by referring to their proper names, we would have been able to create emotions, whenever we merely say *śṛṅgāra* or *karuṇa*. This obviously does not happen (1.4g*A*).

However, what makes Ānandavardhana important in the discussion of *rasa* is his magnum opus, the *Dhvanyāloka*, through which he gave a completely different direction to further intellectual explorations of *rasa*. He shifted the basis of *rasa* to meaning and gave a semantic dimension to the concept of *rasa*. He was emphatic in his assertion that *rasa* is the sole purpose of literature and that any work which does not abound in *rasa* cannot be defined as literature as such. His theory of *dhvani* or suggestion maintained that the core of a *kāvya* or literary work was what it suggested rather than what it denoted or connoted. *Dhvani* was the tertiary layer of meaning that lay beyond the primary and secondary meanings, and this is what gave rise to *rasa* or *rasadhvani*. Ideally, *rasa* cannot be expressed; it had to be suggested.

So Ānandavardhana felt that *rasa* had to be suggested subtly, and this explains why he opposed Udbhaṭa's view that *rasa* can be evoked by uttering its name. According to Ānandavardhana, the most delicate of all *rasa*s is *śṛṅgāra rasa* or the aesthetic emotion of the erotic. It is the most predominant of all *rasa*s because it is more pleasing than the others. He was of the view that poets had to be cautious while dealing with this *rasa*; since desire is an integral element of human life, even a slight flaw could jeopardize the poet's position and destroy the emotion (*Dhvanyāloka* 3.28*A*).

Moreover, there were four impediments to the proper actualization of aesthetic emotion, which the poet had to be careful to address. First of all, a poet should not bring in aesthetic elements which are contrary to the *rasa* under consideration. For instance, philosophical discussions of life and death are inappropriate in lovers' conversations. Imagine lines like "Life is a tale told by an idiot, full of sound and fury, signifying nothing" coming from Romeo when he meets Juliet in the balcony on a moonlit night! It would destroy the *śṛṅgāra rasa*.

Second, a poet should know when and where to stop in his evocation of a *rasa*. If he continues to stimulate a particular *rasa* even after it has reached its high point of intensity, that would play havoc with the *rasa*. Emotions in excess can be counterproductive; for example, a long-drawn-out lament over death can turn a potentially tragic scene into an extremely tedious one. Similarly, if the poet discourses on something completely unrelated to the topic under consideration, *rasa* will slowly ebb away. Inappropriate behavior on the part of the noble characters is another factor that is counterproductive to the *rasa* experience. Ānanda observed that if a woman of noble birth explicitly expresses her sexual desires, that would be against the decorum of the period and disturb the aesthetic relish of the readers. This example might seem politically incorrect to readers today, but we have to keep in mind that Ānandavardhana was writing according to the sociocultural values of his times (*Dhvanyāloka* 3.18–19*K*). However, this was one of the criticisms against D. H. Lawrence's *Lady Chatterley's Lover*, where the aristocratic Constance Chatterley uses four-letter words that were not in keeping with her upbringing and social position.

In all the discussions we have seen so far, *rasa* was believed to belong to the character, actor or the poet. Ānanda held that a poetic composition would be able to evoke *rasa* only if the poet who produces it experiences that *rasa* to the maximum extent possible. Emphasizing this point, Ānandavardhana in his *Dhvanyāloka* referred to the first *kāvya*, the *Rāmāyaṇa* where *kāvya* issued forth from the author's intense grief at the death of a pair of mating birds at the hands of a hunter. Vālmīki, who happens to see a hunter kill a mating bird, curses the hunter out of his intense grief. The intensity of this sorrow makes him spontaneously utter a verse, a form that is outside the realm of ordinary speech. Summing up his observations, Ānanda said that if a poet brims over with *rasa*, poetry will also be laden with *rasa*; if not, it will remain bereft of *rasa* (*Dhvanyāloka* 3.41–42a*A*). *Rasa* here is conceptualized as the passionate intensity with which a writer feels about an incident or person. This is somewhat reminiscent of Wordsworth's definition of poetry as the "spontaneous overflow of powerful feelings."

It is interesting however that Ānandavardhana also considered *rasa* as a figure of speech. But according to him, when *rasa* appears as a figure of speech, it is called *rasavatalaṅkāra*. If a particular aesthetic emotion is subordinate to the primary aesthetic emotion of an event in a *kāvya*, it is called *rasavat* (2.5 *K* and *A*). A case in point is a woman's feeling of anger upon meeting her lover after a long time of separation. Though overwhelmed by her love for him, she may scold him or sulk for having stayed away from her for a long time. In this instance, her feeling of love is expressed through the aesthetic emotion of anger or *raudra rasa*. Therefore, *raudra rasa*, which remains subordinate to *śṛṅgāra rasa*, functions as a *rasavat alaṅkāra* adorning *śṛṅgāra rasa*.

Ānandavardhana also refuted the observation of some critics that *rasavat* occurs only when a sentient entity is portrayed. The critics said that when *rasavat* occurs in the context of inanimate things, what we get is a simile. Ānanda countered this by saying that if that were the case, the figures of speech like similes would be practically non-existent because in *kāvya* a non-sentient thing is often compared to a sentient entity. If the statement that *rasavat* arises only in the case of a sentient entity were true, many great passages will be bereft of simile. Ingalls explains, "The answer to this argument is that great passages of poetry, which everyone recognizes as the paradigms of *rasa*—for example, the description of the oncoming season of rain in the *Rāmāyaṇa*, or Purūravas' apostrophes to nature in the mad scene of the *Vikramorvaśīya*—will lack *rasa* by the objector's criterion" (note to 2.5 e *A*, *245*).

Bhaṭṭa Nāyaka and *Rasa* in the Reader/Spectator

After Ānandavardhana, the next major literary theoretician to deal with the concept of *rasa* is Bhaṭṭa Nāyaka. His major work is *Hṛdayadarpaṇa* which was lost beyond recall. So, we know of his theory only through excerpts quoted by critics like Abhinavagupta or Mammaṭa. We have to be satisfied with a partial understanding of his critical corpus and all the failings that such a partial understanding entails. However, it is safe to say that he was the first to bring the viewer into the *rasa* experience.

Bhaṭṭa Nāyaka argued that *rasa* is not a perceptible product brought forth by the composite working of artistic elements. If *rasa* were produced or manifested in the actor, then it would not have become a "taste" for the spectator. This is because there is no way we can access somebody else's experience through inference. It is also wrong to argue, he said, that *rasa* is *produced* within the spectator. If *rasa* were produced within the spectator, it would again bring about another set of problems. The spectator would be so immersed in one or another state of mind—passion, disgust, shame, etc.—to the point of not being able to enjoy the dramatic performance on stage. That is to say, if *rasa* were internal to the spectator, one would feel actual pain and never again go to the theatre to see sad plays. Second, if *rasa* has to be produced within the spectator, there should be a *vibhāva* (causal factor). During a dramatic performance, what can possibly become a *vibhāva* for the generation of *rasa* in the spectator is another character. But in reality, a character can become the *vibhāva* for only another character. In other words, Sītā can become a *vibhāva* only for Rāma the character, not for the spectator (2.4 *L*).

Since Sītā and the spectator's wife could probably share the property of being a wife, one can argue that the image of Sītā drives home to the spectator's mind thoughts about his own wife, thereby stimulating his *sthāyibhāva*. But Bhaṭṭa Nāyaka ruled out this possibility; there was no point of comparison between an ordinary woman and somebody like Sītā who was the consort of Lord Rāma. For instance, the *śṛṅgāra rasa* in *Uttararāmacarita* is evoked by the romance between Rāma and Sītā; how could the spectator experience this *rasa*, knowing fully well that Sītā is a divine presence who is beyond his mundane sphere of life? Besides, one cannot find incidents similar to everything that is presented in a drama to get his or her stable emotions stimulated. To give a more modern example, we appreciate a film like Francis

Ford Coppola's *Godfather* even without any prior knowledge or experience of the underworld of the mafia and crime.

According to Bhaṭṭa Nāyaka, *rasa* comes into being only when the reader or spectator enjoys it with the help of two elements called *bhāvanā* and *bhoga* which are crucial in the aesthetic experience. The literary language or *abhidhā* as employed by Bhaṭṭa Nāyaka is marked by the presence of figures of speech and poetic merits. *Abhidhā* is endowed with a special power called *bhāvanā* or revelation. This is how he distinguishes between the two: "Rasa is revealed (*bhāvayamāna*) by a special power assumed by words in poetry and drama, the power of revelation (*bhāvana*)—to be distinguished from the power of denotation (*abhidhā*)..." (Gnoli 45). This power which has the special function of "suppressing the thick layer of stupor occupying our consciousness, is a generalization or universalization of the things presented or described" (quoted by Gnoli XXI). During the process of universalization or *sādhāraṇīkaraṇa*, the aesthetic elements such as *vibhāva*, *anubhāva*, and *vyabhicāribhāva* are stripped of their particularities such as "this is the divine figure Sītā," or "she is a queen," or "she is another person's (Rāma's) wife." We have already seen that particularities of characters and emotions are always impediments to the enjoyment of *rasa*. But after the process of universalization, what we get is Sītā emptied of all her particularities, which enables us to experience the stable emotion that Rāma feels for Sītā.

Upon the realization of *rasa*, a third stage known as *bhoga* (aesthetic relish) begins. "The *Rasa*, revealed by this power [of *bhāvanā*] is then enjoyed (*bhuj*) through a sort of enjoyment different from direct experience, from memory, etc."

(Gnoli 46). It is clear that Bhaṭṭa Nāyaka believed that the enjoyment of *rasa* is different from our normal experience of emotions. During the enjoyment of *rasas*, we do not experience the negative effect that the counterparts of these aesthetic emotions—the *sthāyibhāvas*—have on us in our real life. For example, we enjoy *bhayānaka rasa* or *bībhatsā* without being frightened or repulsed. This explains why we enjoy watching horror films or read extremely depressing novels. An aesthetic emotion universalized by the power of *bhāvanā* gives us a sense of pleasure. This experience of universalized emotion is so special that the spectator never thinks that it is somebody else's feeling. There is a complete identification with the emotion that the character feels. However, the experience of these universalized emotions differs radically from real-life emotions. We are traumatized by tragic events in our life; however, reading or watching *Hamlet* gives us supreme pleasure despite its oppressively tragic atmosphere, because it pertains to the artistic realm.

Sādhāraṇīkaraṇa or the process of universalization is at the core of Bhaṭṭa Nāyaka's concept of the *rasa* experience. He also considered the process by which the spectator is able to forget, at least temporarily, their personal and practical interests, and be immersed in another character's experience, as analogical to spiritual experience. As Gnoli explains:

> *Rasa*, the aesthetic experience revealed by the power of revelation (*bhāvanā*), is not noetic in character, is not a perception, but an experience, a fruition (*bhoga*). This fruition is characterized by a state of lysis (*laya*), of rest into our own consciousness, the pervasion of consciousness by

> bliss and light: it belongs to the same order as the enjoyment of the supreme brahman. (xxiii)

This shows how his philosophical perceptions colored his aesthetic concepts. More importantly, it also reveals the seriousness with which our ancient critics approached the idea of art and art experience. Furthermore, Bhaṭṭa Nāyaka differed from many of his contemporaries in his view of the purpose of art. He did not agree that the primary function of art was to instruct; he believed that instruction was secondary to the artistic value of the work (for a detailed reading of Bhaṭṭa Nāyaka's theory, read *Abhinavabhāratī* 270–271; *Kāvyaprakāśa* 56 and 2.4 *L* of *Dhvanyāloka*).

Abhinavagupta and the Experience of Aesthetic Relish

Another major turning point in the history of *rasa* was provided by Abhinavagupta, who wrote a commentary or *Locana* on Ānandavardhana's *Dhvanyāloka*. His commentary on Bharata's *Nāṭyaśāstra* called *Abhinavabhāratī* also further expounded his views on *rasa*.

According to Abhinava, there is a world of difference between *sthāyibhāva* and *rasa*. What we find in the character is *sthāyibhāva* or stable emotion, not *rasa* or aesthetic emotion. What Othello experiences when he is forced to kill Desdemona is the stable emotion of grief. Neither the actor nor the spectator shares it while acting or watching a play. If they were experiencing the *sthāyibhāva* of grief, they would not be able to endure it and would leave the play. What the actor or spectator/reader feels is the aesthetic emotion or *rasa*, which merely resembles the real-world emotion; they are able to enjoy it only because they know that it does not really affect them.

Abhinavagupta observed that actors suggest the stable emotions of the characters with the help of various modes of acting in the course of a dramatic performance. This stable emotion that is suggested comes into contact with the stable emotion of the spectators in such a way that they are stripped of their spatiotemporal or "realistic" aspects. So, if we are watching a play based on the *Rāmāyaṇa*, we cease to think of Sītā as the wife of Rāma but as a woman who is forced to undergo painful experiences. We identify with the character and experience grief which is not of this world but of the temporal world of art. Abhinavagupta agreed with Bhaṭṭa Nāyaka in this conception of "aesthetic emotions" or *rasa*s as distinct from emotions in real life. According to Abhinava, whatever may be the nature of *rasa* vis-à-vis the nature of their counterparts in real life, *rasa* always provided the readers with an *alaukika* or out-of-the-world experience.

The aesthetic experience does not have any practical aspects:

> In aesthetic experience, what happens is … the birth of the aesthetic tasting of the artistic expression. Such an experience, just as a flower born of magic, has, as its essence, solely the present, it is correlated neither with what came before nor with what comes after. This experience is therefore different both from the ordinary experience and from the religious one. (quoted in Gnoli xxxiv)

He also stressed the communal nature of such aesthetic experience, especially when spectators are watching a performance. The several individuals who are watching a performance lose their respective egos or "I"s to form a collective, unique "I," which is distinct from their individual selves. This is somewhat akin to the spiritual experience that arises when a group of devotees take part in a ritual, guided by a common goal and belief. However, the aesthetic experience is different in that here, the individual self is not completely lost; all the emotions and facts of everyday life are present in a transformed manner in the enjoyment of art. As Gnoli explains, "Art is not absence of life—every element of life appears in the aesthetic experience—but it is life itself, pacified and detached from all passions" (XL). For Abhinavagupta, the aesthetic and the religious experience have the same source, because "both are characterized by a state of consciousness self-centred, implying the suppression of any practical desire, and hence the merging of the subject into his object, to the exclusion of everything else" (XLI). This oneness that is achieved with the "object" or the work of art is a state of complete mental independence where you do not have to look outside yourself for bliss. This state of complete beatitude is lysis, repose or *laya*.

This state of repose is accompanied by a sense of wonder which Abhinavagupta terms "*camatkāra*." This term was probably first used by Utpaladeva who was Abhinavagupta's teacher and used again by Bhaṭṭa Nāyaka. This term becomes a distinctive trait of the aesthetic experience as outlined by Abhinavagupta. According to him, *camatkāra* may be defined "as an immersion in an enjoyment (*bhogāveśah*) which can never satiate and is thus uninterrupted..." (Gnoli 59). Since "both the mystical and aesthetic experience imply the cessation of a world—the ordinary, historical world, the *saṃsāra*—and its sudden replacement by a new dimension of reality. In this sense, the two are wonder or surprise" (XLVI). The aesthetic sensibility, then, is nothing but a capacity for wonder (for a detailed reading of these views see, *Abhinavabhāratī* I.272–282).

But Rāmacandra and Guṇacandra in their *Nāṭyadarpaṇa* challenged Abhinavagupta's view that *rasa*, be it *śṛṅgāra* or *bībhatsā*, is always pleasurable. According to them, aesthetic emotions, like actual emotions, could have a negative or positive impact upon people. Since *rasa*s are always an assorted concoction of both pleasant and unpleasant experiences, the responses will also vary. So, while emotions like *śṛṅgāra*, *hāsya*, *vīra*, and *adbhuta* provide the readers with pleasure, *karuṇa*, *raudra*, *bībhatsā*, and *bhayānaka* have the power to unsettle the readers (158).

Abhinavagupta rejected Bhaṭṭa Nāyaka's observation that spectators will not be able to relate to or identify with characters or events that are supernatural or extra-worldly. For instance, Bhaṭṭa Nāyaka said that extraordinary deeds like Rāma's act of building a bridge across the sea will not win a sympathetic response from everybody. However, according to Abhinava, the human mind is characterized by a great variety of latent impressions (*vāsanā*) born out of desires. Consequently, we can identify with anything we see on the stage, however much we are separated from events or characters by birth, place, and time (*Abhinavabhāratī* I.258). This is why we lament the fate of Oedipus, laugh teary-eyed with Chaplin, feel the humiliation of Śakuntalā in Duṣyanta's court and delight in the magical world of Harry Potter.

The *Sahṛdaya*

However, not everybody can experience such aesthetic delight. We have already seen how only a mind with aesthetic sensibility would have the capacity for wonder which is the basic requirement to experience delight. This is a quality that only a *sahṛdaya* can experience. A *sahṛdaya*—literally meaning one whose heart beats in tandem with yours—is the ideal reader or spectator who is receptive to the artistic stimulations presented by the world conjured up by the writer.

This receptivity is a gift you are born with and also a quality that you cultivate. The reading and appreciation of Sanskrit *kāvya* was always an elite business. Along with poets, the readers of Sanskrit *kāvya* were also supposed to be versed in the nuances of literary writing to better appreciate a work. Hence, Lienhard says, "the ability to enjoy *kāvya* presupposed mainly adequate learning and familiarity with the special nature of literary texts" (41). Lienhard adds,

> The reader or listener had a command not only of the literary language, its means of expression and style, but was also familiar with the sources and technique of poetry. . . . He also had a knowledge of metrics, decorative figures (*alaṅkāras*), the theory of the sentiments (*rasa*) and the implied (*dhvani*); indeed, he might even be a specialist in some other branches of science as well. (31)

Viśvanātha's observation in *Sāhityadarpaṇa* about a *rasika* or "a reader capable of enjoying *rasa*" is also important in this context. For Viśvanātha, a *rasika*'s ability to savour *rasa* is simultaneously the result of his predisposition for art (*vāsanā*) that comes not only from this birth but from the previous births as well. In the present birth, one develops this special mindset to enjoy *rasa* through one's constant study of literary works. If the study of literature were not necessary to relish aesthetic emotion, Viśvanātha notes, even the theologians versed in the Vedas and the students of logic would have been able to savor *rasa*. According to him, if we do not consider one's predisposition toward art from the previous birth as an important causal force for being a *sahṛdaya*, we will not be able to explain why some students of *kāvya* are incapable of relishing *rasa*, despite their constant endeavors to do so. Quoting Dharmadatta, Viśvanātha opines that a person without these prerequisites for being a *rasika* remains as insensitive as "the wood-work, the walls and the stones" in the theatre (45).

This reader/viewer is expected to have two major attributes: (i) a rich world of experience, because only a person with varied experience of the world will be able to pick up on the hints in the work of art and make the necessary connections, and (ii) a sensibility (*pratibhā*) that is trained to appreciate poetic beauty. For Abhinavagupta, the essential quality of a responsive reader (*sahṛdayatva*) is their ability to identify with the heart of the poet (*kavihṛdayatādātmyāpattiyogyatā*; *Abhinavabhāratī* 339). The innate sensibility has to be polished so that it becomes mirror-like; only then can it identify with the emotions suggested by the writer and experience the feeling of *rasa* like dry wood catching fire (*śuṣkakāṣṭhāgnidṛṣṭānta*; *Dhvanyāloka* 2.10L). It is evident that Abhinavagupta did not consider the possibility of a resistant reader or subversive reading. This sort of reading, according to him, would be antithetical to the production of *rasa* and hence becomes a futile aesthetic endeavor.

Abhinavagupta emphasized the importance of possessing a finely tuned sensibility because he felt that the realization of *rasa* was not a natural and spontaneous process. There are various aspects that hinder a *sahṛdaya*'s relishing of aesthetic emotions. These *vighna*s or impediments could be located within the spectator or the work of art or external circumstances. These are seven in number:

(i) the unsuitability, that is to say, the lack of verisimilitude;
(ii) the immersion in temporal and spatial determinations perceived as exclusively one's own or exclusively those of another;
(iii) the fact of being at the mercy of our own sensations of pleasure, etc.;
(iv) the defective state of the means of perception;
(v) the lack of evidence;
(vi) the lack of some predominant factor;
(vii) and the presence of doubt (Gnoli 62–63)

Sanskrit poets and literary theoreticians often held the view that an author's worth can be judged only by an able reader. For example, Kālidāsa, in both *Raghuvaṃśa* and *Abhijñānaśākuntala*, talks about the importance of a learned reader in judging the creativity of a poet. In *Raghuvaṃśa*, Kālidāsa says that just as gold is tested with the help of a touchstone so also the heart of a sensible reader functions as a means to judge the quality of a poem (I.10). In *Abhijñānaśākuntala*, he opines that a drama cannot be deemed successful until and unless it is well appreciated by the connoisseurs of art (50). Further emphasizing the importance of the reader in the appreciation of literary works, the 8th century-poet and playwright Bhavabhūti, in his play *Mālatīmādhava*, says that a reader who can properly appreciate his [Bhavabhūti's] poetic merit and who can identify with his creative heart (*samānahṛdaya*) is yet to be born (I.6). According to Rājaśekhara, "Only a good reader can understand the effort and intention of a poet. . . . In the absence of a good reader, all efforts of a poet go in vain" (48). According to Rājaśekhara, a reader's capacity to appreciate a poem is called, *bhāvayatri pratibhā* (46).

Ānandavardhana, in his lost work *Viṣamabāṇalīlā*, opined that the actualization of *kāvya* happens only in the presence of *sahṛdayas* or men of taste just as a lotus blooms when graced by the rays of the sun: "Virtues blossom,/when admired by men of taste/When graced by the sun's rays,/a lotus becomes a lotus [*kamala*]" (quoted in *Dhvanyāloka* 207). In another poem often attributed to Kālidāsa, the speaker makes a strong plea to Lord Brahmā to spare him from the punishment of presenting his poem to an insensitive listener or *arasika* (*arasikeṣu kavitva nivedanaṃ śirasi mā likha mā likha*). Acknowledging the importance of a *sahṛdaya* in the appreciation of a work of art, another anonymous poet declares that the act of a poet appreciating his work of art is as inappropriate as a father appreciating the beauty of his daughter. Although a poet, the poem says, is the creator of a text, its merit has to be ultimately judged by the readers erudite in *kāvyaśāstra* (*kaviḥ karoti kāvyāni svādu jānāti paṇḍitaḥ|sundarāyapi lāvaṇyaṃ patirjānāti no pitā* ||). It is clear that a work of art becomes meaningful only when it succeeds in evoking the desired aesthetic response in the spectator/reader.

Aspects of *Rasa*

What was the function of *rasa*? According to Abhinavagupta, what lay beneath the pleasing veneer of aesthetic emotion is undoubtedly a desire to instruct. For him, *rasa* was a sugar-coated pill for the young princes who were not well-versed in the scriptures or history. Abhinava notes in his commentary on Ānanda's *Dhvanyāloka*,

> Princes, who are not educated in scripture—those works of *śruti* and *smṛti* which consist in commands, like those of a master, to do this or that—and who have not received instruction from history... and who are therefore in pressing need of instruction . . . can be given instruction in the four goals of man only by our entering into their hearts. And what enters into the heart is the relish of *rasa* (*rasāsvāda,* the imaginative experience of emotion). (3.10–14 f *L*)

Besides Abhinavagupta, Bhaṭṭa Nāyaka, Kuntaka, Mammaṭa, and Bhoja shared the same opinion about the didactic function of *rasa*.

Another crucial contribution of Abhinava to the theoretical corpus of *rasa* was his addition of *śānta rasa* to the already existing eight *rasa*s of Bharata. As far as Abhinava was concerned, *śama* is the *sthāyibhāva* of *śānta rasa* and its *vibhāva*s include ascetic practices and association with *yogin*s. The exponents of the Caitanya School like Rupa Goswami came up with another *rasa*, namely *bhakti rasa*. *Bhakti rasa* is supreme bliss that a devotee experiences while watching the emotional bond between Rādhā and Kṛṣṇa.

King Bhoja's conception of *rasa* was also unique. He reduced the number of *rasa*s to just one. According to him, all *rasas* result from *śṛṅgāra* (*Śṛṅgāraprakāśa* I, 2); this explains the title of his work *Śṛṅgāraprakāśa*. Here the idea of *śṛṅgāra* should not be taken in the literal sense of the term. What Bhoja meant by *śṛṅgāra* in this context is the keen desire for something or someone, which leads to various states of mind (*Śṛṅgāraprakāśa* II, 614). Bhoja also went on to argue that the aesthetic emotion of the erotic (*śṛṅgāra rasa*) is the source from which "passion" comes forth. While "passion" generates actual emotions in real life, art with the help of its aesthetic elements produces emotions in a pleasurable manner without negative impact. The argument that *śṛṅgāra* forms the basis for *raudra* may seem counterintuitive, but this resembles the Freudian concept of Eros (represented by the God of Love) as the basic human drive that prompts one to live, whereas Thanatos constitutes the death drive. Like the Freudian Eros, *śṛṅgāra* forms the foundational emotive impulse for Bhoja.

Another major figure who is important in the intellectual discourse on *rasa* in the post-Abhinavagupta period is Viśvanāthadeva. A Vedāntin by his disciplinary affiliation, Viśvanāthadeva brings in a Vedāntic perspective to the idea of *rasa*. He followed the *Upaniṣadic* model of the five sheaths of the self, where the last one is the *ānandamaya kośa* or the "bliss element." The bliss element, says Viśvanāthadeva, is obscured by our inextricable attachment with the phenomenal world. However, during one's experience of aesthetic emotion or *rasa*, one transcends these impediments posed by the material world and eventually achieves the ultimate bliss element (*Sāhityasudhāsindhu* 92–93). The last literary critic to see the idea of *rasa* from a radically new perspective is Jagannātha Paṇḍita. Jagannātha, like his predecessor Viśvanāthadeva, believes that the aesthetic experience is equivalent to the spiritual realization of self. According to Jagannātha, apart from spiritual liberation, aesthetic experience is the only way to break free from the concerns of quotidian life and attain the higher realms of spirituality (*Rasagaṅgādhara* 25).

Conclusion

The *rasa* theory like much of classical literary theory fell into intellectual doldrums since the time of Jagannātha. Although it retained its supremacy in the domain of classical poetics, it did not undergo any significant revision with respect to its foundational concepts. However, this theory which is an analysis of our emotional response to art and literature is of great interest to cognitive science scholars today in the West and India.

A contemporary avatar of *rasa* theory can be seen in Affect theory. What is commonly called Affect theory pays considerable attention to the role of affect or emotions in an attempt to understand their various manifestations in human behavior, culture, and society. According to Marta Figlerowicz, the "Affect theory is grounded in movements or flashes of mental or somatic activity rather than causal narratives of their origins and endpoints" (3). An interdisciplinary field in literary criticism, the Affect theory draws considerable inspiration from the works of psychologist Silvan Tomkins (1911–1999) and his idea of three kinds of affects, namely positive, negative, and neutral affects. He identifies nine primary affects which are reminiscent of the nine *rasa*s. As far as Tomkins is concerned, affect is purely a biological manifestation of emotions. As opposed to remaining deep-seated in a subject's mind, it manifests itself through bodily changes. However, Tomkins's work is primarily in the area of Psychology, while critics like Brian Massumi and Eve Sedgwick Kosofsky deal with the role of emotions in responses to art. Patrick Colm Hogan is another scholar who has worked extensively on the role of emotions in stories and storytelling.

The *rasa* theory continues to be of significance even today, as it explains the alchemy of art, the magic that transforms words on the page or characters on the stage into imaginary worlds that we can inhabit and respond to.

Works Cited

Abhinavagupta. *Abhinavabharatī*. Available at: http://www.columbia.edu/~aso2101/projects/abhinavabharati/abhinavabharati-test/testpage.html#. Accessed July 20, 2015.

Abhinavagupta. *Locana*. In *The Dhvanyāloka of Ānandavardhana with the Locana of Abhinavagupta*. Translated and edited by Daniel Ingalls, Jeffrey Masson, and M. V. Patwardhan, Harvard University Press, 1990.

Ānandavardhana. *The Dhvanyāloka of Ānandavardhana with the Locana of Abhinavagupta*. Translated and edited by Daniel Ingalls, Jeffrey Masson, and M. V. Patwardhan, Harvard: Harvard University Press, 1990.

Bharata. *Nāṭyaśāstram*. Translated (Malayalam) and edited by K. P. Narayana Pisharody, Kerala Sahitya Akademi, 2004.

Bhavabhūti. *Mālatīmadhava*, Government Central Book Depot, 1876.

Bhāmaha. *Kāvyālaṅkāra*. Edited by B. N. Sarma and Baldeva Upadhyay, Chowkhamba Sanskrit Series Office, 1998.

Bhoja. *Śṛṅgāraprakāśa*, Vols 1 and 2, edited by G. S. Josyer, 1955 and 1963.

Daṇḍin. *Kāvyādarśa of Daṇḍin*. Edited by P. Tarkabagisa, Royal Asiatic Society, 1962.

Figlerowicz, Marta. "Affect Theory Dossier: An Introduction." *Qui Parle*, vol. 20, no. 2, Spring/Summer 2012: 3–18.

Gnoli, Raniero. *The Aesthetic Experience According to Abhinavagupta*, Motilal Banarsidass, 1985.

Ingalls, Daniel H.H. "Introduction." *Ānandavardhana, Dhvanyāloka of Ānandavardhana with the Locana of Abhinavagupta*. Translated and edited by Daniel Ingalls, Jeffrey Masson, and M. V. Patwardhan, Harvard: Harvard University Press, 1990, pp. 1–39.

Jagannātha. *The Rasagaṅgādhara of Jagannātha Paṇḍita with the Commentary of Nāgeśa Bhaṭṭa*. Edited by D. Prasad and K. P. Parab, The Nirnaya Sagara Press, 1888.

Kālidāsa. *The Recognition of Śakuntalā*. Clay Sanskrit Library, 2006.

———. *Raghuvaṃśa*. Gopal Narayen & Co., 1922.

Lienhard, Siegfried. *A History of Classical Poetry: Sanskrit, Pali, Prakrit*, Otto Harrassowitz Verlag, 1984.

Pandey, K. C. *Comparative Aesthetics*, Vol I (Indian Aesthetics), Chowkhamba Sanskrit Series, 1950.

Pollock, Sheldon. *The Rasa Reader*, Columbia University Press, 2016.

———. "What was Bhaṭṭanāyaka Saying: The Hermenuetical Transformation of Indian Aesthetics." In *Epic and Argument in Sanskrit Literary Theory*. Edited by Sheldon Pollock, Manohar Publishers, 2010, pp. 143–184.

Rājaśekhara. *Kāvyamīmāṃsa*. Edited by Sadhana Parashar, D. K. Print World, 2000.

Rudraṭa. *Kāvyālaṅkāra*, Nirnaya Sagar Press, 1886.

Udbhaṭa. *Kāvyālaṅkārasārasaṃgraha with the commentary, the Laghuvṛtti of Indurāja*. Edited by Narayana Daso Banhatti, Bhandarkar Oriental Research Institute, 1982.

Viśvanātha. *The Sāhityadarpaṇa*. Translated by J. R. Ballantyne and Pramada Dasa Mitra, Motilal Banarasidas Publishers, 2016.

Viśvanāthadeva. *Sāhityasudhāsindhu*. Edited by Ram Pratap, Bharatiya Vidya Prakashan, 1978.

3

Alaṅkāra

Alaṅkāra has always been an important category of theoretical scrutiny in Sanskrit poetics; an approximate translation of the word would be "figures of speech" or "rhetoric." It is interesting to note that the term *alaṅkāra* was used in Sanskrit poetics in two senses—first as a specific term to signify what was conventionally regarded as figures of speech, and second to denote anything that adds beauty to the poem. *Alaṅkāra* being an important constituent of poetry, the word *alaṅkāraśāstra* in course of time came to represent "literary theory" itself.

The word *alaṅkāra* etymologically means "that which creates beauty." It is derived from the Sanskrit root *kṛ* (to do) with the prefix *alaṃ*, which means "to decorate," "to adorn," etc. The idea of *alaṅkāra* as an ornament implies that there is something to be ornamented. It would be logical to assume then that the thing to be ornamented is the body of the poem. Bimal Krishna Matilal is of the view that we can identify two main theories of *alaṅkāra* in Sanskrit *kāvya*—one, which considers *alaṅkāra* as the special external embellishments (such as *upamā* or *rūpaka*) to the body of poetry, and the other which considers it as everything that adds beauty to a poem. While the idea of ornamentation is relevant to the first theory, the second theory would consider *alaṅkāra* to be beauty itself. Vāmana has used it in these two senses in his

Kāvyālaṅkārasūtravṛtti: "*kāvyam grāhyamalaṅkārāt* (I.1.1) (poetry appears to be attractive to us because of figure of speech)" and later "*saundaryamalaṅkāraḥ* (*alaṅkāra* means beauty" (I.I.2). Bhāmaha, who is considered to be the main proponent of the *Alaṅkāra School*, used the term in this sense. "He implicitly accepted that *alaṅkāra* constitutes the very nature of poetry. This consists in the composition of speech and its meaning in an 'oblique' (*vakra*) manner. It is not only what you say but how you say it" (Matilal 374).

Alaṅkāras are usually divided into two—*śabdālaṅkāra* and *arthālaṅkāra*. *Śabdālaṅkāra* includes all those figures of speech that add to the auditory effect like alliteration, assonance, consonance or pun. *Arthālaṅkāra* is anything that enhances the meaning of a word, like simile or metaphor. The difference in languages makes it difficult for us to draw exact parallels between figures of speech in Sanskrit and English, but there are similarities like the devices of *upamā* and simile or *anuprāsa* and alliteration.

Critics on *Alaṅkāra*

Although Bhāmaha is the name closely associated with the *Alaṅkāra School*, Bharata was the first literary theoretician to define and illustrate *alaṅkāras*. For Bharata, *alaṅkāras* are four in number namely *upamā*, *dīpaka*, *rūpaka*, and *yamaka* (XVII.37). Dramaturgy was the primary concern of Bharata in *Nāṭyaśāstra*, and so he did not analyze the idea of *alaṅkāra* in great detail. Other writers before Bhāmaha had often briefly talked about the idea of figures of speech. A few examples in this respect include a chapter on *alaṅkāra* in *Viṣṇudharmottarapurāṇa* which is of unknown authorship and *Bhaṭṭikāvya* (also known as *Rāvaṇavadha*) by Bhaṭṭi. *Viṣṇudharmottarapurāṇa* contains about 1,000 verses on the topics of *nāṭyaśāstra* and *alaṅkāra*; chapters 14, 15, and 16 are particularly important as far as *alaṅkāra* is concerned. While chapter 14 lists and defines figures of speech in *kāvya*, chapter 15 distinguishes *kāvya* from *itihāsa*, and chapter 17 speaks of *rūpakas* and their 12 varieties. *Bhaṭṭikāvya*, a poem in 22 cantos, was composed primarily for illustrating the rules of Sanskrit grammar. It is divided into four sections. The fourth chapter named *Prasanna-kāṇḍa* is very important from the perspective of *alaṅkāra*. It deals with poetics and illustrates thirty-eight *alaṅkāras*. The order in which *alaṅkāras* are arranged is the same as their order in Bhāmaha's *Kāvyālaṅkāra*, although Bhaṭṭi deviates in a few cases from Bhāmaha. Another major work that deals with *alaṅkāra* in passing is *Agnipurāṇa*. Chapters 328–347 of *Agnipurāṇa* deal with figures of speech such as *yamaka, citra, upamā, rūpaka, sahokti, arthāntaranyāsa, utprekṣā, atiśaya, vibhāvanā, virodha*, and *hetu*.

Practitioners differed from each other with respect to the number of *alaṅkāras*. While Bharata listed only four *alaṅkāras*, they went up to thirty-eight in Bhāmaha's *Kāvyālaṅkāra*. Daṇḍin discussed around thirty-five *alaṅkāras* in his *Kāvyādarśa*. He included *hetu, sukṣma,* and *leśa* in his scheme—the *alaṅkāras* rejected by Bhāmaha. There were forty-one *alaṅkāras* in Udbhaṭa's scheme. He rejected some of the *alaṅkāras* that his predecessors had incorporated and added five more while omitting seven. According to Vāmana, there were thirty-one *alaṅkāras* in his *Kāvyālaṅkārasūtravṛtti*. Rudraṭa listed sixty-six *alaṅkāras*, including the thirty-one new ones that he added. As can be seen, we have to agree with Daṇḍin when he said that *alaṅkāras* are countless and they keep increasing, depending on the ingenuity of the writers (II.1).

Though literary theoreticians invented new linguistic components and considered them to be the soul of *kāvya*, *alaṅkāra* continued to occupy an important role in *kāvyaśāstra*. For instance, Vāmana, despite his predilection for the idea of *guṇa*, maintained that a poem without *alaṅkāra* will not appeal to the minds of readers. According to him, while *guṇas* make a poem charming, *alaṅkāra* adds to poetic beauty (IV.1.1). Hemacandra listed *alaṅkāra* as an important constituent of poetry along with *śabda*, *artha*, and *guṇa* (I.12). For Vāgbhaṭa II, *kāvya* is a linguistic composition marked by the presence of *śabda*, *artha* (signification), *guṇas* (poetic excellence), and *alaṅkāras* (14). In *Candrāloka*, Jayadeva opined that *kāvya* is that special expression characterized by the absence of *doṣas* and the presence of *alaṅkāras* along with other poetic devices (I.7). Vidyānātha in *Pratāparudrīya* saw *kāvya* as that kind of *gadya* (prose) and *padya* (poetry) which is adorned by *guṇa*, *alaṅkāra*, *śabda*, and *artha*, and is bereft of *doṣas* (II.1). At this juncture, it is important to mention the debate between Jayadeva and Mammaṭa on the question of whether *alaṅkāra* is an important constituent for *kāvya*. Jayadeva criticized Mammaṭa for making *alaṅkāra* only an optional element in *kāvya*. Mammaṭa observed that "This [*kāvya*] is the [composition] of word and meaning without faults, qualities, and sometimes without figures of speech" (*Kāvyaprakāśa:* I.4). Criticizing Mammaṭa's stance, Jayadeva asks "Why does not that great scholar who considers a composition without *alaṅkāra* as a *kāvya* opine that the fire is bereft of heat" (I.8).

Ānandavardhana's *Dhvanyāloka* marked a turning point in this extended discussion of figures of speech and rhetoric. For the first time in the history of *kāvyaśāstra,* critical attention shifted from figures of speech and tropes to aesthetic emotion or *rasa*. This does not mean that *alaṅkāra* lost its importance completely. *Alaṅkāra,* as opposed to being the central concern of theoretical analysis, was relegated to the position of a subsidiary, yet important, category. Ānanda's observation bears testimony to it. According to Ānanda, *alaṅkāra*s function like ornaments on a person's body while *guṇa*s function like qualities such as courage (2.6). According to Ānandavardhana, *alaṅkāra*s are "limitless" in number (4.7 b *A*). He is of the view that if carefully used, *alaṅkāra*s can greatly add to the beauty of *rasa*s. Ānanda observed that the employment of figure of speech in poetry should appear natural and effortless; it should be in conjunction with the *rasa* it aims to arouse. Any use of *alaṅkāra*s by force can only destroy the beauty of the poem: "Only a figure which can be composed in the course of one's preoccupation with *rasa* and that requires no separate effort in itself is acceptable as an ornament in suggestive poetry" (2.16 *K*). His discussion of *alaṅkāra* in *Dhvanyāloka* is primarily in connection with the aesthetic emotion of the erotic or *śṛṅgāra rasa*. Ānanda points out that *śabdālaṅkāra*s (figures of speech pertaining to sound) such as *yamaka* can mar the beauty of *śṛṅgāra rasa*. *Yamaka,* where phonetically identical duplicates are repeated, demands a conscious effort on the part of the author, which might result in diverting his/her attention away from the main aim of evocation of *rasa*. Ānanda further says, "A great poet can produce with a single effort some matters that contain *rasa* together with figures of speech. But for composing *yamaka*s and the like, he must make a separate effort even if he is well able to compose them. Therefore these figures cannot play a part subordinate to *rasa*" (2.16 *K*). Ānanda was giving an advisory to the effect that when trying to depict an emotion as powerful as passionate love, it would be disastrous if the poet got caught up in elaborate wordplay.

Bhāmaha

The three pioneering names in the history of *alaṅkāraśāstra* who preceded Ānanda are Bhāmaha, Daṇḍin, and Rudraṭa. For Bhāmaha, the earliest known exponent of *alaṅkāra-śāstra*, it is the presence of *alaṅkāra*s or figures of speech that beautifies language and makes it literary as opposed to ordinary. He defined *kāvya* as a combination of *śabda* and *artha* and believed that *śabdālaṅkāra*s and *arthālaṅkāra*s collectively generate poetic beauty or literariness in *kāvya*. It is significant to note that there were two major views regarding the body of *kāvya*. The first view was that *kāvya* was solely a product of *artha* (signification), and the second, that *kāvya* was constituted exclusively by *śabda* (signifier). Bhāmaha talked about these two camps at great length in his *Kāvyālaṅkāra*. According to Bhāmaha, the first camp argued that *alaṅkāra*s that relate to *artha* (sense) are the cause of poetic beauty. Reproducing the argument of this camp, Bhāmaha says: "Some *ālaṅkārika*s vehemently maintain that only *rūpaka*, etc. constitute its (*kāvya*'s) ornaments. (Because) a damsel's face, though beautiful, does not shine, if it is devoid of ornaments" (I.13). Here the expression *alaṅkāra* denotes *arthālaṅkāra*. The second camp, on the other hand, claimed that only figures of speech pertaining to sound constitute poetic beauty: "Some people are of the opinion that figures of speech like *rūpaka* are external. They maintain that the proper disposition of nouns and verbs constitute the real ornaments of speech" (I.14). This school argues that the beauty of a poem lies primarily in the ornaments of sound. Bhāmaha who wished to strike a balance between these two views, maintained that poetry is the combination of both word and meaning: "Poetry is the combination of both sound and sense" (*śabdārthau sahitau kāvyam;* 1.16). He was also the first literary theoretician to distinguish between *śabdālaṅkāra*s and *arthālaṅkāra*s.

Bhāmaha listed and analyzed thirty-eight *alaṅkāra*s (including the four *alaṅkāra*s identified by Bharata) in his attempt to identify the unique nature of *kāvyaśarīra*. He employed the term *alaṅkāra* to denote all the linguistic techniques and formal devices by which a narrative attains poetic beauty or literariness. He incorporated even the idea of *rasa* under *alaṅkāra*s. He conceived the idea of *rasa* as a trope or verbal expression of emotions. The three emotional tropes that he mentions are *rasavat*, *preyaḥ*, and *ūrjasvi* (III.5–7).

According to Bhāmaḥa, what made *alaṅkāra*s different from other uses of language is its figurative deviation of speech (*vakrokti*) from ordinary language. He initially believed that language which deviated from ordinary usage would fall under the *alaṅkāra* of *atiśayokti*. But later he further developed and modified this idea to conclude that there can be no *alaṅkāra* without *vakratā,* or a deviant, extraordinary use of language. Bhāmaha observed that deviant expression (*vakrokti*) is found in all *alaṅkāra*s and there is no figure of speech [*alaṅkāra*] without this (II.85). Bhāmaha made his point clearer by explaining that if a composition is devoid of the figurative deviation of sense (*vakrokti*), the composition turns out to be mere "news" or *vārtā* and not *kāvya* (II.87). He was of the view that expressions without figurative deviation such as "the sun has set; the moon shines, the birds are winging back to their nests, etc." cannot fall within the category of *alaṅkāra* (II.87). A composition might have words that are elegant, smooth, and clear, but it cannot be considered a *kāvya* if it lacks *vakrokti* (I.34).

What Bhāmaha's theory of *alaṅkāra* shows is that *kāvya* is distinct from other uses of verbal language by the presence of figures of speech which have the quality of *vakratā*. So, his analysis of *kāvyaśarīra* is exclusively concerned with the identification and scrutiny of *alaṅkāra* which presents everything in a striking way through *vakrokti* or deviant utterance. According to Bhāmaha, *atiśayokti* is identical with *vakrokti* or deviant utterance, and all poets should take special care to master this art. In *Kāvyālaṅkāra*, Bhāmaha says, "This [*atiśayokti*] is nothing but *vakrokti*. All meanings appear new by this. Poets should be assiduous in cultivating it. Where is an *alaṅkāra* without this?" (II.85). Matilal observes that "In Bhāmaha's slightly loose terminology, *vakrokti* = *atiśayokti* = *alaṅkāra*" (374). *Atiśayokti* or the device to transcend the ordinary experience pervades all figures of speech and is identical with *vakrokti* or deviant utterance: "Where something transcending ordinary experience is described without reason, it is regarded as the figure *atiśayokti*" (II.81).

According to Daṇḍin, *atiśayokti* "is that great *alaṅkāra* where signification (*vivakṣā*) moves beyond the borders of common perception (*lokasīmātivarttinī*)" (II.214). According to Udbhaṭa, "A statement, with a cause, surprising the common perception of people—the learned consider it to be the *alaṅkāra atiśayokti*" (II.11). Udbhaṭa divided *atiśayokti* into four varieties—"imposition of sameness where there is difference in reality," "imagining difference where there is really no difference," "describing some imaginary thing which is really impossible," and "the reversion of cause and effect to show quickness of effect" (II.11–16). In all these varieties of *atiśayokti*, the ultimate aim is to shatter the reader's common perception about an object or idea. Ānanda subscribed to Bhāmaha's opinion about *vakrokti* and held that *vakrokti* which is identical with *atiśayokti* is the life force of all *alaṅkāras* (3.36 A). Abhinava also subscribed to Bhāmaha's view that *atiśayokti* which was attained through the figurative deviation of speech is the essence of all figures of speech. Abhinava noted:

> That which has been defined as hyperbole is the whole of figured speech, that is, is every sort of figure of speech, for Bhāmaha has said: 'An unusual or striking form of word or meaning (*vakrokti*) is considered an ornament (*alaṅkṛti*) of poetic utterance.' For the 'bent' (*vakra*) form of a word or of a meaning (*ukti*) is its presentation in an unusual or striking form (*lokottīrṇena rūpeṇa*) and this constitutes the ornament of a figure of speech (*alaṅkārasyālaṅkāraḥ*). Now hyperbole is precisely the property of being unusual or striking (*lokottaratā*). Hence hyperbole is a common property of all figures of speech. Thus . . . it is by this hyperbole that a meaning which has been worn out by everyone's use of it can be given new variety and interest. (3.36 *L*)

Although this seems to be a rather exaggerated emphasis on hyperbole or exaggeration, there is no denying the fact that it is the unordinary use of ordinary language that constitutes the essence of the poetic. For instance, the beauty of Yeats's "The Song of Wandering Aengus" is this quality of hyperbole:

> Though I am old with wandering
> Through hollow lands and hilly lands,
> I will find out where she has gone,
> And kiss her lips and take her hands;
> And walk among long dappled grass,
> And pluck till time and times are done,
> The silver apples of the moon,
> The golden apples of the sun. (68)

But this emphasis on *atiśayokti* was not shared by all critics. Daṇḍin, who is the second-most influential exponent of the *Alaṅkāra School*, particularly disagreed with Bhāmaha's observation that *vārtā* or report cannot serve as the ornament of poetry. Daṇḍin employed the term *svabhāvokti* to designate what Bhāmaha calls *vārtā*. According to Daṇḍin, *svabhāvokti* is a figure of speech. This is, in fact, the first *alaṅkāra* he dealt with in *Kāvyādarśa*. He maintained that *svabhāvokti* (he also calls it *jāti*) which is also found abundantly in *śāstras* is well appreciated by connoisseurs of art as an *alaṅkāra* (II.8).

Kuntaka is perceived as the last prominent critic in the *Alaṅkāra School*. It is not surprising that Kuntaka, who espoused *vakrokti*, should agree that the essence of poetry is *alaṅkāra* or ornamental speech which differs from ordinary use of language. According to Kuntaka, *svabhāvokti* or "the presentation of an idea or entity in the way they are popularly presented or perceived in the society" [*svabhāvasyapadārthadharmalakṣaṇasya parispandasya uktirabhidhā*] does not have any space within the ambit of *kāvya* (I.11). Instead of re-creating or re-presenting the dominant conception about the identity of an entity (*svabhāva*), a poet should be concerned about *vakrokti* or figurative deviation. Kuntaka's approach was more holistic; according to Matilal, Kuntaka believed that "a poem is a whole; its beauty, or even the means for its beautification, cannot be separated from it" (376).

Alaṅkāra in Practice

Despite occupying a central position in the discussion of poetics, *alaṅkāra* often came with what appears to be a statutory warning to not employ it to excess. Ānandavardhana repeatedly emphasized the need to subordinate *alaṅkāra*s to the *rasa* that they should help in producing. According to Raghavan, Ānandavardhana exhorted poets to exercise *samīkṣā* (discrimination) in the use of *alaṅkāra*s and formulated the following principles to be adhered to with respect to *alaṅkāra*:

(i) *Alaṅkāra*s must be ancillary—*aṅgabhūta*.
(ii) They must never become main—*pradhāna* or *aṅgin*.
(iii) The main theme shall always be kept in view and figures, in consequence, must be taken and thrown away in accordance with the requirements of the main idea.
(iv) They must not be too much elaborated or overworked.
(v) Even if they are worked out, a good poet must take care to give them, on the whole, the position of *aṅga* only. (Raghavan 243; for a detailed reading, see *Dhvanyāloka* 2.15–2.19g)

What Ānandavardhana is stressing is that the *alaṅkāra* should appear natural and spontaneous, and not forced; nor should an excessive obsession with wordplay drown the meaning of the poem. Kṣemendra would say that poets should exercise *aucitya* in the matter of using *alaṅkāras*.

A poet's greatness can be judged on the basis of this discretion in the use of figures of speech. In the *Sundarakāṇḍa* of the *Rāmāyaṇa*, Vālmīki describes the beautiful women following Rāvaṇa as *vidyullatā* or streaks of lightning. This becomes even more apt when you consider the implied comparison of Rāvaṇa to a dark thundercloud, merely hinted at through *ghanaṃ* (the cloud) (5.18.15). In the same chapter, the grief-stricken Sītā is compared to a crescent moon hidden by an autumnal cloud, indicating her natural lustre that is temporarily overcast. Later, Sītā sitting under the *śiṃśupa* tree in the Aśoka grove is described thus: "Sitting in that manner she resembled a coiled serpent queen, the star Rohiṇī overshadowed by a smoking comet [that is Rāvaṇa]" (5.19.9). The analogy between a demure Sītā and a coiled serpent appears to be rather ill-suited, but it becomes a beautiful simile when we consider that she proves to be the undoing of Rāvaṇa; like the coiled serpent, she was just biding time to strike.

Kālidāsa is another classical poet who was reputed for his beautiful similes that added to the richness of his works. In *Abhijnānaśākuntalaṃ*, a series of beautiful similes are employed to describe the pristine beauty of Śakuntalā. She is compared to a "flower unsmelled" (*anāghrātaṃ puṣpaṃ*) and to "new wine as yet unsavored" (*madhu navam anāsvāditarasaṃ*) (115).

However, used in excess, figures of speech can become a liability. According to Dr Johnson, this is one fatal flaw that could be found in Shakespeare: "A quibble is to Shakespeare, what luminous vapors are to the traveller; he follows it at all adventures, it is sure to lead him out of his way, and sure to engulf him in the mire" (9). For instance, Sonnet 135 where he plays upon the word "will" has sent critics and poetry lovers into a tizzy regarding meaning:

> Whoever hath her wish, thou hast thy Will,
> And Will to boot, and Will in overplus; (279)

The same can be said of John Donne and the other metaphysical poets' elaborate play on what are called "conceits."

Repeated use of the same image can also lead to clichéd metaphors and similes that fail to arouse the intended effect. The standard salutation of kings and warriors in classical Sanskrit as "*puruṣarṣabha*" or "bull among men" is a case in point. This fascination with ornate language was not restricted to poetry in Sanskrit. Padmini Rajappa in her translator's introduction to Bāṇabhaṭṭa's *Kādambarī* notes how Bāṇa's prose becomes dense with long compounds and how he too "gets lured by the tempting charms of the Sanskrit language only to lose his way in verbal mazes" (x).

While we are discussing the use and abuse of *alaṅkāra*s, it is also pertinent to debate whether *svabhāvokti* can constitute good poetry or not. It will not, if we go by what theorists like Bhāmaha and Kuntaka said. However, the problem here is the distinction between a bare reporting of facts and lines that are deceptively simple yet suggestive of meaning beyond the surface. For example, consider the concluding stanza of Frost's famous "Stopping by Woods on a Snowy Evening": "The woods are lovely, dark and deep,/ But I have promises to keep/And miles to go before I sleep/ And miles to go before I sleep." (279). The lines appear to be merely stating facts, but they are suggestive of a much larger philosophical meaning in the context of the poem. The woods become a metaphor for the temptations that can distract you from the task before you. What would appear to be *svabhāvokti* is an *arthālaṅkāra* that becomes a good example of *dhvani.*

There could also be instances where unadorned prose would actually be more suitable than ornate statements. According to Matthew Arnold, a single line from the poem "Michael" conveys the silent grief of a father who has lost his only son and captures Wordsworth's poetic genius: "And never lifted up a single stone." As Arnold points out, "There is nothing subtle in it, no heightening, no study of poetic style, strictly so called, at all; yet it is expression of the highest and most truly expressive kind." He agrees that many would describe his style as "bald" but according to Arnold, it "is bald as the bare mountain-tops are bald, with a baldness which is full of grandeur," because Wordsworth was skilled in combining "profound truth of subject with profound truth of execution."

Equating ornate, rhetorical lines with poetry becomes all the more difficult when it comes to modernist poetry and free verse. The language of poetry does not differ much from everyday language in much of contemporary verse. For instance, look at the opening stanza of Alice Walker's "Working Class Hero":

My brothers knew
The things you know.
I did not scorn
learning them;
It's just my mind
Was busy being trained
For "Other Things":
Poetry, Philosophy, Literature.
Survival, for a girl. (24)

There is not a single word or line that appears to be "poetic" or striking in its extraordinary usage of words. Would Bhāmaha permit this to be considered poetry?

If such plain statements can be considered poetic, the converse can also be held true. Lines that revel in wordplay without much concern for meaning can also be defined as poetry. As Raghavan observes: "There is simply beautiful poetry, which is nothing but the poet's desire to express taken shape" (244). Walter de la Mare's poem "Silver" which plays upon the alliterative use of the consonant "s" can be taken as an example:

Slowly, silently, now the moon
Walks the night in her silver shoon;
This way, and that, she peers, and sees
Silver fruit upon silver trees; (108)

The poem is but a description of a night-time world that turns silver when touched by the magic of moonlight, beautiful yet without any deeper layers of meaning; nobody can deny that this is poetic.

Conclusion

Of all the concepts in Sanskrit poetics, *alaṅkāra* is perhaps the one that is most difficult to adapt to contemporary times, mainly due to the changing definitions of what constitutes poetic language. The huge disparity in time and culture between the classical age of Sanskrit and our times is undoubtedly a reason for this. We have different evaluative standards for poetry and literature; we do not think of literature as a hermetically closed-off territory which exists purely according to aesthetic criteria. There is a predominant school of critical thought which believes that poetry instead of writing about "lilacs" and "poppy-petalled metaphysics" should talk about the "blood in the street" (Pablo Neruda). The classical idea of poetic language embellished with *alaṅkāra*s obviously would not apply to this concept of poetry and literature. There is also moreover the distinct feeling that literature should speak the language of the masses, and not an elitist and exclusive language.

However, we should not forget that despite such concepts, figurative language is still the hallmark of literature and poetry. It might not be as ornamented as the classical literary works of yore, but it does mark itself out of the ordinary, as can be seen in Nobel laureate Bob Dylan's famous "Blowin' in the Wind":

> How many roads must a man walk down
> Before you call him a man?
> How many seas must a white dove sail
> Before she sleeps in the sand?
> How many times must the cannon balls fly
> Before they're forever banned?

The answer, my friend, is blowin' in the wind
The answer is blowin' in the wind.

Works Cited

Abhinavagupta. *Locana*. In *The Dhvanyāloka of Ānandavardhana with the Locana of Abhinavagupta*. Translated and edited by Daniel Ingalls, Jeffrey Masson, and M. V. Patwardhan, Harvard University Press, 1990.

Ānandavardhana. *The Dhvanyāloka of Ānandavardhana with the Locana of Abhinavagupta*. Translated and edited by Daniel Ingalls, Jeffrey Masson, and M. V. Patwardhan, Harvard: Harvard University Press, 1990.

Arnold, Matthew. "Wordsworth." *Essays in Criticism*, Second Series. https://archive.org/details/essaysincriticis00arnorich/page/122/mode/2up. Accessed August 12, 2019.

Bharata. *Nāṭyaśāstram*. Translated (Malayalam) and edited by K. P. Narayana Pisharody, Kerala Sahitya Akademi, 2004.

Bhāmaha. *Kāvyālaṅkāra*. Edited by B. N. Sarma and Baldeva Upadhyay, Chowkhamba Sanskrit Series Office, 1998.

Daṇḍin. *Kāvyādarśa of Daṇḍin*. Edited by Premachandra Tarkabagisa, Royal Asiatic Society, 1962.

Dylan, Bob. n.d. https://www.azlyrics.com/lyrics/bobdylan/blowininthewind.html. Accessed August 12, 2019.

Frost, Robert. "Stopping by Woods on a Snowy Evening." *Collected Poems of Robert Frost*, Halcyon House, 1939.

Hemacandra. *Kāvyānuśāsana*. Edited by Rasiklal C. Parikh, Mahavira Jaina Vidyalaya, 1938.

Jayadeva. *Candrāloka of Jayadeva*. Edited by A. S. Vetal, Chowkamba Sanskrit Series Office, 1932.

Johnson, Samuel. *Preface to Shakespeare*. Edited by Berts and Fischer, 2008.

Kālidāsa. *The Recognition of Sakuntala*. Translated and edited by Somadeva Vasudeva, Clay Sanskrit Library, 2006.

Kuntaka. *Vakroktijīvita*. Translated by Krishnamoorthy, Karnatak University, 1977.

Mammaṭa. *Kāvyaprakāśa of Mammaṭa*. Edited by G. Jha, Bharathiya Vidya Prakashan, 1966.

Mare, Walter de la. "Silver." *A Book of Rhymes*, Constable and Company, 1920, p. 109.

Matilal, Bimal Krishna. "Vakrokti and Dhvani: Controversies about the Theory of Poetry in the Indian Tradition." *Abhinavagupta: Reconsiderations*. Edited by Makarand Paranjape, Samvad Foundation, 2006, pp. 372–380.

Neruda, Pablo. "I'm Explaining a Few Things," https://www.poetryinternational.org/pi/poem/22618/auto/0/0/Pablo-Neruda/IM-EXPLAINING-A-FEW-THINGS/en/tile. Accessed August 23, 2020.

Raghavan, V. "Use and Abuse of *Alaṅkāra*." *Indian Aesthetics: An Introduction*. Edited by V. S. Seturaman, Macmillan, 2005, pp. 235–244.

Rajappa, Padmini, "Introduction." *Kādambarī* by Bāṇa, Penguin, 2001, pp. ix–xxvii.

Shakespeare, William. "Sonnet 135." *Shakespeare's Sonnets*. Edited by Barbara A. Mowat and Paul Werstine, Washington Square Press, 2004, p. 279.

Udbhaṭa. *Kāvyālaṅkārasārasaṃgraha with the commentary, the Laghuvṛtti of Indurāja*. Edited by Narayana Daso Banhatti, Bhandarkar Oriental Research Institute, 1982.

Vāgbhaṭa II. *Kāvyānuśāsana*. Nirnaya Sagar Press, 1915.

Vālmīki. valmiki.iitk.ac.in. 2000. Accessed December 13, 2017.

Vāmana. *Kāvyālaṅkārasūtravṛtti*. Translated (Malayalam) and edited by E. Easwaran Nambootiri, Kerala Bhasha Institute, 2000.

Vidyānātha. *Pratāparudrīya*. Edited by K. S. Ramamurthi and S. R. Matha, Oriental Research Institute, 1933.

Walker, Alice. "Working Class Hero." *The World will Follow Joy: Turning Madness into Flowers*, The New Press, 2013, pp. 24–28.

Yeats, William Butler. "The Song of Wandering Aengus." *The Wind among the Reeds*. Franklin Mathews, 1899, pp. 15–16.

4

Rīti, Guṇas, and Doṣas

We have seen how the tradition of classical Sanskrit poetics was consistently debating the aims and methods of poetic composition. The metaphor of the body was very important to the *ālaṅkārikas* who conceived of *alaṅkāras* as ornaments that decked up the body of poetry. Vāmana, who followed Bhāmaha and Daṇḍin, was unlike them in that he thought about the 'soul' of poetry rather than the body of poetry; he believed that *rīti* is the soul of poetry—*rītirātmā kāvyasya*. Although *rīti* is usually translated as "style," it would be better to understand it as diction. What we mean by style today is the individualistic use of language by a particular writer as in the statement "Style is the man." It is also very common to talk about the minimalist style of Hemingway or the flamboyant style of Rushdie. However, *rīti* is not style in this sense of the word; it cannot be related to one particular writer but is indicative of the choice of words that are used in writing. So, you can choose an ornate style which has high-sounding bombastic words, or a simple style with ordinary words—this is the way in which *rīti* as style should be understood. V. K. Chari points out: "There was no conception of period style or any notion of personal style (style as the signature of its author)" (133).

Rīti can be understood in terms of the structure of word forms and collocations, and also on the basis of certain qualities. These qualities were called *guṇas* by the Sanskrit theoreticians. Vāmana, who was a proponent of *rīti*, said: "The speciality of style is to be defined by its quality" (Chari 139). Since *rīti* cannot be evaluated separately from the idea of *guṇa*, these two concepts are discussed in conjunction here. This would also involve a glimpse of *doṣa*, which is a flaw that can also be defined as the absence of *guṇa*.

The origins of the idea of *rīti* can be traced back to Bharata who in his *Nāṭyaśāstra*, described four *vṛtti*s—*kaiśikī, sātvatī, ārabhaṭī*, and *bhāratī*. Of these, only *bhāratī* had anything to do with language while the others were connected to various aspects of performance. Bharata also had categories called *pravṛtti*s, which were based on the regional variations of language, behavior, and cultural practices. These were *avanti, dākṣinātya, pāñcālī*, and *ugramāgadhī*, representing the styles of the west, south, east, and north of India respectively. The idea was that the characters should speak a language that suited the region and culture they came from. The idea of *rīti* was an evolution from Bharata's concepts of *vṛtti* and *pravṛtti* (see chapter XXII of *Nāṭyaśāstra* for a detailed reading of the idea of *vṛtti*).

Bhāmaha, Daṇḍin, and Kuntaka used the term "*mārga*" instead of *rīti*. There were three prominent *rīti*s at that time—*vaidarbhī, pāñcālī*, and *gauḍī*. Bhāmaha did not think much of *mārga*/*rīti;* he was more concerned with the way language was used, irrespective of the style. He mentioned *vaidarbhī* and *gauḍī*, but he rejected outright the very classification of *rīti* and did not subscribe to the idea that *vaidarbhī* was superior and *gauḍī* was inferior. According to Bhāmaha, there was hardly any difference between *vaidarbhī* and *gauḍī*. He opined that "this nomenclature is due to unintelligent people following blindly the lead of others" (I.36).

He observed that "Even *gauḍīya* is superior if it has *alaṅkāras*, is devoid of vulgarity, has full and proper meaning, and is simple. There is no separate thing as *vaidarbhī*" (I.36).

In *Kāvyādarśa,* although Daṇḍin mentions *mārgas* such as *pāñcālī, avantikā, lāṭīya,* and *magadhī*, he scrutinized only two *mārgas* namely *vaidarbhī* and *gauḍī*, citing the reason that only these two are discernible (I.40). Like Bhāmaha, Daṇḍin also saw *kāvya* as a distinct linguistic entity and focused on the scrutiny of *kāvyaśarīra* to tease out its characteristics. But unlike Bhāmaha, Daṇḍin did not see individual *alaṅkāras* as the sole means of the beautifying principle. According to him, it was the combination of both *guṇas* and *alaṅkāras* that constituted literariness. So, he dealt with both *guṇas* and *alaṅkāras* in his *Kāvyādarśa.* Daṇḍin identified ten *guṇas*, such as *śleṣa* (synthesis), *prasāda* (perspicuity), *samatā* (smoothness), *samādhi* (concentration), *ojas* (grandeur), *padasaukumārya* (delicacy of a word), *arthavyakti* (clarity of meaning), *udāratā* (depth), *kānti* (splendor), and *mādhurya* (sweetness) (I.41–102). He considered these *guṇas* as qualities that are to be necessarily present in a *kāvya* and connected them to *mārgas* (1.40). According to Daṇḍin, all the ten *guṇas* can be perceived only in *vaidarbhī mārga*, while *gauḍī* contains some of them (I.42). Daṇḍin was, in fact, adding one more layer to Bhāmaha's scrutiny of the peculiarities of *kāvyaśarīra* by analyzing in detail the idea of *guṇa*. Although Daṇḍin referred to all the ten *guṇas* that Bharata mentioned, he conceptualized many *guṇas* differently. He also believed that even *gauḍī* and *vaidarbhī*, despite being clearly distinguishable, vary from writer to another. In other words, innumerable variants of *gauḍī* and *vaidarbhī* can be found (I.100). Daṇḍin also points out that even Sarasvatī, the goddess of speech, is incapable of counting the *mārgas* existing in this world (I.101). It is worth noticing that Daṇḍin's approach takes cognizance of the fact that a lot of subjectivity goes into the choice of style and diction, which was a departure from the norm.

Udbhaṭa borrowed the idea of *vṛtti* from Bharata and developed the idea of a style that depended on diction. A style that had harsh-sounding words that were difficult to pronounce was called *paruṣa*; words that were soft and pleasing constituted *komalā*, and a middle path was termed *upanāgarikā* (*Kāvyālaṅkāra-sāra-saṃgraha* I.4–6).

Vāmana's Contribution

Vāmana's *Kāvyālaṅkārasūtravṛtti* has five divisions (*adhikaraṇas*), and each division has two or three chapters (*adhyāya*). The first division discusses the functions of *kāvya*, the second deals with the *doṣas* or defects of words and sentences; the third discusses *guṇas*; the fourth is about *alaṅkāras*, and the fifth is about rules of prosody and grammar.

Vāmana's discussion of *rīti* appears in the first part. According to him, a *rīti* where all the *guṇas* are properly knit together serves as the soul of *kāvya* (I.2.5). He thought of *rīti* as *viśiṣta pada racanā* or a special arrangement of words (I.2.7). According to Vāmana, *rītis* are three in number, namely *vaidarbhī, gaudīyā*, and *pāñcālī* (I.2.9). Vāmana also reminds the readers that these styles are named after these places primarily because these varieties are mainly employed by writers from these places. Of all these three styles, Vāmana considered *vaidarbhī* as the most appropriate diction to compose poetry as it contained all the twenty *guṇas*. He praises *vaidarbhī* by saying that it is as sonorous as the sound of the musical instrument *vīṇā* (*vipañcīsvarasaubhāgyā*) (I.2.11). *Gaudīya* is characterized by the presence of only two qualities namely *ojas* and *prasāda*. *Mādhurya* and *saukumārya* are the only qualities associated with *pāñcālī*. Vāmana warns aspiring poets against practising the art of composing poems in any style other than *vaidarbhī*. Vāmana mentions other styles only to distinguish *vaidarbhī* from the rest (I.2.12–18).

The important contribution made by Vāmana was that he connected the ten *guṇas* that Bharata mentioned to *śabda* (sound) and *artha* (meaning), thus effectively making it twenty *guṇas*. As Chari explains: "Although style is defined by Vāmana primarily as having to do with the structuring of words, its application is not believed to be limited to the sounds alone; stylistic features belong, by extension, to meanings as well" (139).

Vāmana believed that just as a painting evolved from initial lines on the canvas, a poem developed from one of the three *rītis* (I.2.13). *Vaidarbhī* was the most preferred style for Vāmana because it had all the merits and he believed that only this style was capable enough to express the inexpressible truth of poetry (I.2.11). S. K. De explains:

> ... *Vaidarbhī* is the complete or ideal one which unifies all the poetic excellences, whereas the other two encourage extremes. The one lays stress on the grand, the glorious or the imposing, the other on softness and sweetness, whereby the former loses itself often in bombast, the latter in prolixity. (198)

De is of the view that these styles which derive their names from regions could have been developed from "an empirical analysis of the prevailing peculiarities of poetic expression in different places and furnishes another proof of the general *a posteriori* character of the discipline itself" (198).

Rudraṭa added one more *rīti* namely *lāṭīyam* to Vāmana's list which comprised *vaidarbhī, pāñcālī*, and *gauḍī* styles. Mammaṭa called diction *vṛtti*. Like Udbhaṭa, he divided *vṛtti*s into three categories—*paruṣa, komalā*, and *upanāgarikā*. He opined that they were equal to Vāmana's three poetic dictions. Like Daṇḍin much before him, Kuntaka's term for *rīti* was *mārga*. According to him, *mārgas* were three in number, such as *sukumāra, vaicitrya*, and *madhyama*.

Refuting Vāmana's view that *rīti* is the soul of poetry, Ānandavardhana used the term *saṃghaṭanā* to refer to what Vāmana called *rīti*. According to Ānanda, "It was persons unable to analyze the true nature of poetry . . . who propounded the doctrine of styles" (3.46 *K*). Ānanda continues to observe: "The *Vaidarbhī, Gauḍī*, and *Pāñcālī* styles were set up by persons unable to give a clear idea of the true nature of poetry, for this true nature, which we have analyzed by using the concept of *dhvani*, appeared to them unclearly" (3.46 *A*). Although he rejected the primacy attributed by Vāmana to *rīti*, he borrowed the idea of the dual classification of poetry into body and soul. His argument was that *rīti* dealt only with the syntactics of poesy and did not really analyze the true nature of literary creation. Moreover, the choice of style was dependent on the *rasa* to be conveyed; it is fallacious to claim that one particular style is the most appropriate. This is also the reason why Ānandavardhana selected three—*mādhurya, ojas*, and *prasāda*—out of the ten *guṇa*s outlined by Vāmana and classified *saṃghaṭanā* into three on the basis of those three *guṇas*. The three *saṃghaṭanā*s were *asamāsa* (that which lacks in compounds), *madhyama samāsa* (that which has compounds of medium length) and *dīrgha samāsa* (that which has long compounds) (3.5).

When the speaker (this could be either the poet himself or a character invented by the poet) is under the sway of a predominant *rasa*, only the uncompounded *saṅghaṭana* or a *saṅghaṭana* employing compounds of medium length should be used. But in *karuṇa rasa* and love-in-separation (*vipralambha-śṛṅgāra*), only the uncompounded *saṅghaṭana* is allowed. This is because compounds which can often create ambiguity in meaning delays our perception of meaning and mars the beauty of delicate *rasas* such as *karuṇa* and love-in-separation. On the other hand, in the presentation of other *rasa*s such as *raudra*, etc., a texture of medium-length compounds can be used. Sometimes, to describe the action of a hero who is brave and arrogant, even texture of long compounds can be considered (3.6 h *A*). Ānandavardhana saw *saṃghaṭanā* and *guṇa* as two separate things. As we have already seen, he thought that *alaṅkāra*s function like ornaments on a person's body while *guṇa*s are qualities like courage (2.5g). He subordinated the ideas of *alaṅkāra* and *guṇa* to *rasa*. Ānandavardhana was also against the view that a good poetic composition should contain all the *guṇa*s because according to him, *guṇa* has to be modified according to the *rasa* that is portrayed. *Śṛṅgāra-rasa* has the quality of sweetness (*mādhurya*) predominant in it whereas *raudra* has the quality of *ojas* (ibid.: 2.7–9).

Guṇa

There is one aspect of style or *rīti* that has to be specifically mentioned here. Unlike its Western counterpart, the Indian concept of style also seemed to incorporate *artha* or meaning. *Rīti* was the proper way of organizing words, but this organization depended on the idea that had to be expressed. As De explains, "… *Rīti* is not, like the style, the expression of poetic individuality, as it is generally understood by Western Criticism, but it is merely the outward presentation of its beauty called forth by a harmonious combination of more or less fixed literary 'excellences'" (198). These excellences are the *guṇas*. Vāmana considered them to be essential elements that made up the *rīti*.

Although Vāmana discussed the concept extensively, it was Bharata who had first mentioned it. However, Bharata defined it by absence rather than presence, or that *doṣas* are the absence of *guṇas*. He said that *guṇas* like *mādhurya* come from the absence of *doṣas*—(*guṇā viparyayādeṣāṃ mādhuryairdāryalakṣaṇāḥ*; XVII. 92). Bharata was also the first one to say that *guṇas* had to be coordinated with the *rasa*. Bhāmaha did not give much importance to *guṇas*. His discussion of *guṇas* (he did not even name them *guṇas*) was limited to *mādhurya* and *prasāda*, the two *guṇas* that Bharata had already mentioned in *Nāṭyaśāstra* (II.1–2). But Bhāmaha did not consider them to be essential qualities of *kāvya*.

Vāmana in *Kāvyālaṅkārasūtravṛtti* talked about ten *guṇas* namely, *ojas, prasāda, śleṣa, samatā, Samādhi, mādhurya, Saukumārya, udāratā, arthavyakti, kānti*. These are the same as listed by Daṇḍin earlier, but Vāmana applied it to *śabda* (the word) as well as *artha* (meaning). So, each *guṇa* had an application to sound as well as sense in the following way:

(i) *Ojas*—Compactness of word structure;
Maturity of conception

(ii) *Prasāda*—Flexibility of structure;
Clarity of meaning

(iii) *Śleṣa*—Smooth combination of words;
Unity of ideas

(iv) *Samatā*—Similarity of word construction;
Coherence

(v) *Samādhi*—Symmetry of words;
Comprehension of meaning

(vi) *Mādhurya*—Words without long compounds;
Striking expression

(vii) *Saukumārya*—Lack of harsh sounds;
Absence of unacceptable ideas

(viii) *udāratā*—Liveliness of words;
Absence of vulgarity

(ix) *Artha-vyakti*—Explicitness of words;
Explicitness of ideas

(x) *Kānti*—Richness of words;
Prominence of *rasa*s

(De 200–201)

Vāmana did not consider *alaṅkāra*s to be of equal importance. He made a clear-cut distinction between *guṇa* and *alaṅkāra*, which was a different approach from that of Bhāmaha, Daṇḍin, and Udbhaṭa. Vāmana used the term *alaṅkāra* in its broader sense of beauty; beauty was a necessary attribute for a poetic work, but that need not necessarily arise from poetic figures of speech. The function of *alaṅkāra*, on the other hand, is only to enhance the beauty of *kāvya* which is already beautified by the presence of *guṇa*s (3.1.1). "The *rīti* and its constituent *guṇa*s come in as a *sine qua non* in the production of this beauty, but the poetic figures only contribute to its heightening"—this was Vāmana's stance on the matter (De 201). The major difference between *guṇa*s and *alaṅkāra*s was that *guṇa*s were permanent while *alaṅkāra*s were not (*Kāvyālaṅkārasūtravṛtti* III.4.3); a poem could be beautiful even without figurative language but it could not do without the *guṇa*s that help to create a good *rīti*. Vāmana's concept of *kānti* as an *artha-guṇa* was a major advancement from the previous theoretical position of *alaṅkāra* for this brought *rasa* into the remit of a formalistic perception of literary beauty.

Ānandavardhana's schema considers *guṇa*s as dependent on *rasa*. He defined *guṇa* on the basis of the mental changes effected by the evocation of *rasa* (2.7–10). There are three identifiable mental states in the experience of *rasa*—*druti* (softening of the heart), *dīpti* (excitement), and *vikāsa* (expansion); so Ānandavardhana acknowledged only three *guṇa*s, namely, *mādhurya*, *ojas*, and *prasāda*. The *druti* that you experience in *śṛṅgāra rasa* was termed *mādhurya* (2.8); the *dīpti* felt during *raudra rasa* as *ojas* (2.9); and *prasāda* is the ability of a *kāvya* to communicate its *rasa*s to the reader (2.10). Only *mādhurya* and *ojas* were distinctly different from each other as they were attached to particular *rasa*s; *prasāda* could occur with any *rasa*. The *guṇa*s could not coexist simultaneously. For example, *ojas* and *mādhurya* could never occur at the same time (3.6 I *A*). He disagreed with Vāmana on this issue.

Doṣa

If there are qualities that enhance the beauty of a literary work, there should be contrarian aspects that affect it adversely. These are called *doṣa*s or flaws that have to be avoided. In what is perhaps a departure from Western classical tradition, most of the theorists starting with Bharata paid a lot of attention to this negative aspect of poetic creation. Bharata defined *guṇa* as the absence of *doṣa*, but there were later theorists who maintained that both these concepts could not be determined outside the overarching domain of *aucitya*. For instance, double entendre bordering on obscenity can be seen as a flaw in the language of Falstaff, but it is only appropriate in a character like him. Thus, a precise definition of what is a merit or a flaw is a problem; they appear to be contextual and contingent on the *rasa*.

However, the working definition for *guṇa* and *doṣa* was the following—a factor that enhanced *rasa* was a *guṇa* and that which reduced it was a *doṣa*. The main impact of a *doṣa* was felt on *rasa*, and one of the main causes for a *doṣa* was lack of propriety or *aucitya*. Failure to keep propriety could occur through various channels—technical as well as natural. A writer should have good command over language, grammar, and prosody, without which he would not be able to use the right word in the correct form in the right place. However, this was technical knowledge that could be gained through proper education. Other elements of poetic creation like plot structure, characterization, use of figurative language, and the evocation of *rasa* require a judicious exercise of *aucitya*. This ability is called genius and cannot be acquired through learning; one has to be born a genius. The harmful effect of a *doṣa*, if inadvertently committed, could be overcome by the natural talent of a poetic genius. It is clear that the theorists of those days believed that creative work was the product of inspired genius and not a combination of 99 percent perspiration and 1 percent inspiration!

Nevertheless, they believed in identifying pitfalls and warning potential authors against them. Faults can occur in a literary work in many ways. Anything that adversely affects the meaning and hinders the proper enjoyment of the work can be counted as a fault. It can prevent, delay, or destroy aesthetic appreciation. Bharata outlined ten *doṣa*s that had to be avoided:

(i) *Gūḍhārtha,* which is employing an uncommon word or a roundabout way to describe a common idea. Periphrastic or circumlocutory words baffle the reader and delay the process of enjoyment.
(ii) *Arthāntara* or that which describes what is unnecessary.
(iii) *Arthahīna* or absurd words.
(iv) *Bhinnārtha,* which denotes the use of obscene and crude words.
(v) *Ekārtha,* or repeating the same idea in other words; tautology.
(vi) *Abhipluthārtha,* where there is no connection between words or phrases in a sentence.
(vii) *Nyāyādapeta* or illogical words.
(viii) *Viṣama* occurs in poetry when poetical meters are mixed up.
(ix) *Visandhi* occurs when syllables or words that cannot be joined together are juxtaposed.
(x) *Avarṇasvarayojana* or cacophony. (*Nāṭyaśāstra,* XVII 80–91)

Bharata's categories encompass the word, word meaning, sentence, and sentence meaning; in short, it ranges from syntax to semantics. Latter-day critics also acknowledged these as poetic faults. Vāmana, for instance, followed

Bharata's footsteps and similar to the *guṇa* categories came up with twenty *doṣa*s under the four aspects that Bharata had identified. This method of identification of faults at the different levels of words and sentences was followed by most critics including Mammaṭa and Bhoja. Ānandavardhana and Kṣemendra, however, differed slightly in their conceptual definition of a *doṣa*. According to Ānandavardhana, any aspect that hindered aesthetic enjoyment was a *doṣa* while to Kṣemendra, anything that was inappropriate was a *doṣa*. Ānandavardhana saw *doṣa*s arising out of two different problems—lack of *vyutppatti* (formal training) on the part of a poet or lack of *pratibhā* (inherent poetic genius). Lack of formal training could make a poet err in terms of apt usage of words and sentences but this flaw could be covered up by poetic genius. Ānanda notes,

> For a poetic fault is of two kinds: it may be due to the poet's lack of mature judgement (*avyutpatti*) or it may be due to his lack of skill (*śakti*). A fault that is due to lack of mature judgement may be concealed by the poet's skill and so never be noticed. But a fault that is due to the poet's lack of skill will appear immediately. (*Dhvanyāloka* 3.6 e *A*)

The ancient theoreticians subscribed to the view that genius is all. We can believe this if we think of the magic that Shakespeare could produce even though he knew "little Latin and less Greek."

Formal or Semantic Feature?

How are we to evaluate the contributions made by these theorists of *alaṅkāra* and *rīti*? One of the major drawbacks of this approach was that it did not take the reader into consideration. It can be seen that all the discussions on figurative language and style were from the poet's perspective; in fact, the elaborate explanations of figures of speech, style, merits, and defects read almost like a user's manual intended for would-be poets. In many respects, it comes close to what we refer to as stylistics and rhetoric in the contemporary world.

Nonetheless, *rīti* marks a radical departure in the history of Sanskrit poetics. It was this school that started off the inquiry into the distinctive mark of a literary work and located it in the language of literature. This line of argument that it is the different use of language that distinguishes literature from mere reporting was to eventually lead to Kuntaka's concept of *vakrokti*.

However, there is still some confusion regarding the *Rīti School*—was it purely a formalist school? According to proponents of *rīti*, what distinguished poetic language from everyday language was the different and striking way in which it was used (a concept that was developed more fully by Kuntaka through his concept of *vakrokti*). So, they were more concerned about the form and manner of poetry than its content. Chari explains:

> Conspicuousness was to be achieved either by highlighting the structural (phonological/syntactic) elements of language through patterning or by lexical or semantic deviation (consisting of some "twist" or straining of the logic of thought, called vakrokti, or "crooked expression"). Thus, what these critics conceived of as "poetic form" applied to the whole "linguistic body" of poetic utterance, as distinguished from its "content of thought." "Poetic form"

does not mean that the city is u
inting at is the artificiality and s
words like "unreal," "brown," and "
gestion constitutes *dhvani.*
mary argument in *Dhvanyāloka* was
tituent of literariness in *kāvya* is *dhvan*
ealing extensively with the nature and
f *dhvani*, was composed mainly to establish
efuting the argument of his detractors that
exist and what Ānanda considers *dhvani* was
ed under other categories such as *alaṅkāra*
agnum opus *Dhvanyāloka* systematically
ese objections that were raised against the
ani and convincingly established that this was
that distinguished fine poetry from inferior
Ānandavardhana demarcated *dhvani* from
cts of poetic language like *alaṅkāra, guṇa,*
en systematically went on to exemplify why
re significant concept:

> ight contend that poetry is nothing more than
> odied in word and meaning. The means of
> this pair that lie in sound, such as alliteration,
> hat lie in meaning, such as simile, are well
> o well known are [those qualities] such as
> hich possess certain properties of phoneme and
> t. The *vṛtti*s which have been described by some
> er such names as *upanāgarikā*, and which are
> t in function from these [figures and qualities]
> ached our ears. So also the styles [*rīti*s] such as
> What is this thing called *dhvani* that it should
> these? (1.1a, *A*)

> is thus "style" or *manner* of expression (*bhaṅgi-bhaṇiti*, in Kuntaka's language). (Chari 141)

Chari's argument is that *rīti* or style is a function of language, but that function is not of expressing meaning. So, style is a formalistic feature (142). However, Vāmana went one step ahead of the *ālaṅkārikas* and incorporated *rasa* as an *artha-guṇa*. This rather complicates the debate about *rīti* being a formalist device because *rasa* is not strictly an aspect of form.

Conclusion

It was this apparent emphasis on form rather than content that proved detrimental to the school of *rīti*, *guṇa*, and *doṣa*; they cannot be said to have made a contribution comparable to *dhvani* or even *vakrokti* in the domain of Sanskrit poetics. It could not hold out against the intellectual onslaught of the *dhvani* school and its formidable leaders Ānandavardhana and Abhinavagupta. The enumeration and sometimes mind-numbing cataloguing of various styles or qualities and flaws were difficult, if not redundant. The ever-expanding list of *rīti* and *guṇa*s as outlined by different theorists down the ages shows us that these were dynamic attributes which could not be pinned down and solidified. However, it is to our early theoreticians' credit that the merits and defects they have identified still find a mention in our principles of good writing; the list of merits and flaws are still applicable to writers of not merely good literature, but writing in general. Perhaps this is where the problem lies—that the rightful place of these schools is in the field of stylistics and not poetics.

Works Cited

Ānandavardhana. *The Dhvanyāloka of Ānandavardhana with Locana of Abhinavagupta*. Translated and edited by Daniel Ingalls, Jeffrey Masson, and M. V. Patwardhan, Harvard University Press, 1990.

Bhāmaha. *Kāvyālaṅkāra*. Edited by B. N. Sarma and Baldeva Upadhyay, Chowkhamba Sanskrit Series Office, 1998.

Chari, V. K. *Sanskrit Criticism*. Motilal Banarsidass Publishers, 1993

Daṇḍin. *Kāvyādarśa of Daṇḍin*. Edited by Premachandra Tarkabagisa, Royal Asiatic Society, 1962.

De, Sushil Kumar. "Introduction." *Vakroktijīvita*, by Kuntaka, Firma K. L. Mukhopadhyay, 1961, pp. i–lxi.

Rudraṭa. *Kāvyālaṅkāra*. Nirnaya Sagar Press, 1886.

Udbhaṭa. *Kāvyālaṅkārasārasaṃgraha with the Commentary, the Laghuvṛtti of Induraja*. Edited by Narayana Daso Banhatti, Bhandarkar Oriental Research Institute, 1982.

Vāmana. *Kāvyālaṅkārasūtravṛtti*. Translated (Malayalam) and edited by E. Easwaran Nambootiri, Kerala Bhasha Institute, 2000.

This, of course, does not imply that *dhvani* was something that Ānandavardhana originally invented. Long before Ānanda wrote *Dhvanyāloka*, writers of *kāvya* had already used the possibility of poetic suggestion to its optimum. It is evident from the various cases of *dhvani* that Ānanda cites from the works of his predecessors such as Vālmīki and Kālidāsa.

The idea of *dhvani*, though in a different sense, was first used by the grammarians. Ānandavardhana himself acknowledged this in his *Dhvanyāloka*:

> The preeminent men of knowledge are the grammarians, for all the sciences rest on grammar; and they gave the name *dhvani* to the sounds of speech that are heard. In the same manner other wise men, who know the true essence of poetry have followed the example of the grammarians by giving the title *dhvani* to that verbal entity which contains a mixture of denotative and denoted elements and which is designated "as a poem". (1.13 l A)

What Ānandavardhana refers to here is the concept of *sphoṭa* propounded by the master grammarian Bhartṛhari. According to grammarians like him, we understand the meaning of a sentence only through the last sound that is uttered. So, what we hear and register is not a complete set of sounds, but the last sound which is born of other sounds, much like the echo left by a ringing bell. It is this echo that is called *sphoṭa*. *Dhvani* too is like *sphoṭa* because the suggested meaning arises out of other meanings and lingers in our minds like an echo.

Ānandavardhana's theory of *dhvani* was a combination of two concepts—the teleological hermeneutic model and the aesthetic concept of *rasa*. According to the teleological hermeneutic model proposed by *mīmāṃsakas*, a sentence might have a hidden meaning. For instance, a sentence might not explicitly instruct the reader but could implicitly have a didactic purpose. This happens through an extra semantic function called *bhāvanā*. Using the power of *bhāvanā*, the reader can infer something extra-textual from a sentence. The sentence "There are thieves on the way," is explicitly a mere statement of a fact but the reader will read an implicit warning into it, which is that she should be careful while going that way. Similarly, the sentence "There are sharks in the water," also warns readers "Do not swim here." Both implicit meanings are drawn from extra-textual factors. Drawing inspiration from *mīmāṃsaka*'s concept of *bhāvanā*, Ānandavardhana observed that an ideal poem is that which always suggests something more than what it explicitly denotes. The suggested element can be a thing or a fact (*vastu*), a figure of speech (like an *alaṅkāra*) or an aesthetic emotion (*rasa*). For Ānanda, *rasa* is the ultimate aim of poetry; so, even if a poetic composition suggests a meaning or thing, it will eventually result in the suggestion of *rasa*.

Ānandavardhana is important in the intellectual history of *dhvani* primarily because he was the first critic to systematically theorize the concept of *dhvani*. Therefore, his *Dhvanyāloka* can rightly be called the *lakṣaṇa-grantha* (the rule book) of *dhvani*. According to this work, what primarily distinguishes *kāvya* from other uses of language is the presence of *dhvani*. This does not mean that Ānandavardhana did not pay attention to linguistic devices such as *alaṅkāra*

> is thus "style" or *manner* of expression (*bhaṅgi-bhaṇiti*, in Kuntaka's language). (Chari 141)

Chari's argument is that *rīti* or style is a function of language, but that function is not of expressing meaning. So, style is a formalistic feature (142). However, Vāmana went one step ahead of the *ālaṅkārika*s and incorporated *rasa* as an *artha-guṇa*. This rather complicates the debate about *rīti* being a formalist device because *rasa* is not strictly an aspect of form.

Conclusion

It was this apparent emphasis on form rather than content that proved detrimental to the school of *rīti*, *guṇa*, and *doṣa*; they cannot be said to have made a contribution comparable to *dhvani* or even *vakrokti* in the domain of Sanskrit poetics. It could not hold out against the intellectual onslaught of the *dhvani* school and its formidable leaders Ānandavardhana and Abhinavagupta. The enumeration and sometimes mind-numbing cataloguing of various styles or qualities and flaws were difficult, if not redundant. The ever-expanding list of *rīti* and *guṇa*s as outlined by different theorists down the ages shows us that these were dynamic attributes which could not be pinned down and solidified. However, it is to our early theoreticians' credit that the merits and defects they have identified still find a mention in our principles of good writing; the list of merits and flaws are still applicable to writers of not merely good literature, but writing in general. Perhaps this is where the problem lies—that the rightful place of these schools is in the field of stylistics and not poetics.

Works Cited

Ānandavardhana. *The Dhvanyāloka of Ānandavardhana with Locana of Abhinavagupta*. Translated and edited by Daniel Ingalls, Jeffrey Masson, and M. V. Patwardhan, Harvard University Press, 1990.

Bhāmaha. *Kāvyālaṅkāra*. Edited by B. N. Sarma and Baldeva Upadhyay, Chowkhamba Sanskrit Series Office, 1998.

Chari, V. K. *Sanskrit Criticism*. Motilal Banarsidass Publishers, 1993

Daṇḍin. *Kāvyādarśa of Daṇḍin*. Edited by Premachandra Tarkabagisa, Royal Asiatic Society, 1962.

De, Sushil Kumar. "Introduction." *Vakroktijīvita*, by Kuntaka, Firma K. L. Mukhopadhyay, 1961, pp. i–lxi.

Rudraṭa. *Kāvyālaṅkāra*. Nirnaya Sagar Press, 1886.

Udbhaṭa. *Kāvyālaṅkārasārasaṃgraha with the Commentary, the Laghuvṛtti of Induraja*. Edited by Narayana Daso Banhatti, Bhandarkar Oriental Research Institute, 1982.

Vāmana. *Kāvyālaṅkārasūtravṛtti*. Translated (Malayalam) and edited by E. Easwaran Nambootiri, Kerala Bhasha Institute, 2000.

5

Dhvani

Like the theoretical positions that we saw in the previous chapters, Ānandavardhana's theory of *dhvani* was also an attempt to answer the age-old question of what constitutes literariness in *kāvya*. *Dhvani* means suggestion or resonance; simply put, it is the ability of a word, a sentence, or a literary composition to suggest a meaning, a *rasa* or an *alaṅkāra* beyond what is explicitly stated. It should also be clarified that *dhvani* lies in the tertiary level beyond denotation and connotation. The traditional example for *dhvani* is the Sanskrit phrase, *gaṅgāyāṃ ghoṣaḥ* or the village on the Ganga. This is considered to be an example of *dhvani* because primarily it means "a village on the Ganga." But this primary meaning of "on the Ganga" literally does not make sense because you cannot have a village on a river. So what it means is that it is situated on the banks of the Ganga; this constitutes the secondary meaning. Beyond that, it suggests the pristine and sacred nature of the village. This feeling is evoked because of the proximity of the village to the sacred river Ganga. The literal meaning of the phrase—its denotation—does not convey this. At the secondary level, what it connotes could probably be the location of the village. The tertiary level of suggestion is evoked because we know that the Ganga is holy and so by extension, the villages situated on its banks would also be holy. Similarly, T. S. Eliot's description of London as an "Unreal city/Under the brown fog of a winter dawn" (72) in *The Wasteland* does not mean that the city is unreal. What these lines are hinting at is the artificiality and sterility of the city through words like "unreal," "brown," and "winter." This hint or suggestion constitutes *dhvani*.

Ānanda's primary argument in *Dhvanyāloka* was that the major constituent of literariness in *kāvya* is *dhvani*. *Dhvanyāloka*, dealing extensively with the nature and characteristics of *dhvani*, was composed mainly to establish this claim by refuting the argument of his detractors that *dhvani* does not exist and what Ānanda considers *dhvani* was already subsumed under other categories such as *alaṅkāra* or *rīti*. The magnum opus *Dhvanyāloka* systematically addressed all these objections that were raised against the primacy of *dhvani* and convincingly established that this was the sole quality that distinguished fine poetry from inferior compositions. Ānandavardhana demarcated *dhvani* from the other aspects of poetic language like *alaṅkāra*, *guṇa*, or *rīti*, and then systematically went on to exemplify why *dhvani* is a more significant concept:

> Here some might contend that poetry is nothing more than what is embodied in word and meaning. The means of beautifying this pair that lie in sound, such as alliteration, and those that lie in meaning, such as simile, are well known. Also well known are [those qualities] such as sweetness, which possess certain properties of phoneme and arrangement. The *vṛttis* which have been described by some writers under such names as *upanāgarikā*, and which are not different in function from these [figures and qualities] also have reached our ears. So also the styles [*rītis*] such as *vaidarbhī*. What is this thing called *dhvani* that it should differ from these? (1.1a, *A*)

This, of course, does not imply that *dhvani* was something that Ānandavardhana originally invented. Long before Ānanda wrote *Dhvanyāloka*, writers of *kāvya* had already used the possibility of poetic suggestion to its optimum. It is evident from the various cases of *dhvani* that Ānanda cites from the works of his predecessors such as Vālmīki and Kālidāsa.

The idea of *dhvani*, though in a different sense, was first used by the grammarians. Ānandavardhana himself acknowledged this in his *Dhvanyāloka*:

> The preeminent men of knowledge are the grammarians, for all the sciences rest on grammar; and they gave the name *dhvani* to the sounds of speech that are heard. In the same manner other wise men, who know the true essence of poetry have followed the example of the grammarians by giving the title *dhvani* to that verbal entity which contains a mixture of denotative and denoted elements and which is designated "as a poem". (1.13 l A)

What Ānandavardhana refers to here is the concept of *sphoṭa* propounded by the master grammarian Bhartṛhari. According to grammarians like him, we understand the meaning of a sentence only through the last sound that is uttered. So, what we hear and register is not a complete set of sounds, but the last sound which is born of other sounds, much like the echo left by a ringing bell. It is this echo that is called *sphoṭa*. *Dhvani* too is like *sphoṭa* because the suggested meaning arises out of other meanings and lingers in our minds like an echo.

Ānandavardhana's theory of *dhvani* was a combination of two concepts—the teleological hermeneutic model and the aesthetic concept of *rasa*. According to the teleological hermeneutic model proposed by *mīmāṃsakas*, a sentence might have a hidden meaning. For instance, a sentence might not explicitly instruct the reader but could implicitly have a didactic purpose. This happens through an extra semantic function called *bhāvanā*. Using the power of *bhāvanā*, the reader can infer something extra-textual from a sentence. The sentence "There are thieves on the way," is explicitly a mere statement of a fact but the reader will read an implicit warning into it, which is that she should be careful while going that way. Similarly, the sentence "There are sharks in the water," also warns readers "Do not swim here." Both implicit meanings are drawn from extra-textual factors. Drawing inspiration from *mīmāṃsaka*'s concept of *bhāvanā*, Ānandavardhana observed that an ideal poem is that which always suggests something more than what it explicitly denotes. The suggested element can be a thing or a fact (*vastu*), a figure of speech (like an *alaṅkāra*) or an aesthetic emotion (*rasa*). For Ānanda, *rasa* is the ultimate aim of poetry; so, even if a poetic composition suggests a meaning or thing, it will eventually result in the suggestion of *rasa*.

Ānandavardhana is important in the intellectual history of *dhvani* primarily because he was the first critic to systematically theorize the concept of *dhvani*. Therefore, his *Dhvanyāloka* can rightly be called the *lakṣaṇa-grantha* (the rule book) of *dhvani*. According to this work, what primarily distinguishes *kāvya* from other uses of language is the presence of *dhvani*. This does not mean that Ānandavardhana did not pay attention to linguistic devices such as *alaṅkāra* and *guṇa*—formal devices that his predecessors had previously identified as the distinguishing marks of *kāvya*. He merely disagreed with the primacy accorded to such features. According to Ānandavardhana, *alaṅkāra*s function like ornaments on a person's body, while *guṇa*s are qualities like courage (2.5 g). However, the soul of *kāvya*, for him, was undoubtedly *dhvani*.

Meaning, according to his concept, is of two types—literal (*vācya*) and suggestive (*pratīyamāna*). *Dhvani* is that ability of a signifier, a set of signifiers, a meaning, a sound, or a gesture to suggest (*pratīyamāna*) something other than what it explicitly presents (1.2 and 4). These elements which help to evoke suggestion are called *vyañjaka*s. Although Ānandavardhana classified *vyañjaka*s under a wide range of linguistic and non-linguistic elements, his intensive discussion of *vyañjaka* and *dhvani* is limited to the linguistic and emotive realms. According to Ānandavardhana, *vyañjaka* within the linguistic field covers a wide variety of elements such as a *pada* (word), a *vākya* (sentence), a *varṇa* (phoneme), a *padāṃśa* (a part of a word), a *saṃghaṭanā* (texture), an *alaṅkāra* (figure of speech), an *aṅgya* (gesture), a *sup* (case endings), a *tiri* (personal endings of a verb), *vacana* (grammatical number), *saṃbandha* (relationship indicated through the genitive), *kāraka* (complement of the verbal action such as agent, object, locus, etc.), a *kṛt* (primary suffix attached to the verb root), *sandhi* (compounds), and so on (3.16 *K*). During the process of suggestion, what a *vyañjaka* explicitly represents recedes into the background and another aspect that is not conventionally associated with it comes to the view of a *sahṛdaya* (a sensitive reader).

Different Forms of *Dhvani*

Ānandavardhana divided the whole realm of *dhvani* into two broad categories:

(i) *avivakṣita-vācya-dhvani*
(ii) *vivakṣitānya-paravācya-dhvani*

In *avivakṣita-vācya-dhvani*, a word abandons its primary meaning completely and then comes to suggest a new meaning that is not conventionally associated with it. According to Ānandavardhana, the term *avivakṣita-vācya* means "that instance of *dhvani* where the literal meaning is not intended" (2.1 *A*). The word is the *vyañjaka* or "suggestor" in the case of *avivakṣita-vācya-dhvani*.

Avivakṣita-vācya-dhvani is again divided into two, depending on the way the *dhvani* is evoked:

(i) *atyanta-tiraskṛta-vācya*
(ii) *arthāntara-saṃkramita-vācya*

The category of *atyanta-tiraskṛta-vācya* is that type of *dhvani* where the literal sense (*abhidhā*) of the word is completely negated. In *arthāntara-saṃkramita-vācya*, the literal meaning retains certain elements of its primary sense but suggests a new meaning that is not conventionally attributed to it (2.1). It goes without saying that if we completely negate the primary meaning of a term, it is impossible to generate a new meaning out of it. Therefore, Ānandavardhana's division of *avivakṣita-vācya-dhvani* into *atyanta-tiraskṛta-vācya* and *arthāntara-saṃkramita-vācya* is not on the basis of whether a word completely negates its primary meaning or not, but on the degree to which it retains its primary meaning. It is admittedly difficult to precisely decide the extent to which a word has retained its primary meaning. There are overlaps between the two sub-categories, and distinguishing one from the other is extremely problematic.

Ānandavardhana has given a few examples to illustrate his idea of *dhvani*. The following is an example of *atyanta-tiraskṛta-vācya* variety of *dhvani*:

> Though the sky is filled with drunken [*matta*] clouds,
> and the woods with *arjunas* thrashing in the downpour,
> these black nights too when the moon has lost its *pride* [*ahaṅkāra*],
> carry off my heart. (2.1 d)

According to Ānandavardhana, this Prākrit verse which describes a monsoon night incorporates *dhvani* in such words as "drunken" (*matta*) and "pride" (*ahaṅkāra*). The word "drunken" (*matta*) means "state of inebriation due to the use of some intoxicant." Since the condition of inebriation is applicable only to a sentient entity, the conventional meaning of the word "drunken" (*matta*) is impossible in this context because a cloud, being a non-sentient thing, cannot get intoxicated. So, the word "drunken" gets extended to suggest one of the characteristics associated with a drunkard (as opposed to denoting the state of inebriation), which is "the act of wandering around aimlessly." Thus, the word "drunken" undergoes an incorporeal transformation, i.e., the physicality of the word does not change, but it takes on a new meaning which is not conventionally associated with it. The same process happens in the case of the word "pride" (*ahaṅkāra*). The word "pride" literally means "a feeling of pleasure or satisfaction that you get when you or people who are connected with you have done something well or own something that other people admire." This is a quality typical of a sentient creature, especially a human being. But this quality is attributed to the moon which is a non-sentient thing. Hence the literal meaning of the term "pride" (*ahaṅkāra*) gets blocked and the word expands its conventional semantic ambit to incorporate another meaning—glory (a positive quality which people can pride on). So, the sentence means that the moon has lost its glory. Therefore, it is an example of *atyanta-tiraskṛta-vācya*.

Now let us look at the second variety of *dhvani* under *avivakṣita-vācya—arthāntara-saṅkramita-vācya dhvani*. Here the word retains certain elements of its primary sense and then suggests a new meaning that is not conventionally attributed to it. A classic example of this variety of *dhvani* is *nagaraṃ praviśanti kuntāḥ* (the spears enter the city). In this example, the word "spear" does not mean "a weapon with a pointed tip"; rather it means "soldiers who wield spears," or spearmen. Here the word "spear" retains its primary meaning to a greater degree because the persons here referred to are "spearmen," not "swordsmen" or "bowmen." So, the word *kuntāḥ* maintains certain aspects of its primary meaning, yet shows a new meaning that is not conventionally associated with it. The following is another example of *arthāntara-saṃkramita-vācya* that Ānandavardhana quotes in *Dhvanyāloka*:

Virtues blossom
When admired by men of taste
When graced by the sun's rays
a lotus becomes a *lotus* [*kamala*]. (2.1 b)

This verse which Ānandavardhana takes from his own *Viṣamabāṇalīlā* refers to the point at which a *kāvya* attains perfection. The speaker says that just as a lotus reaches the pinnacle of its beauty only when the sun shines on it, so also poetic qualities shine forth only when they are appreciated by a connoisseur of art or *sahṛdaya*. In the given example, the suggestive word is "lotus" (*kamala*) in its second occurrence. The word "lotus" is conventionally used to refer to a flower but this meaning does not make any sense in the line, "the lotus becomes a lotus." So, the second "lotus" acquires another layer of meaning, which is "the actualization of all qualities that are supposed to be present in a lotus." In other words, the word "lotus" here means "a state of perfection." Thus, this line comes to mean that it is only when graced by the rays of the sun that a lotus reaches a state of perfection.

To make the point clearer, let us have a look at a few modern examples of *avivakṣita-vācya-dhvani*. The following example from Stephen Spender's "Not Palaces," which describes the eye as it perceives a landscape, is a case in point.

> Eye gazelle, delicate wanderer,
> Drinker of horizon's fluid line. (64)

Here *dhvani* is evoked by the connection between the eye and the gazelle which drinks water. We know that the "eye" is incapable of drinking. Therefore, in this context, the primary meaning of the word "drinker" gets blocked, and the focus shifts to the idea of an "experience," which is where the act of seeing is. Thus, the word "drinker" abandons its primary meaning and goes on to suggest a new unconventional meaning—somebody who sees a sight. The desultory nature of the gaze is accentuated by the metaphorical comparison to the gazelle that casually drinks from the stream. The term "fluid line" refers to the stream-like appearance of the horizon, and the word "drink" is aptly used to suggest the act of synesthetically experiencing the "taste" of that "fluid line." The lines, on the whole, suggest the grace and fluidity of movement of the eyes as they wander over the horizon; this suggestion is not overtly done but through the subtle use of appropriate words.

Another example that will illustrate the idea even further is from Shakespeare's *The Merchant of Venice*—"How sweet the moonlight *sleeps* upon this bank" (V.1.54). By ascribing the act of sleeping to a non-human element like moonlight, Shakespeare has successfully moved away from the primary meaning of sleep to focus on the usual posture that somebody adopts while sleeping, which is to lie flat on a surface. The words "sweet" and "sleep" do not allow the reader to wonder how moonlight can sleep; instead, they coax her into enjoying the silent and calm beauty of a moonlit night.

According to Ānandavardhana, both these varieties of *avivakṣita-vācya-dhvani* operate with the help of secondary meanings of words. In fact, his examples for *atyanta-tiraskṛta-vācya* and *arthāntara-saṃkramita-vācya dhvani* seem to correspond to metaphor and metonymy respectively. However, this does not mean that all secondary meanings or metaphor and metonymy, automatically become *dhvani*. He pointed out that some secondary usages become so clichéd that they appear to be prosaic to us. Ānanda says, "Secondary usage can also be found [in instances that are entirely] without suggestiveness" (3.33 j *A*). For instance, it is the secondary meaning that is operational in the usage "hands of a clock," but it is not *dhvani* because it has become part of our everyday language. According to Ānanda, a secondary usage becomes an instance of *dhvani* only when it is not part of the existing linguistic convention. A case in point is the word *lāvaṇya.* Ānanda observes that words such as *lāvaṇya*, which are used idiomatically in a sense other than their proper sense, are never instances of *dhvani*. The word *lāvaṇya*, which literally means "salty" is also used figuratively by means of secondary usage to mean "charm" or "beauty." Even when the word *lāvaṇya* is used in the secondary sense to mean "charm" or "beauty," it cannot be considered an instance of *dhvani* because this secondary usage has lost its newness and is already a part of the existing linguistic convention. Ānanda observes, "Words such as *lāvaṇya*, which are used idiomatically in a sense other than their proper (etymological) sense, are never instances of *dhvani*" (1.16 k).

Abhinavagupta too agreed with this definition of *dhvani*. Quoting Kumārilabhaṭṭa's *Tantravārttika*, he said,

> As has been said, 'some cases of secondary usage, being idiomatic, so far as their force is concerned are just like direct denotation.' Such words, although used in a sense different from their etymological sense, do not carry any *dhvani* and we cannot speak of *dhvani* in such cases. (1.16 *L*)

For Ānandavardhana, secondary usage sometimes functions only as an *upalakṣaṇa* (adventitious mark) of *dhvani* (1.19 *K*). An *upalakṣaṇa* denotes a sign or symbol that incidentally helps us to identify a thing; it functions only temporarily under certain conditions. For example, "the first house east of the lake" where the location (east) is the *lakṣaṇa* (here the word means a characteristic mark) of a washerman's house. An *upalakṣaṇa* of this house would be "the house on the roof of which a crow is sitting." This is an *upalakṣaṇa* because the crow that sits on the house may fly away at any time and hence it cannot be considered a permanent marker to identify the washerman's house. According to Ānanda, this secondary usage is not a *lakṣaṇa* or a characteristic mark of *dhvani* because it is too broad a category. After all, crows do not exclusively sit on washerman's houses; the crow sitting on the washerman's house is incidental and temporary and is an aspect that is broad enough to apply to all houses. (For this example on *upalakṣaṇa*, see n10 on 1.1 e A in Ingall's translation of *Dhvanyāloka*. Abhinava also briefly comments on this in 1.14 *L.*) Similarly, if we define an apple as anything red and round, that will eventuate in the fallacy of "too broad" because all that is red and round cannot be an apple. The planet Mars is also red and round. According to the aforesaid definition, Mars should also be considered an apple. Therefore, this definition is faulty. These examples point to the fact that *avivakṣita-vācya-dhvani* does not occur in all the instances where secondary usage occurs. If a secondary usage needs to become an *avivakṣita-vācya-dhvani*, it should operate in such a way that it produces a new meaning which is not yet a part of the linguistic convention.

Vivakṣitānya-paravācya

The expression *vivakṣitānya-paravācya* means "the literal meaning (*vivakṣita*) understood in a different way (*anyaparavācya*)" (2.1 A). In *vivakṣitānya-paravācya dhvani*, the literal meaning, although it is intended, moves on to suggest something which is not explicitly presented. *Vivakṣitānya-paravācya* is broadly divided into two:

(i) *saṃlakṣya-krama-vyaṅgya*
(ii) *asaṃlakṣya-krama-vyaṅgya* (2.2)

This division is on the basis of the process through which we arrive at the suggested meaning. In *asaṃlakṣya-krama-vyaṅgya*, we are not conscious of the movement from the literal to the suggested meaning. Only *rasadhvani* falls within the ambit of *asaṃlakṣya-krama-vyaṅgya*. In *saṃlakṣya-krama-vyaṅgya*, which is also known as *anuraṇana-rūpa-vyaṅgya-dhvani* (suggested sense appearing like a reverberation), we are conscious of the movement that takes place from the literal meaning to the suggested meaning. In other words, we perceive the literal sense first, and then after a momentary interval, the suggested sense dawns on us. *Saṃlakṣya-krama-vyaṅgya* is divided into two varieties—*śabda-śakti-mūla* and *artha-śakti-mūla* (2.20 K).

Śabda-śakti-mūla is that variety of *dhvani* where a word or a set of words implies a figure of speech. In *artha-śakti-mūla-dhvani*, the meaning of words acts as suggestor. The following is an example of an *alaṅkāra* (figure of speech) being suggested by the power of words (*śabdaśakti*). Ānandavardhana takes this example from Mayūra's *Sūryaśataka*:

> *... dattānandāḥ prajānām samucitasamayākṛṣṭasṛṣṭaiḥ payobhiḥ*
> *pūrvahne viprakīrṇā diśi diśi viramatyahni saṃhārabhājaḥ*
> *dīptāṃśordīrghaduḥkhaprabhavabhavabhayodanvaduttāranāvo*
> *gāvo vaḥ pāvanānāṃ paramaparimitāṃ prītimutpādayantu.*
> (IX.1)

In the actual context given in the text, this verse is about the rays of the sun:

> Giving joy to all creatures,
> by their absorption and release of water [*payobhiḥ*],
> scattering to all directions in the morning

and disappearing [*samhāra*] at the close of day;
they are a ship for crossing
the sea of transmigration, the source of our long pain
May these rays [*gāvo*] of the blazing sun engender
in your purified selves unmeasured bliss. (2.21 e)

However, the word *gāvo* can also mean cows, and so the same verse can denote another meaning, although the new meaning does not fit in the context of the poem. The pun gives rise to the second meaning which alludes to cows which gather in one place after roaming around various places the whole day. This second meaning is possible because the word *payobhi* can mean both water and milk; *saṃhāra,* both "disappear" and "gather in one place" and *gāvo,* both "rays" and "cows." The following is the second meaning which can be arrived at:

Giving joy to their progeny
By their absorption and release of milk [*payobhi*],
scattering to all directions in the morning
And gathering in one place [*samhāra*] at the close of day:
they are a ship for crossing
the sea of transmigration, the source of our long pain
May these cows [*gāvo*] engender
In your purified selves unmeasured bliss. (2.21 e)

In the example given above, the contextual meaning and the non-contextual meaning are literal. However there is an implicit connection between the contextual meaning (the meaning related to the clouds) and the non-contextual meaning (the meaning related to the cows) in the sense that a parallel can be drawn between the clouds wandering in the sky and cows roaming around various places, on the basis of the common function that they perform—that is, both of them give joy to people. This connection is that of a subject and tenor (*upamāna* and *upameya*). Therefore, what is suggested is the figure of speech called *rūpaka* or metaphor where a connection is drawn between two dissimilar objects in such a way that this connection between the two has to be understood from the context.

Similarly, puns which lead to equivocation can result in two different meanings. Although he used it as an exercise in deconstruction, Jim Powell has pointed out how in the following haiku, the word "pines" can be interpreted as verb or noun, and how the meaning can change:

> How mournfully the wind of
> Autumn pines
> Upon the mountainside as day
> Declines. (26)

The second variety under *saṃlakṣya-krama-vyaṅgya* is *artha-śakti-mūla dhvani*. In this variety of *dhvani*, a fact—other than the literal meaning of the words—is suggested by the primary meaning (2.22). Unlike *avivakṣita-vācya-dhvani*, where the literal meaning of the word is abandoned to suggest a new meaning by the secondary usage of words, *artha-śakti-mūla dhvani* does not make use of the possibilities of the secondary usage to generate the suggested meaning. On the other hand, in *artha-śakti-mūla*, the literal meaning is retained; the suggested meaning is created solely by the power of primary meaning and context. However, Ānandavardhana says that this variety is different from the literal sense. He uses a verse from *Sattasaī* to illustrate this. The speaker of this verse is a woman who tries to prevent a mendicant from venturing into her romantic retreat on the bank of the Goda River. A religious mendicant was always frightened away from a house by the family dog and he used to wander around freely along the banks of Goda River to gather flowers for his *pūjā*. The young wife of this house was in the habit of secretly meeting her lover in a thicket on the riverbank. Now she fears that the mendicant who comes along the riverbank will become a hindrance to her tryst with her lover. To prevent the mendicant from coming to the thicket thereby interrupting her love-making, the clever woman says these words to the mendicant.

> Go your rounds freely, gently monk;
> the little dog is gone.
> Just today from the thickets by the Goda
> came a fearsome lion and killed him. (1.4 b)

The verse literally means that the mendicant is free to roam around the banks of the Goda River. But this positive statement hides a threat; the old man who was afraid of the small dog is now told that he can wander around in a place where there is a fearsome lion. What the verse suggests is not a permission, but a prohibition that he should not walk along the banks of the Goda River. Thus, the verse negates its literal meaning and suggests a new meaning. Ānandavardhana explains various sorts of *vastudhvani* where the literal meaning contradicts its suggested meaning—permission becomes a prohibition or a prohibition is permission. Although he demonstrates only a few instances of *vastudhvani*, he says that "Other differences of the suggested meaning from the literal are possible along these lines. We have merely indicated the general direction" (1.4 g *A*).

Rasadhvani

When a verse suggests a *rasa*, that becomes *rasadhvani*. According to Abhinavagupta, the commentator of Ānanda's *Dhvanyāloka*, the very first benedictory verse in *Dhvanyāloka* is an example of *rasadhvani*:

Of Madhu's foe
Incarnate as a lion by his will,
May the claws, which put the moon to shame
In purity and shape,
By cutting off his devotees' distress
grant you protection. (I.1)

This benedictory verse has as its subject Narasiṃha, the man-lion incarnation of Viṣṇu. The legend has it that Viṣṇu incarnated as Narasiṃha in order to destroy the demon king Hiraṇyakaśipu to remove the distress of his devotee Prahlāda. According to Abhinavagupta, "The heroic flavor (*vīrarasa*) is suggested by our apprehension of energy (*utsāha*), an apprehension furnished by the association of God, who is constantly exerting himself [on behalf of humankind], with the characteristic of clarity of purpose and diligent resolve" (1.1 e *L*).

The following is another example of *rasadhvani* that Ānanda cites:

Her face was bowed in shyness
in the presence of our elders
and she forced back the grief
that gave motion to her breast.
But did not the mere corner of her eye,
lovelier than a startled deer's,

> somehow, as it dropped a tear,
> tell me not to go? (3.4. b *A*)

The woman who looks at her man in the presence of elders cannot tell him not to go; her goodbye is tinged with the sadness of separation which is suggested by the image of tears dropping from the corner of her eyes.

Similarly, this verse from a *puram* poem that is spoken by the widow of a brave warrior:

> The horse
> Of our good man,
> Who was father in our house
> To a little son
> With a tuft of hair
> Like a plume on a steed,
> It did not come back. (Ramanujan 179)

These lines evoke *karuṇa rasa* or the pathos of loss experienced by a wife and mother without directly alluding to sorrow. Likewise, Lear's famous "Pray you, undo this button" (V.3.309) when he has a dead Cordelia in his arms evoke *karuṇa rasa* without any direct reference to death.

Different Forms of Poetic Composition

It is clear from the above examples that Ānandavardhana considered *dhvani* to be the determining factor of the nature of a *kāvya*. He was of the view that both the expressed meaning and suggested meaning of a poetic composition should be valid:

> The suggested sense, which has been described as comparable to the charm of a beautiful woman, has been called *dhvani* when it predominates (over the expressed meaning).

> But now a type of poetry is envisaged where this sense is subordinated, the expressed meaning being more beautiful. This is called *guṇībhūta-vyaṅgya-kāvya*. (3.34 *A*)

In *guṇībhūta-vyaṅgya-kāvya,* the suggested elements always remain subordinate to what is explicitly stated. According to Ānanda, the subordination of the suggested element "to the principal sense of the sentence is like a king's following after his servant in the servant's wedding procession" (3.34 *A*). In some cases, both *dhvani* and *guṇībhūta* can appear in a combination. In such instances, the readers should understand the element that predominates and then call it appropriately either *dhvani kāvya* or *guṇībhūta-vyaṅgya-kāvya*. The following is an example of *guṇībhūta-vyaṅgya-kāvya*:

> Knowing that her gallant had set his heart
> on a rendezvous, the subtle lass
> smiled and *to show her meaning* folded
> the petals of the lotus in her hand. (2.22 a; emphasis added)

According to Ānandavardhana, in the poem, the readers are expressly told that there is a suggestiveness in the girl's folding up the lotus blossom with which she is playing. Therefore, Ānanda opines that suggestiveness in the poem is subordinated to the explicit meaning. As lotuses close their petals at sundown, she means that he is to meet her at that time. The suggestion is the fact that her lover should come at night which makes it a *vastudhvani.* We arrive at the suggested meaning immediately. This remark indicating that there is a suggestion in the act of folding the petals ruins the concealed nature of poetic suggestion. Abhinava's commentary on this passage is noteworthy. According to Abhinava,

> It is true that no one word in these three lines, even in connection with its neighbors, has the power of denoting the sense of 'evening,' and to that extent the suggestiveness of the stanza is not undone. However, we are expressly told that the sense is suggestive of some other sense and thereby the very life of suggestion, which consists of the charm of something being said in a hidden manner, is destroyed. (2.22a *L*)

In the previous example of *guṇībhūta-vyaṅgya-kāvya*, the suggested element is a fact. Since the poet vividly states that there is a suggested element in the girl's act of folding the petals, suggestion loses its charm. To put it in the words of Abhinavagupta, the suggested sense here no longer appears like a "treasure buried beneath the earth" (since the poet tells the readers that the girl means something more than what she does). According to Ānandavardhana, seen from the point of view of *rasa*, even this sort of a *guṇībhūta-vyaṅgya-kāvya* can eventually turn out to be a *dhvani kāvya* provided it suggests any other element such as a *rasa* or an *alaṅkāra*. Ānanda says, "This type of poetry also, where the suggestion is subordinated, may take on the nature of *dhvani* when regarded from the viewpoint of its final meaning if that meaning is a *rasa* …" (3.40 *K*).

Standing in contrast to *dhvani-kāvya* is what Ānanda calls *citra-kāvya*. According to Ānandavardhana, a literary composition which looks beautiful because of its novelties of literal sense and expression but fails to suggest a *rasa* or a fact or a thing as its final meaning is called a *citra-kāvya*.

For Ānanda, it is not real poetry, but just an imitation of poetry like a *citra* or painting. *Citra-kāvya* is of two types namely, *śabda-citra* (verbal poetry of display), and *artha-citra* (semantic poetry of display). Semantic *citra* which extensively uses figures of speech like poetic fancy carry no suggested sense and fails to suggest anything because of the predominance of the literal meaning. Similarly, in verbal *citra-kāvya*, the emphasis is on wordplay without suggestion. Anticipating criticism from his detractors, Ānanda says that people who deny the existence of *dhvani* may point out that poetry cannot be about nothing; anything that a poet mentions in the poem can turn out to be a *vibhāva* or stimulant for some *rasa* (3.41–42 *K*). It can be argued that even nonsense verse like Edward Lear's or Lewis Carroll's *Jabberwocky* is evoking a *rasa*:

> Twas brillig, and the slithy toves
> Did gyre and gimble in the wabe:
> All mimsy were the borogoves,
> And the mome raths outgrabe. (224)

It could be argued that despite being nonsensical, this verse evokes *hāsya rasa*. He observed that although it is true that ultimately a poetic composition results in *rasa*, the purport (*tatparya*) of the poet is particularly important. In the above verse, Carroll was aiming at producing a comic effect, so the poem becomes effective in that sense. If the poet is not properly charged with emotion and does not have the intention of producing a *rasa*, a poetic composition will turn out to be a *rasābhāsa*, an imitation of *rasa* bereft of aesthetic emotion. Ānanda states,

> For the meaning of the words in a poem is greatly strengthened by the author's intention. By force of the inherent capability of the literal sense there may be an apprehension of *rasa*, even though the author had no intention of revealing it; but that apprehension will be very weak. In this way too we may regard such a composition as without *rasa* and so assign it to the area of *citra*. (3.41–42 a)

This appears to lead us to a tricky area where we are asked to go deeper into the realm of the poet's intentions. It is significant that this is an aspect of literary appreciation that Western critics like Wimsatt and Beardsley termed the "intentional fallacy," warning that a literary work should not be read according to what the author intended it to be. However, what Ānandavardhana seems to be pointing to is the practical fact that an author who is not fired up by the desire to evoke *rasa* and does not share that passion will be insincere in his effort and produce a *citra-kāvya*. Intention, according to him, seems to indicate not the effect that the author seeks to create through the work, but the seriousness with which s/he approaches the work. So, Carroll's "Jabberwocky" will not be a *citrakāvya* because his intention in writing it was to evoke the *hāsya rasa* through his verbal games.

The Reader's Role

An important element in the actualization of *dhvani* is a sympathetic reader. Ānanda observed that in the absence of a responsive and sympathetic reader—who he calls a *sahṛdaya*—it is impossible to arrive at the suggested meaning. In *Dhvanyāloka*, he noted, "It [*dhvani*] is not understood by the mere knowledge of grammar and dictionaries. It is understood only by those who know the true knowledge of poetic meaning" (1.7 K). The true knowledge of poetic meaning here means the ability to move beyond the conventional meaning of a word. In his commentary on this aspect, Ānanda continues,

> [T]his [suggested sense] is understood only by those who know the nature of poetic meaning. If this meaning were denotative, one would get to it by knowledge of literal, denotative meanings, and the words that convey them. But this meaning is beyond the range of those who have taken pains only on the definitions of words and who have paid no attention to the poetic meaning, just as the character of the notes (*svaras*) and *śrutis*, etc. is beyond the range of those who know the definitions of music but are not good singers. (1.7 *A*)

Privileging the position of the reader further, Ānandavardhana says that a reader's actualization of *dhvani* need not always depend on whether the author or speaker intends *dhvani* in a particular context. According to Ānandavardhana, even if the author or speaker does not intend suggestive meaning in a particular context, a *sahṛdaya* has the freedom to come up with *dhvani*. He says,

> A suggested sense which is revealed by word and meaning, if it is a specific intention, becomes a *vivakṣita* [something that the speaker wishes to convey], when it is revealed as the *tātparya* [final sentence meaning]. However, this alone will not explain the term *dhvani*, which covers an immense area, because it is insufficient. Rather, it is a suggested element in any of the three forms, [*vastu*, *alaṅkāra* or *rasa*], *whether in the form of a speaker's intention or not*, if it is suggested as

> the final sentence meaning, that justifies the term *dhvani*, as we said in defining *dhvani* in terms of the aforesaid types of suggestiveness. (3.33 m; emphasis added)

The gist of what Ānanda says is that if a reader can "create" the possibility of *dhvani* in a context—irrespective of whether the speaker/author intends it or not—that suggestive meaning, which the *sahṛdaya* creates on his own, will fall in the ambit of *dhvani*. Daniel H. H. Ingalls explains the words of Ānanda: "The *vyaṅgya* need not be intended by the speaker. A naive girl, to give an example not seldom used in Sanskrit poetry, may make a suggestion of which she is quite unaware and which she is so far from intending that she would avoid if she were" (3.33 m A notes 2). This can be better explained with the help of an example from Shakespeare's *King Lear* where the mentally deranged Lear asks his companion Fool to unbutton his dress upon feeling suffocated: "Pray, undo my button" (5.3.309). This request, being the words of an anguished father who sees the body of his beloved daughter, is on the surface banal but suggests the depth of the misery that asphyxiates him. A creative reader can turn these words into an instance of *avivakṣita-vācya-dhvani* and say that what Lear wants the Fool to do is not just undo a few buttons but save him from the ailments of his physical existence by unbuttoning and removing the apparel of his life. It is of no consequence to speculate whether Shakespeare intended this range of meanings.

Conclusion

Dhvani has posed a conundrum for critics and literature aficionados alike, precisely because it is so hard to define and identify. This tertiary level of meaning that Ānandavardhana spoke of is the outcome of deep analysis and interpretation of literary works. There is no denying that this is a very subjective process which depends on a host of individualistic factors like the reader's cultural values, belief systems, and other inclinations. It is also completely contextual. The examples that Ānandavardhana has given as examples of *dhvani* are bound to befuddle readers today, because literary and cultural symbols are not static and change with the times. For instance, the image of a girl folding the petals of a lotus will not be understood as sending out a message that she is free to meet in the evening. Ānandavardhana also felt that *dhvani* was contextual:

> A denotative power is the very self of each individual word, bound to it from the time of our first understanding the word, for the word is never known without it. But suggestiveness is not bound to the word, but accidental, for our apprehension of it is conditioned by context, etc. and it is not apprehended in the absence of those conditions. (3.33 l A)

This would obviously make it difficult for readers to fully appreciate artistic works from other cultures.

It is also confusing as to what exactly the tertiary meaning implies. It is very clear that *dhvani* is not metaphor, metonymy, pun or irony. This is an evanescent concept which can be defined only negatively as to what it is not, rather than what it is. Abhinavagupta was right when he remarked that if we are expressly told that the sense is suggestive of something, then the beauty of suggestion or indirect allusion, is destroyed. In short, *dhvani* is inexplicable and ineffable.

However, nobody would deny the importance of Ānandavardhana's concept of *dhvani* as a distinctive feature which marks a literary work. The beauty of a literary composition lies in both what it expresses as well as what it does not express, the hidden meaning that we read into lines that suggest "thoughts that do often lie too deep for tears" (Wordsworth, "Ode on Intimations of Immortality").

Works Cited

Abhinavagupta. *Locana*. In *The Dhvanyāloka of Ānandavardhana with the Locana of Abhinavagupta*. Translated and edited by Daniel Ingalls, Jeffrey Masson, and M. V. Patwardhan, Harvard University Press, 1990.

Ānandavardhana. *The Dhvanyāloka of Ānandavardhana with the Locana of Abhinavagupta*. Translated and edited by Daniel Ingalls, Jeffrey Masson, and M. V. Patwardhan, Harvard University Press. 1990.

Carroll, Lewis. *Through the Looking-glass: And What Alice Found There*. Macmillan and Co., 1875.

Eliot, T. S. "The Waste Land." *The Waste Land and Other Poems*. Broad View Press, 2011, pp. 63–84.

Powell, Jim. *Derrida for Beginners*. Orient Longman, 2000.

Ramanujan, A. K. *Poems of Love and War*. Columbia University Press, 2011.

Shakespeare, William. *The Merchant of Venice*. Maple Press, 2013.

———. *King Lear*. Penguin Books, 1999.

Spender, Stephen. *Collected Poems 1928–1953*. Faber and Faber Ltd., 1959.

Wordsworth, William. "Ode on Intimations of Immortality." https://poets.org/poem/ode-intimations-immortality-recollections-early-childhood. Accessed September 10, 2019.

6

Vakrokti

We have seen how *rasa* was an overarching concern for almost all the major practitioners and theoreticians of literature in Sanskrit. However, the status attributed to it varied from one individual to the other. If evocation of *rasa* was of primary importance to Bharata, it was but one of the many embellishments that a literary work should have to somebody like Bhāmaha or Daṇḍin. Nonetheless, nobody ever disputed the primacy of this aesthetic experience that was unique to literature and the arts. This question of the function of literature or *kāvya* naturally led to an exploration of the various aspects of its nature and composition. What is the distinctive trait of a *kāvya* that sets it apart from ordinary linguistic expressions? Are there features which are immediately discernible and unique to a *kāvya*? One distinctive feature that naturally arose was language. For instance, "the rose is red" will not under ordinary circumstances be thought of as poetry; but "my love is like a red, red rose" will strike you as poetic. The reason is the way the language has been used. It connects an ordinary expression like "red rose" in a very different and extraordinary way that makes you sit up and take notice. Ancient Indian theorists of poetry termed this *vakrokti* (which literally means "deviant use of language") and maintained that this is one distinctive feature that helped you to recognize a *kāvya* when you saw or read it. The Sanskrit word *vakrokti* is a portmanteau word composed of two words namely *vakratā* and *ukti* meaning respectively "deviant" and "utterance." So, the word *vakrokti* literally means deviant utterance or a "striking usage" (Pollock, *The Rasa Reader*).

It has been mentioned earlier that in Sanskrit *kāvyaśāstra*, Bhāmaha was the first literary theoretician to use the term *vakrokti* to denote the idea of figurative deviation of speech although it was Kuntaka in the 10th century to deal with it in extenso, connecting it to almost all the aspects of *kāvya*. Before Bhāmaha, Bharata had employed the idea of deviant utterance in his *Nāṭyaśāstra* without using the term *vakrokti* per se. Bharata used the term *lakṣaṇā* to refer to what his successors would call *vakrokti*. Bhāmaha used the term *vakrokti* with regard to his discussion of the figure of speech *atiśayokti*. According to Bhāmaha, *atiśayokti*, and *vakrokti* were coterminous with each other (*Kāvyālaṅkāra* II.85). For him, the figure of speech *atiśayokti* is the treatment of an idea or entity in such a way that they transcend the familiar way in which they are usually perceived and presented. The following is an example of *atiśayokti*, which Bhāmaha cites in *Kāvyālaṅkāra*: "If the loose skin of waters drops down like the slough of serpents, then it will become the white garments on the limbs of ladies sporting on in the water" (II.83). In this example, Bhāmaha provides us with an uncustomary equation to perceive water. The dominant conception about water is that it is a colorless, odorless, liquid which forms water bodies such as rivers, oceans, ponds, and so on. In the example given above, Bhāmaha is, in fact, breaking the conventional image of water by visualizing it as the dress worn by women. We see a similar unconventional image when Ted Hughes describes a snowdrop as "Brutal as the stars of this month, /Her pale head heavy as metal" (56). The stereotypical associations of purity and innocence with the snowdrop are completely destroyed here where adjectival expressions like "brutal" and "heavy as metal" convey a sinister feeling. "Brutal" is also not an adjective one would usually associate with stars; this is a striking and unusual way to perceive an ordinary object.

Bhāmaha's observation was that *atiśayokti,* which similarly rules out all familiar equations of perception and presentation, pervades all figures of speech (*alaṅkāra*) and is identical with *vakrokti* or deviant utterance: "This [*atiśayokti*] is nothing but *vakrokti.* All meanings appear new by this. Poets should be assiduous in cultivating it. Where is an *alaṅkāra* without this?" (II.85). He opined that the prosaic expressions which verbatim reiterate the familiar way we view entities without any *vakratā* should not be considered an ornament of speech or *alaṅkāra.* For him, the matter-of-fact expressions without any *vakratā* are mere *vārtā* (report), not an *alaṅkāra.* He was specifically referring to an *alaṅkāra* that was known as *svabhāvokti* when he observed, "'The sun has set; the moon shines, the birds are winging back to their nests.' What kind of poetry is this? This is called *vārtā*" (II.87). While describing five kinds of *kāvya,* Bhāmaha reiterated that *kāvya* in any form, be it a *kathā* or *kāvya* or *mahakāvya* becomes meritorious only if it is marked by figurative deviation (*yukta vakrasvabhāvoktyā sarvamevaitadiṣṭyate*) (I.30). According to Bhāmaha, a composition which is clear, smooth, and elegant but devoid of deviant utterance can at most be only music (not *kāvya*) (I.34).

Daṇḍin, Bhāmaha's successor, divided the realm of speech into two broad categories, namely *vakrokti* and *svabhāvokti*

(II.363). But Daṇḍin, whose treatment of the concept of *vakrokti* ended with this brief observation, was more interested in the ontology of figures of speech in general as opposed to exclusively dealing with the idea of *vakrokti*. The same holds true for his successor Vāmana who saw *vakrokti* as only one of many *śabdālaṅkāras* or figurative deviations of speech. According to him, *vakrokti* is the secondary usage based on similarity (*sadrśya-lakṣaṇā-vakrokti*) (IV.3.8).

The first major literary work that avowedly made a claim to consistently make use of the possibilities of *vakrokti* in *kāvya* was the 9th-century Kashmiri poet Ratnākara's *Vakroktipañcāśikā*. This short poem portrayed Goddess Pārvatī's quarrel with her husband Śiva and Śiva's attempts to assuage her anger through the skilful employment of *vakrokti*. Śiva playfully evades Pārvatī's complaints by intentionally taking them in a sense unintended by her, thereby forcing her to concede to his position and reconcile with him. Other poems modeled on Ratnākara's skilful use of *vakrokti* in *Vakroktipañcāśikā* include Śivarāma's *Lakṣmī-sarasvatī-saṃvāda* and the anonymous *Raṃbhā-śuka-saṃvāda* and *Girijā-kamala-vivāda*. *Lakṣmī-sarasvatī-saṃvāda* portrayed the verbal fencing between Lakṣmī and Sarasvatī, the rival wives of Viṣṇu and Brahmā. *Rambhā-śuka-saṃvāda* dealt with the dialogue between the ascetic Śuka and the celestial woman Raṃbhā, who came to earth to seduce him. *Girijā-kamala-vivāda* was in the form of a dialogue between Pārvatī and Lakṣmī.

The 9th-century Kashmiri critic Rudraṭa is credited with empolying the term *vakrokti* for the first time as a separate poetic figure. For Rudraṭa, *vakrokti* is an *arthālaṅkāra* (figurative language that adorns the meaning) which played on the meaning. He divided it further into two broad categories namely *śleṣa-vakrokti* and *kāku-vakrokti*. *Śleṣa-vakrokti* is *vakrokti* based on pun, whereas *kāku-vakrokti* is *vakrokti* based on the tone of voice. According to Rudraṭa, "A sentence uttered in one sense by a speaker and then taken in another sense by a listener because of the double meaning of the words is called *śleṣa vakratā* (*vakratā* of pun)" (II.15). Sometimes there is a change in the meaning of a sentence because of a change in the speaker's intonation. It is called *kāku vakratā* or *vakratā* of tone (II.16).

Ānandavardhana, a colleague of Rudraṭa in the court of King Avantivarman, also referred to the concept of *vakrokti* in his *Dhvanyāloka*. In the third *udyota* of *Dhvanyāloka*, Ānanda subscribed to Bhāmaha's opinion about *vakrokti* and held that *vakrokti*, which is identical with *atiśayokti*, is the very life force of all *alaṅkāras* (3.36 A). In *Dhvanyāloka*, Ānandavardhana laid a lot of emphasis on the importance of *vakrokti*. Ānanda reproduces a verse of Manoratha in this respect. According to Manoratha, says Ānanda, only an imbecile will term a piece of writing bereft of content, ornament, and *vakrokti* (*vakrokti-śūnya*) an ideal *kāvya* (1.1 c). Abhinavagupta's commentary on this passage is also important in this context. In his commentary, Abhinava opined that *vakrokti* is identical with sublime *saṃghaṭanā* (*vakrokti utkṛṣṭa saṃghaṭanā*), which meant a beautiful arrangement of words; he, too, felt that the absence of *vakrokti* amounts to the absence of beauty (I.1 c L). Bhoja in his *Sarasvatīkaṇṭhābharaṇa* divided the whole world of speech into three—*vakrokti, rasokti*, and *svabhāvokti* (*vakroktiśca rasoktiśca savabhāvoktiśca vāṅmayaṃ* V.8).

In *Kāvyaprakāśa*, Mammaṭa treated *vakrokti* in both its narrow and broad senses—as a figurative deviation of speech and as a general term for the essential quality of all kinds of *alaṅkāras*. In its narrow sense, Mammaṭa like Rudraṭa before him, conceived the idea of *vakrokti* as a *śabdālaṅkāra*, dividing it into the two categories of *śleṣa-vakrokti* and *kāku-vakrokti* (IX.1). Like his predecessors, Bhāmaha, Ānandavardhana, and Abhinavagupta, Mammaṭa also saw the concept of *vakrokti* in a broader sense as the essence of all *alaṅkāras* by quoting Bhāmaha's celebrated dictum that *atiśayokti* is as same as *vakrokti* and no *alaṅkāra* can exist without it (458). Likewise, Ruyyaka, who shared the opinion of Mammaṭa first saw it as a category of *śabdālaṅkāra*, and later considered it as the life force of all *alaṅkāras* (228).

For Viśvanātha (X.11) and Viśveśvara (145), *vakrokti* was a mere ornament of sound whereas Jayadeva, Appayya Dīkṣita, and Devaśaṅkara Purohita treated *vakrokti* as an *arthālaṅkāra* that had more to do with meaning than sound (Jayadeva 106; Dīkṣita 259; Devaśaṅkara Purohita 305–306). Considering *vakrokti* as the ultimate locus of literariness in *kāvya*, many practising poets called themselves unparalleled experts in the employment of *vakrokti*. For instance, the poet Kavirāja in his *Rāghavapāṇḍavīya* named himself, Subandhu, Bāṇabhaṭṭa, and Kavirāja as the only three experts in the employment of *vakrokti*. He asks: "Subandhu, Bāṇa, and Kavirāja are the only three masters of deviant utterance. Can there be a fourth one?" (1.41). Later in the early 13th century, Vidyāmādhava added his own name to the list. In his *Pārvatīrukmiṇīya*, a work modeled on Kavirāja's *Rāghavapāṇḍavīya*, Vidyāmādhava remarks: "Bāṇa, Subandhu, Kavirāja and I, the erudite scholar Vidyāmādhava, are the only four masters of deviant utterance in this world. There will never ever be a fifth one" (I.15).

We can see that although Bhāmaha had laid the foundation for the idea of *vakrokti*, and his followers such as Daṇḍin, Rudraṭa, Ānandavardhana, and others took it up in their literary theory, nobody made *vakrokti* the primary focus of their inquiry. For them, *vakrokti* always remained an individual figure of speech or an essential characteristic pervading all figures of speech. We find a detailed enquiry into the ontology of *vakrokti* only in *Vakroktijīvita* of the 10th-century Kashmiri critic Kuntaka. In Kuntaka's opinion, what can be called the hallmark of *kāvya* is *vakrokti*—the art of delineating an idea or an entity in a fashion which is characteristically different from the way we usually perceive it. He contends that "sound" and "sense" in literature necessarily need to be adorned by the ornament *vakrokti*. Kuntaka defined *vakrokti* as the "unique charm which marks it off from other modes of composition [*prasiddha-prasthāna-vyatireki*]" (313). He primarily saw *vakrokti* as the portrayal of sound and sense in a deviant form so that the familiar, ordinary, objects around us appear different. This is somewhat similar to the concept of defamiliarization that was propounded by Viktor Shklovsky, the Russian Formalist, in the 20th century:

> The purpose of art is to impart the sensation of things as they are perceived and not as they are known. The technique of art is to make objects 'unfamiliar,' to make forms difficult, to increase the difficulty and length of perception because the process of perception is an aesthetic end in itself and must be prolonged. (12)

According to Kuntaka, what made a narrative a verbal art was the presence of *alaṅkāra*, and the only *alaṅkāra* or ornament that could adorn a poem was *vakrokti*:

> Both these refer to words and meanings which deserve to be looked upon as the subjects of ornamentation for the enhancement of their appeal. 'What then is this ornament?' one might ask. The answer is that though they are two in number, they have only one common ornament. What exactly is this ornament? 'Artistic turn of speech' is the reply. It stands for a charming and novel utterance peculiar to poetry and distinct from familiar usage. It is the very index of the artistic turn that a master-poet's speech takes. In other words, artistic utterance itself is the ornament in question. (307)

Kuntaka clearly differentiated *vakrokti* and *svabhāvokti,* maintaining that *svabhāvokti* is nothing more than the description of objects in nature and would not qualify to be a part of poetry.

Instead of re-creating or re-presenting the dominant conception about the identity of an entity (*svabhāva*), Kuntaka, like Shklovsky much later, was concerned with the creative transformation of the existing structures and he never aimed to reproduce the known and the familiar:

> The gist is:—The poets do not give existence to things non-existent in the world; only they endow such superior and original excellences to things which merely existed before, that a unique appeal of beauty to connoisseurs is invariably brought about. . . . Things in the world have mere existence. But they are given such heightened extraordinary beauty or shade of charm that they began to appear as if they are entirely new. Their natural state is completely concealed and a new splendor comes to be attached to them making one think that

> they were invented right then for the first time. It is this fact which confers the title of 'Creators' on the poets. (415)

Shklovksy was later to say that art would break the "automatism of perception" (11) or the habitual way in which we see the world around us. It is only through poetry that we are jolted out of our usual stupor to see that a red rose is a loved one. For instance, we have a different perspective of the withering effect of a completely natural phenomenon like frost on flowers through Emily Dickinson's poem, "Apparently with no Surprise":

> Apparently with no surprise
> To any happy Flower
> The Frost beheads it at its play—
> In accidental power—
> The blonde Assassin passes on—
> The Sun proceeds unmoved
> To measure off another Day
> For an Approving God (666–667)

This natural world is not benign and is not meant to refresh you with its panoramic views; it has "accidental power" that can behead innocent lives and is completely indifferent to destruction and death. Dickinson makes us look at the world with awe and respect. According to Kuntaka, this deviance from the ordinary to gain an extraordinary perception of the objects around us is what constitutes literariness.

Six Categories of *Vakratā*

However, extraordinary use of language can happen at various levels—at the level of the word, the sentence or the work as a whole. This is why Kuntaka divided *vakratā* into six broad categories in his *Vakroktijīvita* (313). The divisions were:

(i) *varṇa-vinyāsa-vakratā*
(ii) *pada-pūrvārtha-vakratā*
(iii) *pada-parārtha-vakratā*
(iv) *vākya-vakratā*
(v) *prakaraṇa-vakratā*
(vi) *prabandha-vakratā*

Varṇa-vinyāsa-vakratā is the skilful employment of consonants to form alliteration and consonance (359). *Pada-pūrvārtha-vakratā* is manipulation of words (369–370). *Pada-parārtha-vakratā*, also known as *pratyaya-vakratā*, is the artistic deviation of the terminal part of a word which decides tense, number, gender, etc. of a signifier (401). *Vākya-vakratā* is the figurative deviation at the sentence level and is concerned with all the three aspects of *kāvya* namely *rasa*, *alaṅkāra*, and *svabhāva* (321). *Prakaraṇa-vakratā* is artistic deviation through episodes that make up a plot (537). *Prabandha-vakratā* is the deviant utterance at the level of plot (569).

According to Kuntaka, *varṇa-vinyāsa-vakratā* is employed with the specific intention of using syllables distinctly different from the conventional way in which they are employed (*prasiddha prasthāna vyatireki*; 313). Kuntaka said,

> One, two or more syllables used again and again at short intervals constitute three forms of 'art in the arrangement of syllables' [*varṇa-vinyāsa-vakratā*]. Here, 'syllable' stands for 'consonant,' following general usage. The idea is that 'art in the arrangement of syllables' is the same as art in

> the arrangement of consonants; and it is usually regarded as three-fold: (1) only one consonant closely repeated, (2) two consonants closely repeated and (3) many consonants closely repeated. (359)

An example of this sort of *vakratā* is the famous word coined by James Joyce to indicate the sound of thunder in his *Finnegans Wake*: "*Bababadalgharaghtakamminarronnkonnbronntonnerronntuonnthunntrovarrhounawnskawntoohoohoordenenthurnuk*" (1).

The second variety, *pada-pūrvārtha-vakratā,* is again divided into nine categories, which are the various ways in which words can be joined in an extraordinary way. They are: *rūḍhi-vaicitrya-vakratā* (use of the word in such a way that it abandons its primary meaning and expresses a new meaning which is not conventionally associated with it) (369–370); *paryāya-vakratā* (use of an appropriate synonym) (373); *upacāra-vakratā* (metaphorical usage) (381); *viśeṣaṇa-vakratā* (conveying meaning through adverbs, adjectives and epithets) (384); *saṃvrti-vakratā* (use of pronouns) (386); *vṛtti-vakratā* (grammatical use of compounds) (390); *bhāva-vakratā* (mixing of tenses) (391); *liṅga-vaicitrya-vakratā* (different use of gender) (392); and *kriyā-vaicitrya-vakratā* (different use of the root of a verb) (395).

Of these, *liṅga-vaicitrya-vakratā* and *kriyā-vaicitrya-vakratā* have further subdivisions. These were primarily meant for the Sanskrit language which has genders for all nouns; this cannot be understood in the context of a language like English which does not follow this system. For instance, *liṅga-vaicitrya-vakratā* could be achieved either by using different genders for the same object, or by attributing a feminine gender to an object that has another gender. The example

Kuntaka gave was from Kālidāsa's *Raghuvaṃśa*, where Rāma attributes the female gender to a creeper (*latā*) who showed him the way to Sītā, when he was searching for her after Rāvaṇa abducted her (393). Kālidāsa, chooses a noun with female gender to denote the creeper because they were tender-hearted enough to show the way to a forlorn lover; this, according to Kuntaka, is a different use of the word "*latā*" and so evokes pleasure in the reader. Similarly *kriyā-vaicitrya-vakratā* also has five varieties namely *karturatyanta-raṅgatva-vakratā* (suggesting an idea through the performance of an action which is in some way associated with that idea), *kartāntara-vaicitrya-vakratā* (attributing an ability to an object which it is usually not able to perform), *kriyā-viśeṣaṇa-vaicitrya-vakratā* (deviant utterance through the employment of adverbs), *upacāra-manohārita-vakratā* (metaphorical superimposition of a quality upon an object) and *karmādi-saṃvrti-vakratā* (concealment of an action or direct object) (395).

The third variety namely *pada-parārtha-vakratā* has six subdivisions such as *kāla-vaicitrya-vakratā* (deviant use of tense) (399); *kāraka-vakratā* (artistic deviation through the reversal of subject, instrument of action, case, etc.) (401); *saṃkhyā-vakratā* (artistic deviation of numbers) (402); *puruṣa-vakratā* (artistic deviation through the transposition of *uttama*, *madhyama*, and *pradhama* or the first, second, and third persons) (404); *upagraha-vakratā* (artistic deviation through the skilful use of *ātmanepad* and *parasmaipad* forms) (405); and *pratyaya-vakratā* (artistic deviation through affixes) (405).

Vākya-vakratā can roughly be translated as diction, or the appropriate use of words to best describe the subject matter at the sentence level. Kuntaka believed that subjects which despite being decorated with all sorts of poetic ornaments did not have inherent beauty could not be depicted in poetry. It is bound to appear insipid like a painting done on a flawed canvas. *Vākya-vakratā* depends on the poet's craft or their skill with words. According to Kuntaka, the whole conventional category of *alaṅkāra* is subsumed in the category of *vākya-vakratā.* Kuntaka in the first chapter of *Vakroktijīvita* observes, "And art in a whole sentence admits a thousand varieties. In it is included the whole lot of Figures of Speech" (321).

For Kuntaka, *prakaraṇa-vakratā* and *prabandha-vakratā* constitute an important category in the realm of *vakrokti.* According to him, many sentences or *vākya* make a *prakaraṇa* or an episode, and many episodes make a *prabandha.* In the context of these two varieties of *vakratā,* Kuntaka was discussing how descriptions of certain episodes can lend beauty to the work as a whole. *Prakaraṇa-vakratā,* says Kuntaka, is divided into ten categories (according to some scholars, this has only nine divisions) (651). The first is *pariṇāma-gopana-vakratā;* this means the interpolation of certain episodes that can shed more light on the inner workings of characters (540). Soliloquies like that of Prince Hal in Shakespeare's *Henry IV Part I,* where he says "I know ye all, and will awhile uphold/The unyoked humor of your idleness" (I.2.185–186) is an example. This scene gives us an insight into a hitherto unknown aspect of the profligate prince's character, a pointer to his later evolution into a serious and responsible king. *Utpādya-lāvaṇya-vakratā* is the way in which an already existing story is given novelty through the addition or deletion of episodes (540).

Kālidāsa took up the thread of the Śakuntalā story from the *Mahābhārata* and in his *Abhijñānaśākuntala*, added the episode of Durvasa's curse of memory loss on Duṣyanta. This made the story completely different from the story in the epic, adding to its charm.

Upakāryopakartṛtva-vakratā ensures that each component of the story adds to the total effect as a whole (556). In the film *Sholay*, Jai is shown as flipping a coin to help arrive at decisions in difficult situations. This is a seemingly irrelevant detail, but when the last scene reveals that the coin has the same image on both sides so that Jai always wins, we realize that this had much to do with the character of Jai. Thus, even a trivial component is woven into the story as a whole.

Abhidheyāvarttana-vakratā is the way in which the same episode is depicted in different ways, with different effects (547). An example can be seen in the Japanese author Ryonosuke Akutagawa's short story "In the Bamboo-grove" adapted by the famous director Akira Kurosawa into the film *Rashomon*. The same incident of the murder of a young samurai is recounted by four different people with different results.

When a sub-plot is elaborated in a way that it contributes to the main *rasa* and thus becomes a crucial element in the main storyline, it is called *kathopakāraka-vastu-vinyāsa-vakratā* (555–556). The Ophelia–Hamlet relationship in *Hamlet* is not merely an addition of love interest in the play; it does not disturb the overall *karuṇa rasa* with *śṛṅgāra* but is, in fact, an emphasis on the troubled nature of Hamlet's personality.

Elements that appear extraneous to the story are sometimes described in great detail, appearing to be digressions. However, if they are linked to the main storyline with a view to enhancing the grandeur of the work as a whole, it constitutes *kathā-vaicitrya-vakratā* (556). The chapters on whaling in *Moby Dick* or the chapters describing the architectural splendor of Notre Dame Cathedral in *The Hunchback of Notre Dame* are examples of this.

Sometimes the author lavishes so much attention on one particular episode that it stands out with a *rasa* on its own without however hindering the effect of the work as a whole. The Falstaff scenes in Henry IV are examples of this. It is called *aṅgirasa-niṣyanda-vakratā* (559).

An episode that has no apparent connection with the main storyline is described, only to eventually link it up in a very significant way to the main story. This is *vastvantara-vaicitrya-vakratā*, which we can discern in the handkerchief episode in Othello (561).

Prakaraṇāntara-vakratā is relevant only in the context of a play and refers to the incorporation of a play within a play (564). Examples can be found in Bhavabhūti's *Uttararāmacarita* and Shakespeare's *Hamlet*. Bhavabhūti makes his character Vālmīki write and enact a play before a Rāma who is traumatized by the memory of his abandonment of Sītā. Like in *Hamlet*, the play depicts reality as it deals with the plight of the abandoned Sītā. The thin line separating reality and the magical world of the play blurs as the real Sītā herself appears, and a repentant Rāma is reunited with her. The play within the play usually had a specific purpose, much like the way Shakespeare used it later.

Finally, there is *aṅgāṅgi-sāṃgatya-vakratā*, which denotes the continuity and coherence of episodes in the totality of the work (569).

After devoting attention to the various constituent elements of a work starting with the word to incidents in the story, Kuntaka turns to the work as a whole or *prabandha* (569). How do you make the work as a whole striking? *Prabandha-vakratā* also has seven varieties. Of these, *rasāntara-vinyāsa-vakratā* is the way in which a story can be made new by changing the generally accepted *rasa* of a well-known story (569). Adaptations or retellings demonstrate this sort of *vakratā.* Jean Rhys's *Wide Sargasso Sea* which is told from the perspective of Bertha Mason, the madwoman in the attic in *Jane Eyre,* is not merely changing the story but also changing the *rasa.* Bertha's perspective brings in *karuṇa rasa,* while Charlotte Bronte's story has *śṛṅgāra rasa* because of the Jane–Rochester romance.

Sometimes the story is tweaked by the author so that the hero is made to look better than his original. For instance, Bhāravi's *Kirātārjunīya* ends with Arjuna winning the battle against Śiva who is disguised as a tribal. It does not go on to describe the war with the Kauravas or the ups and downs that occur in Arjuna's life, thus ensuring that the hero's image is not tarnished. Such modification is termed *nāyakotkkarṣa-nibandhana-vakratā* (570–571).

Prāsaṃgika-kathārasa-nibandhana-vakratā is the way in which the author transforms what is generally deemed to be a digression from the main story into an interesting event in the main plot in such a way that it becomes inevitable for the main story (573). Kuntaka reminds us that this should be done carefully without adversely affecting the main *rasa.* The Bassanio–Portia love story in *The Merchant of Venice* is a case in point. Bassanio's wooing of Portia takes up the major part of the play, almost making us forget the main plot of Antonio's debt to Shylock. However, Shakespeare's deft touch justifies the detailed portrayal of Portia by eventually making her the valiant rescuer of Antonio from his preposterous bond to Shylock.

Aneka-phala-sambatti-vakratā refers to the manipulation of the plot to enhance the glory of a hero by showing him achieving a lot of subsidiary feats besides his ultimate goal (574). The Vikram–Vetal stories, adventures of Sindbad the sailor or Robin Hood are examples of these. The use of appropriate titles for the work as a whole is also thought of as a form of *vakratā,* called *kāvya-nāma-vakratā* (575). Kuntaka thought that titles that convey the gist of the story, like *Abhijñānaśākuntala* or *Mudrārākṣasa* added to the beauty of the work. Contemporary works like *Harry Potter and the Prisoner of Azkaban* or *The Handmaid's Tale* are examples for this.

Retelling of a familiar story in such a way that it appears new, makes *anyonya-vailakṣaṇya-vakratā* (576). Mahasweta Devi's short stories like "Kunti and the Nishadin," or "Souvali" are examples for this. It can be seen that this *vakratā* refers to all forms of adaptations. Kuntaka paid attention to and approved of the modified versions of popular stories from epics like the *Rāmāyaṇa* and the *Mahābhārata*.

A writer can make use of the work to convey his ideas on ethics and morality; this constitutes *nayopadeśa-vakratā* (577). Albert Camus' *The Outsider* (*The Stranger*) would be a perfect example of this. Meursault in the novel is the prototype of the absurd man as outlined by Camus in his essay *The Myth of Sisyphus*. Although there is a danger of such type of works to descend into propaganda, Kuntaka thought it legitimate to utilize art to propagate the values one believed in.

Pleasant Modification

There is a possibility that this process of presenting a familiar structure in a defamiliarized way can shock the readers, as opposed to surprising them. In the theoretical position of *vakrokti*, Kuntaka's attempt, despite his avowed aim of effecting a change in what the reader expects from a story, is to ensure a pleasant experience for the reader. According to Kuntaka, though *kāvya* is generally defined as the special combination of *śabda* and *artha* marked by the presence of deviant utterance, it should ultimately be pleasing to the reader. He was of the view that, "Poetry is that word and sense together enshrined in a style revealing the artistic creativity of the poet on the one hand and giving aesthetic delight to the man of taste on the other" (*tadvidāhlādakāriṇi*; 292). Deviation from the existing value system of the reader is the primary cause for the artistic tool of *vakratā* turning into an unpleasant experience. Therefore Kuntaka, like his predecessors such as Bhāmaha, Daṇḍin, and Ānandavardhana, was extremely mindful of social decorum and never allowed any sort of deviant approach to *kāvya* that challenged the propriety of the period. He insisted that the readers should not have to encounter a situation that differs radically from their value system. Kuntaka said: "There is no other cause for a breach in sentiment except indecorum" (*anaucityādṛte nānyadrasabhaṅgasya kāraṇam*; 446). An example for this would be the deviant (*vakratā*) representation of a putative noble character as an inferior figure lacking in prowess and moral integrity. Kuntaka would obviously frown at retellings like Nina Paley's *Sita Sings the Blues* where Rāma is shown as a heartless husband who abandons his pregnant wife.

Citing the reason that any representation of an event which is at war with the readers' beliefs, ideas, and values can create a discomfort in them, Kuntaka insisted that the writers should strictly conform to social propriety. In the *Rāmāyaṇa*, upon hearing the cry of Rāma who has gone to catch the golden deer, his brother Lakṣmaṇa goes in search of him. But in the drama *Udāttarāghava*, this plot is rewritten in such a way that it is Rāma who goes to rescue Lakṣmaṇa. This change was made to conform to the social propriety of the period which held that it would be highly improper for a man of great prowess and courage like Rāma to be rescued by his younger brother Lakṣmaṇa (323). Despite his attempts to defy prevalent stereotypes and social value systems, Kuntaka however never was critical of the decorum of the society he belonged to and never shocked the readers out of their comfort zone. As far as Kuntaka was concerned, the aim of *kāvya* was to impart pleasure to the reader. Hence, even when he approved of artistic attempts to challenge the dominantly conceived *svabhāva* of entities, Kuntaka made sure that these changes did not force the readers to alter their beliefs or ethical values.

Conclusion

Kuntaka did not usher in any revolutionary ideas into the world of Sanskrit *kāvya*; in fact, at times he seems to be closely following in the footsteps of his predecessors like Ānandavardhana. But the emphasis he laid on the extraordinary use of the ordinary by artists makes him remarkably similar to the Formalists of the 20th century. He is also perhaps the most "modern" of all the ancient theorists because he provides a framework to study adaptations and retellings which are so much in vogue today.

Works Cited

Abhinavagupta. *Locana*. In *The Dhvanyāloka of Ānandavardhana with the Locana of Abhinavagupta*. Translated and edited by Daniel Ingalls, Jeffrey Masson, and M. V. Patwardhan, Harvard University Press. 1990.

Ānandavardhana. *The Dhvanyāloka of Ānandavardhana with the Locana of Abhinavagupta*. Translated and edited by Daniel Ingalls, Jeffrey Masson, and M. V. Patwardhan, Harvard University Press. 1990.

Bhāmaha. *Kāvyālaṅkāra*. Edited by B. N. Sarma and Baldeva Upadhyay, Chowkhamba Sanskrit Series Office, 1998.

Bhoja. *Sarasvatīkaṇṭhābharaṇa*. Edited by Pandurang Jawaji, Nirnayasagar Press, 1934.

Daṇḍin. *Kāvyādarśa of Daṇḍin*. Edited by Premachandra Tarkabagisa, Royal Asiatic Society, 1962.

Dickinson, Emily. *The Complete Poems of Emily Dickinson*. Edited by Thomas H. Johnson, Little Brown and Company, 1942.

Dīkṣita, Appaya. *Kuvalālyananda*. Edited by Subramanya Sharma, P. R., Banarjee Press, 1903.

Hughes, Ted. "Snowdrop." *Lupercal*. Faber and Faber, 1960.

Jayadeva. *Chandrāloka of Jayadeva*. Edited by A. S. Vetal, Chowkamba Sanskrit Series Office, 1932.

Joyce, James. *Finnegans Wake*. Oxford University Press, 2012.

Kavirāja. *Raghavapāṇḍaviya*. Edited by Pandit Sivadatta, Nirnaya Sagar Press, 1897.

Kuntaka. *Vakroktijīvita*. Translated and edited by Krishnamoorthy, Karnataka University Press, 1977.

Mammaṭa. *Kāvyaprakāśa of Mammaṭa*. Edited by Ganganath Jha, Bharathiya Vidya Prakashan, 1966.

Pollock, Sheldon. *The Rasa Reader*. Columbia University Press, 2016.

Purohita, Bahatta Devasankara. *Alaṅkāramañjuṣā*. Edited by Sadashiva Lakshmidhara Katre, Oriental Manuscript Library, 1940.

Rudraṭa. *Kāvyālaṅkāra*. Nirnaya Sagar Press, 1886.

Ruyyaka. *Alaṅkārasarvasva of Rājanaka Ruyyaka with the commentary of Jayaratha*. Edited by Girijaprasad Dvivedi, Nirnaya Sagar Press, 1898.

Shakespeare, William. *Henry IV*. Oxford University Press, 1994.

Shklovsky, Viktor. "Art as Technique." *Russian Formalist Criticism: Four Essays*. Translated and edited by Lee T. Lemon and Marion J. Reis, University of Nebraska Press, 1965.

Vāmana. *Kāvyālaṅkārasūtravṛtti*. Translated (Malayalam) and edited by E. Eswaran Nambootiri, Kerala Bhasha Institute, 2000.

Viśvanātha. *The Sāhityadarpaṇa*. Translated by J. R. Ballantyne and Pramada Dasa Mitra, Motilal Banarasidas Publishers, 2016.

Viśveśvara. *Camatkāracandrikā*. Edited by Sarasvati Mohan, Meharchand Lacchmandas, 1972.

7

Aucitya

The concept of *aucitya* or propriety had always been central to the treatment of literature in Sanskrit *kāvyaśāstra*, although it evolved into a comprehensive theoretical concept only by the 11th century with Kṣemendra's *Aucityavicāracarcā*. According to Pollock,

> Propriety came to function as a critical standard in literary judgement at a relatively early date, and by the time of its most complete exposition in the eleventh century, it had become an all-embracing category of fitness, 'the life force pervading the limbs of a literary text', in regulating the use of everything from particular preverbs, particles, and individual words . . . to figures of speech, aesthetic moods (*rasa*), and the argument of the work as a whole. (*The Language of the Gods*, 198)

A review of some major texts that became landmarks in the intellectual history of Sanskrit *kāvyaśāstra* will clearly show the importance of *aucitya* in Sanskrit poetics. The Sanskrit word *aucitya* can be translated into English as "propriety" and is associated with what the classical Greeks termed "decorum." In Sanskrit literary theory, the idea of *aucitya* was concerned with almost all aspects of literature right from diction to form, content, and characterization. It can also be defined as the judicious use of the poetic devices that are available to the writer—like the word, sentence, or image—to foreground the subject and attain the aim of aesthetic relish or *rasa*.

The beginning of the idea of *aucitya*, just like many other literary concepts in Sanskrit literary science, can be traced back to Bharata's *Nāṭyaśāstra*. Bharata considered the *nāṭya* to be an imitation of the world (*lokavṛttānukaraṇaṃ*) and therefore opined that it should closely follow the ways and manners accepted in the society (I.85). Emphasizing the importance of *aucitya*, he instructed that the characters in a drama must put on costumes that befit their age, must follow a gait that suits their costume and must speak according to their gait (XIV.62). Bhāmaha, Daṇḍin, Vāmana, Viśvanātha, Mahimabhaṭṭa, and Hemacandra also discuss the concept of *aucitya*, but they touch upon it in the context of their discussion of *kāvya doṣa*s or the improper elements in literature that can ruin the beauty of *kāvya*. To them, *aucitya* essentially meant the avoidance of *doṣa*s.

Ānandavardhana can rightly be called the first author to reflect systematically upon the concept of *aucitya,* though it was Kṣemendra who later considered it a special category of theoretical reflection. In *Dhvanyāloka,* Ānanda emphasized the importance of *aucitya* in literature, by saying that

> a poet who follows the system of Bharata and others, who studies the work of great poets of the past, and who gives rein to his own genius, must still be attentive and exert the greatest care not to relax or depart from the proprieties of the *vibhāva*s and other factors of *rasa*. (3.10–14 c *A*)

Mahimabhaṭṭa likewise considered *aucitya* as the most essential component of *rasa*: "Impropriety is the only cause for the spoiling of *rasa*/Composing a work in conformity with propriety is the very *Upaniṣad* of *rasa*. (31).

In *Vakroktijīvita*, Kuntaka treated *aucitya* as an unavoidable component in a poetic composition and thought that a poet should not slacken his concern for social propriety in the process of writing. Kuntaka's discussion about the idea of *aucitya* in *Vakroktijīvita* appears primarily in connection with his criticism against the concept of *ūrjasvin* which literary theoreticians like Udbhaṭa considered a figure of speech. *Ūrjasvin* being the indecorous representation of *rasa*s and *bhāva*s (402), Kuntaka outright ruled out the view that *ūrjasvin* is an *alaṅkāra*. He stated that an improper composition of various constituent elements (*vibhāva*s, *anubhāva*s, and, so on) prevents the proper nourishing of *rasa* (404). He firmly believed that a *rasa* marked by impropriety could not serve as an ornament (405). Repeating the stance of both Ānandavardhana and Mahimabhaṭṭa on propriety, Kuntaka stated: "There is no other cause for a breach in sentiment except indecorum. The highest secret about sentiment is conformity to well-known considerations of decorum or propriety" (404). Mammaṭa in *Kāvyaprakāśa* cautioned the poets that impropriety or *anaucitya* creates the aberration of emotion (*rasābhāsa*) (72).

Bhoja was being conscious of *aucitya* when he mentioned social mores in his *Śṛṅgāraprakāśa*, the famous treatise on literary science. Bhoja declared in the seventh chapter of *Śṛṅgāraprakāśa* that, he as a king, would not overstep the boundaries of the prevailing social order of his society: "I hereby pray to the omnipotent God to ensure that while I am composing this book, there would be no transgression of the established order, the practice of the social orders and the four life stages" (I, 257). In what appears to be a succinct definition of *aucitya*, Bhoja further stated:

> Words suitable for each character, Characters befitting the whole story, The culmination of *rasa* at the right time and no deviation from the story line, a neat organization of component parts and the incorporation of suitable words. These are the virtues which will win the attention of the erudite audience. (II, 461)

In his *Sarasvatīkaṇṭhābharaṇa*, Bhoja identified six kinds of propriety such as *viṣayaucitya* (propriety of subject), *vācyaucitya* (propriety of speech), *deśaucitya* (propriety of place), *samayaucitya* (propriety of time), *vaktṛviṣayaucitya* (propriety of using language according to the status of the speaker), and *arthaucitya* (propriety in the use of language according to the subject matter) (942–949).

Bhānudatta in his *Rasataraṅgiṇī (The River of Rasa)* notes: "[I]mpropriety must by all means be carefully avoided" (329). According to him, "There is nothing that destroys *rasa* more than impropriety. Composing in a way that keeps to the canons of propriety is the priceless secret of *rasa*" (331). As far as Bhānu is concerned, "Impropriety causes disruption whereas propriety confirms the currency of the general state of affairs" (331).

Kṣemendra differed from all the other literary theoreticians who dealt with the idea of *aucitya,* in that he became the first to deal with the idea of *aucitya* as a separate and systematic body of knowledge by connecting it with almost all aspects of poetry. However, it would be wrong to describe this work as innovative or original because Kṣemendra was merely collating Ānandavardhana's ideas on the subject and explaining them in a simpler way with exemplifications. He saw *aucitya* as the soul of *kāvya* (*aucityam rasasiddhasya sthiraraṃ jīvitam kāvyasya*; I.5). He compared a poem that does not conform to the standards of propriety to a person who ends up looking bizarre by wearing ornaments in an eccentric manner. Kṣemendra observed:

> An embellishment is a (real) embellishment if applied at the proper place; merits are always (real) merits when they are not divested of propriety. Put at a proper place, ornaments could beautify, otherwise they do not even deserve to be called ornaments. Similarly merits, if they do not fall short of propriety, are merits, otherwise they are blemishes. Wherefore he says—Who do not suffer mockery by (putting on) the girdle-string around the neck, the radiant necklace around the waist, the anklets on hands, the bracelets on feet, and (by showing) might against the prostrated and compassion towards foes? Similarly neither figures of speech nor the merits look charming without propriety. (I.6)

Kṣemendra went on to list twenty-seven forms of *aucitya* pertaining to elements such as *pada* (word), *vākya* (sentence), *kriyā* (verb), *liṅga* (gender), *guṇa* (poetic merits), *alaṅkāra* (figure of speech), *rasa* (aesthetic emotion), etc. He also exemplified each of these aspects with good and bad examples—basically it was a "to do" list along with "what not to do" while composing a poem. It says a lot about his objectivity when we take note of the fact that he has cited his own verse as an example for *anaucitya*!

As explained by Kṣemendra, *aucitya* encompassed various aspects of a work starting from the word, to style, content, and genre. Bharata was emphasizing the importance of *aucitya* when he instructed that the characters in a drama must put on costumes that befit their age, must follow a gait that suits their costume and must speak according to their gait (XIV.62). This idea of *aucitya* like the concept of *rasa* was not disputed by poets and critics alike after Bharata; in fact, all of them in their various ways supported this overarching aspect of literary architectonics. All of them were convinced of the necessity of harmony among the various constituents of the artistic work, so much so that it was not only literary critics but poets also who expressed this view. For instance, Māgha in his *Śiśupālavadha*, compared the wisdom of a king choosing the right policy to that of a poet choosing the right style for his work (II, 83). This is the essence of the literary concept of *aucitya*. However, the first to use the term in poetry was Yaśovarman in his *Rāmābhyudaya* (8th century) and the first to mention it in poetics was Rudraṭa.

Functions of *Aucitya*

In *kāvyaśāstra*, the concept of *aucitya* functioned in two ways. First, it set models for the representation of each character-type and emotion and encouraged the creative writers to follow them devotedly. Second, it persuaded the writers to avoid the representation of situations or issues that went against the accepted practices of the time. The tendency to prescribe the ideal model for the representation of each character-type and emotion starts from Bharata's *Nāṭyaśāstra* onwards. In the sixth chapter of *Nāṭyaśāstra*, Bharata talks about the ideal manner in which each emotion has to be enacted according to the nature of the various character types. For example, he insisted that the source of *śṛṅgāra-rasa* should always be a young (*yuvaprakṛti*) heterosexual couple (*strīpuruṣahetuka*) belonging to the noble category (VI.49). Besides character attributes, there is also a detailed manual on the gestures and gait of characters according to their social status—nobility (*uttama*), middle class (*madhyama*), and the lower class (*adhama*)—as well as gender. For instance, Bharata said that in the expression of *hāsya rasa* (the comic emotion) the noble characters (*uttama*) can have laughter (*vihasitaṃ*) and gentle smile (*smitaṃ*). The middling characters (*madhyama*) may be allowed broad smile (*vihasitaṃ*) and laughter of ridicule (*upahasitaṃ*). It is only the low (*adhama*) characters who resort to *apahasitaṃ* (silly laughter) and *atihasitaṃ* (boisterous laughter) (VI.64). Bharata's exposition likewise extends to other emotions, paying minute attention to even the movements of eyebrows.

It is interesting to note how the gestural and behavioral aspects tie up with aspects of character as well. According to Bharata, an *uttama* female character should always be unperturbed by anything unpleasant. She should not speak harshly to her lover, should not retain her anger for long, and should not conceal the mistakes she has committed. Being compliant with the dominant social order, she is always desired by men. A *madhyama* female character, on the other hand, is always short-tempered, reciprocates the love of whoever loves her, is jealous of her rivals in love, and is good at the art of love-making. An *adhama* woman's character does not agree with the general conception of how an ideal woman is supposed to behave. She will express her anger without thinking about the propriety of place and time, will not conform to the code of conduct, and will be harsh and proud (XXXIV 6–8; Vol. II). Bharata's dictum is that a creative writer should unfailingly and appropriately ascribe these qualities to each character-type during their representation in *nāṭya*. In other words, a creative writer cannot represent an *uttama* character with the qualities of an *adhama* character and vice versa. Juliet in *Romeo and Juliet* cannot speak in double entendre like her Nurse or behave like her; that would be a violation of the rules of propriety.

There are also directives regarding a hero's behavior; how a scene of lovemaking should be depicted; how a heroine should behave toward her guilty lover; how male characters of different character traits such as *catura* (clever), *uttama* (noble), *madhyama* (middling character) *adhama* (degenerate or low-born) and *saṃbravṛttaka* (a lover who is indifferent to fear and anger) should behave in front of a courtesan (XXV.36–43); how the friend of a lover should act (XXV.5) and so on. This tendency of setting appropriate models for the representation of different character-types and aesthetic emotions runs through the length and breadth of the entire *kāvyaśāstra* tradition. Dhanañjaya's *Daśarūpaka*, Bhānudatta's *Rasamañjarī* and *Rasataraṅgiṇī*, Vidyānātha's *Pratāparudrī*ya, and Bhoja's *Śṛṅgāraprakāśa* are a few other texts that give directives in this manner.

Closely related to this tendency of setting models for each character-type and aesthetic emotion was the attempt to sanitize situations in which an otherwise noble character commits an occasional act of impropriety. This was often implemented on the ground that any violation of the existing moral and social order will result in *rasābhāsa* or the semblance of *rasa*. *Rasābhāsa* is that situation wherein a particular *rasa* fails to come into being—despite the presence of all the components congenial for its production—because the emotion is presented in an indecorous manner or is directed toward an improper object.

The history of *rasābhāsa* can be traced back to the 9th-century critic Udbhaṭa's *Kāvyālaṅkāra-sāra-saṃgraha.* According to Udbhaṭa, "Any sentiment or feeling that is developed in an improper and objectionable manner is called *rasābhāsa* or *bhāvābhāsa*" (IV.4–5). Udbhaṭa also used the term *ūrjasvin* to denote what he newly called *rasābhāsa.* According to Udbhaṭa, *ūrjasvin* is "the composition of sentiments [*rasas*] and feelings [*bhāvas*] wherein an action transgresses propriety (*anaucityapravarttānām*) because of anger, desire and so on" (IV. 5). The example given by Udbhaṭa for *ūrjasvin* is Śiva's indecorous advance toward Pārvatī before their marriage. A classic example of *rasābhāsa* that Abhinavagupta cites in his commentary on Ānandavardhana's *Dhvanyāloka* is Rāvaṇa's love for Sītā (54). According to Abhinavagupta, since Sītā is another man's wife and a divine being, Rāvaṇa's advances toward Sītā are highly improper and do not generate *śṛṅgāra rasa* although Rāvaṇa does everything that one is supposed to do to express erotic emotion. Abhinavagupta says, "*Rasa* appears when a stable state of mind (*cittavṛtti*), constantly directed toward a proper object, is aesthetically relished. The improper variety (*ābhāsa*) of *rasa* or *bhāva* appears when either of them is directed toward an improper object, as when Rāvaṇa's love is directed toward Sītā" (1.4 g *L*).

Through *rasābhāsa*, the literary theoreticians primarily aimed to give the writers of *kāvya* a clear idea about the elements that they should necessarily avoid in the representation of an ideal situation or character-type. Ānandavardhana, for example, explained about the importance of avoiding the improper representation of *śṛṅgāra rasa* in the case of characters of the upper class (*uttama*) like kings and gods. Ānandavardhana observed,

> Accordingly, whether in the literature of performance or in poetry which is not performed, the description of vulgar sexual enjoyment between characters of the upper class, kings, and ladies, is highly indecent, just like the description of the sexual enjoyment of our parents. Precisely, the same charge appears within the sphere of the gods. Furthermore, sexual intercourse is not the only form of love-in-enjoyment (*saṃbhoga-śṛṅgāra*). Other forms such as the interchange of glances and the like are possible and can be used in writing of upper-class characters. Thus that which is appropriate to the character is to be followed in treating of sexual desire (*rati*) just as of energy. (3.10–14 b *A*)

As far as Ānanda was concerned, any impropriety of *vṛtti* or *vyavahāra* (behavior and code of conduct) is a hindrance to *rasa*. Therefore, he was of the view that if the poet "observes a pattern in the story that goes against the *rasa*, he should eliminate it, and bring in some other story appropriate to the *rasa* by his invention" (3.10–14 e *A*). Ānandavardhana also believed that it was wrong to attribute moral flaws to great characters; according to him, that would only ruin the greatness of the noble characters. He wrote, "Thus, if we assign a type of love to characters of the upper class by recourse to what is appropriate to the lower class, how ridiculous will be the result! Even in India what is appropriate in love differs according to the three classes of men" (3.10–14 b *A*).

In *Pratāparudrīya*, Vidyānātha also asked poets to avoid the representation of situations and character-types that are indecorous. He maintained that "Incidents that do not have propriety should not be represented on the stage" (III.20–21). Vidyānātha's discussions of *anaucitya* and *rasābhāsa*, like his predecessor Ānanda's, were also in connection with *śṛṅgāra rasa*. Vidyānātha opined that *rasābhāsa* in connection with *śṛṅgāra* occurs "[i]f the love is one-sided as in the case of Rāvaṇa's love for Sītā; if it is presented in connection with animals and lower-caste people, and if a woman loves many men" (132). According to Bhānudatta, the situations that eventuate in *rasābhāsa* of *śṛṅgāra rasa* include the unappeasable anger of a heroine; a man's love for more than one woman (until and unless they are his wives); a woman who is in love with more than one man; love for an elderly woman; the lesser degree of passion experienced by one of the pair; or the desire felt only by the man (*Bouquet of Rasa* 33; *River of Rasa* 333, 259)

Jagannātha in *Rasagaṅgādhara* gave a long list of situations that are to be eliminated from the gamut of *kāvya* (101–102). These lists of "to be avoided" situations and behavior appear preposterous to us today, mainly due to our changed cultural contexts. Nonetheless, what these observations reveal is the close connection that exists between any form of art and the sociocultural contexts that engender it. A closer analysis, would however, point to a similarity in inhibitions that artists hold even in contemporary times. For instance, an open depiction of overt sexuality or violence is considered unacceptable in Indian theatres or films even today. It is not surprising that our ancestors who thought long and deeply about the nature of art and its function should also have thought of what could not or should not be represented in art. The Greek theatrical concept of decorum shared this view of *aucitya* when they insisted on not representing death on stage.

These observations show that the idea of *rasa*, as conceived by Sanskrit literary theoreticians, was also closely associated with the socially accepted values and customs through the concept of *aucitya*, and that the creative writers were supposed to remove anything that countered the moral ethos of the period. *Aucitya* was particularly observed, when poets borrowed stories from other well-known sources such as the *Rāmāyaṇa* and *Mahābhārata*. Bhoja in his *Śṛṅgāraprakāśa* chronicled a lot of "self-censoring" incidents from the past where the poets, by rewriting the occasional acts of impropriety committed by an otherwise *uttama* character, re-fashioned older texts according to the prevalent notions of *aucitya*. For example, in the *Rāmāyaṇa*, Daśaratha exiles Rāma to keep the word he has given to his wife Kaikeyī. But in the play *Nirdoṣadaśaratha*, this event is radically revised in such a way that Rāma is exiled not by Daśaratha and his wife Kaikeyī, but by two magical creatures who impersonate Daśaratha and Kaikeyī. In Bhavabhūti's *Mahāvīracarita*, Rāma has a fair duel with Vālin, as opposed to the original plot in which Rāma treacherously kills Vālin by shooting an arrow at him from behind a tree. In the *Mahābhārata*, Bhīma drinks the blood of Duḥśāsana after killing him. Considering that such a heinous act is unbecoming of a high-born character like Bhīma, Bhaṭṭa Nārāyaṇa in his *Veṇīsaṃhāra*, revises this scene in such a way that Duḥśāsana's blood is drunk not by Bhīma, but by a demon who has possessed him. In *Harivaṃśa*, Māyāvatī is presented as the reincarnation of the wife of Kāma, the lord of love, and her lover Pradyumna as Kāma himself, in contrast to the original story where Pradyumna falls in love with Māyāvatī who is his preceptor's wife. Such a change is made because *śṛṅgāra* with one's guru's wife was socially unacceptable. In Kālidāsa's *Abhijñānaśākuntalaṃ*, Duṣyanta's failure to recognize Śakuntalā is because of Durvasa's curse, which is a radical departure from the original story in the *Mahābhārata* where Duṣyanta deliberately spurns her in open court. Yet another major work that Bhoja refers to in connection with the revision of the plot is *Calitarāma*. *Calitarāma* portrays Rāma's return to Ayodhyā after his victory over Rāvaṇa and recovery of his wife Sītā. But in this version of Rāma's story, Rāma spurns Sītā because he was deceived by a posse of his surviving enemies led by a demon named Lavaṇa. In Mātrarāja's *Tāpasavatsarāja*, which is an emendation of Bhāsa's *Svapnavāsavadattaṃ*, the minster lies to king Udayana that queen Vāsavadattā perished in the fire. He lies to the king not because he held a grudge against the king, but because he wanted to save the king who is enamored by Vāsavadattā to the point of neglecting his kingly duties (II; 460).

In *Vakroktijīvita*, Kuntaka also referred to such emendations of plots. The drama *Udāttarāghava* by Māyurarāja has already been mentioned, where it is Rāma who goes to rescue Lakṣmaṇa. Such a revision of the plot was justified on the ground that it is highly improper for a man of great prowess and courage like Rāma to be rescued by his younger brother Lakṣmaṇa (323).

***Aucitya* in Diction**

These restrictions on elements which countered the existing notions of propriety were applicable not only to the representation of character-types and situations, but also to the very diction of *kāvya*. Literary theoreticians starting from Bhāmaha instructed the authors to avoid terms that were considered taboo. According to Bhāmaha, writers should always stay away from such faults as *śrutiduṣṭa* (offensive to ear), *arthaduṣṭa* (improper or objectionable meaning), and *kalpanāduṣṭa* (objectionable construction wherein joining of words give rise to an objectionable sense) (I.46–59). Bhāmaha gave a list of words and expressions that are to be avoided, like *varcas* (excrement), *saṃbādha* (vulva), *dharṣita* (seduce/outrage), *udgāra* (vomiting), or *reta* (semen); word combinations like *hiraṇyaretāḥ* (because one part of this expression contains the taboo word for semen, '*retāḥ*'); or sentences like "*sa saśauryābharaṇo yathā*" (because the sentence has the word '*yābha*' which is an indecorous term for sexual intercourse)" (I.49).

Daṇḍin also held the same opinion. According to him, the expression—"Hey maiden, why don't you love me who loves you a lot?"—is *grāmya* (uncouth and unpolished) as it explicitly expresses a man's desire for a woman (I.63). He was also against any explicit representation of *saṃbhoga-śṛṅgāra* (love-in-union) and the employment of taboo terms referring to love-making (I.64). Like Bhāmaha, Daṇḍin pointed out that a poet should always be careful about the conjoining of words in a sentence so that it does not generate any obscene connotation or double entendre.

It should also be borne in mind that *anaucitya* or impropriety cannot be equated with what was culturally offensive. In the case of degenerate characters (*adhama*) like Rāvaṇa, impropriety was very much acceptable. Creative writers often employed the impropriety of the inferior characters (*adhama*) as a way to differentiate them from the law-abiding noble characters (*uttama*). Pollock points out that the presence of impropriety "as such does not enfeeble literature, as if, since 'the sole aim of literature' is *rasa*, when 'real rasa' is not present, the true aim of literature is not attained. How, after all, could one have the *Rāmāyaṇa* without Rāvaṇa?" ("The Social Aesthetics" 211).

This flexibility with respect to characterization applied to diction also. Chari points out that Sanskrit poeticians periodically listed the poetic virtues (*guṇa*) that aided in the realization of *rasa*, and poetic faults (*doṣa*) that impeded the process of *rasa*. However, the governing principle in determining a *guṇa* or *doṣa* was *aucitya*, because, "Different excellences characterized different poetic styles and were suitable to different types of poetic composition. Further, *doṣa*(s) themselves were thought to be *anitya* (transitory) as there could be cases of *doṣa-guṇa*—of *doṣa*(s) turning out to be *guṇa*(s) under certain circumstances" (Chari 61). According to this definition, any word or behavior that is inappropriate would be a *doṣa*. This is quite logical, considering the dynamic nature of social and cultural mores. A woman character like Mahasweta Devi's Dopdi (in "Draupadi"), defiantly flaunts her maimed and tortured naked body before her tormentors. But a century back, this would have been unthinkable and unrepresentable; the culture of those days would have construed this as a *doṣa*, arguing that a woman would not behave in this manner.

Aucitya and Decorum

It is clear that the Indian concept of *aucitya* corresponds to the Greek and Roman classical concept of decorum. Aristotle in his *Poetics* emphasizes the need for the poet to aim for the "necessary or the probable" (XV, 55) in characterization as well as diction. He also frowned upon showing death on stage. Decorum was the guiding principle of Cicero's *De Oratore* as well as Horace's *Ars Poetica*. So, classical literature in general—Greek, Roman, and Sanskrit—seems to be under the sway of this insistence on the "right thing to do." It can be argued that this all-encompassing concept of *aucitya* acted like an inhibiting force, discouraging authors to challenge and overthrow prevalent notions of the acceptable in literature.

Decorum or *aucitya* operated in two ways: one, as a guiding principle for the inclusions and exclusions that are part of the creative process; two, as a set of unwritten rules that outlined the limits of the representable in literature. The first concept appears to operate even today for authors and artists everywhere. Authors carefully choose their words, locales, and characters. "Big Brother is watching you" is simple and direct but the simplicity is belied by the menace it conceals; these words are appropriate for the message that Orwell wished to convey. The Sundarbans almost becomes a character in Amitav Ghosh's *The Hungry Tide*, and the novel, or a character like Fokir could not have evolved the way it has in any other locale. Here, Ghosh has displayed *aucitya* in depicting a character like Fokir against the background of the tide country.

The second concept of *aucitya* also is not unknown to us today. It is the general perception of what is acceptable or unacceptable that decides the cases of book bans. Lawrence's *Lady Chatterley's Lover* was thought to be unfit for respectable society because of the profusion of four-letter words. This was considered culpable obscenity in England in the 1920s when the novel was published. Interestingly, Ānandavardhana had a very different stance on obscenity in literature. The eighth *sarga* of Kālidāsa's *Kumārasambhava*, which was considered by many critics to be obscene because it contained explicit descriptions of the physical intimacy of Śiva and Pārvatī, was exonerated by him; Ānanda observes that this section in *Kumārasambhava* "does not appear as vulgarity because it is concealed by his skill. An example is the description of [Śiva's] enjoyment of Pārvatī in the *Kumārasambhava* ... it will appear in conclusion by positive and negative examples that this fault can be concealed by poetic skill" (3.6 e *A*). This becomes all the more significant when we think of Ānandavardhana frowning on the depiction of sexual enjoyment of *uttama* characters. Nonetheless, according to critics like Ānandavardhana and Abhinavagupta, there are no fixed standards of propriety. The poet was expected to exercise his discretion in matters of diction or characterization. If the language used is expected of the character in his/her social circumstances, then that is acceptable in literature even if it is not in respectable society. So, Lawrence was right in giving coarse language to the game-keeper Mellors in his novel, while it does not suit Lady Chatterley.

Conclusion

However, it would be wrong to assume that *aucitya* was merely an inhibitory force. The above discussion also points to the fact that *aucitya* was not always based on what was socially acceptable, but what was artistically consistent. Kṣemendra was not completely wrong or archaic in his assumption that this is the overarching artistic principle behind good art in all its variety. Although postmodernism has exploded generic and stylistic literary conventions, the notion of propriety still holds true for literary works of this ilk. John Barth could not have written his *Lost in the Funhouse* in the style of an epic; Salman Rushdie and other postcolonial writers "chutnify" their English because it is appropriate to a non-English speaking readership. *Aucitya* is the artistic principle that all good artists who are also skilled craftsmen abide by even today.

Works Cited

Abhinavagupta. *Locana.* In *The Dhvanyāloka of Ānandavardhana with the Locana of Abhinavagupta.* Translated and edited by Daniel Ingalls, Jeffrey Masson, and M. V. Patwardhan, Harvard University Press, 1990.

Ānandavardhana. *The Dhvanyāloka of Ānandavardhana with the Locana of Abhinavagupta.* Translated and edited by Daniel Ingalls, Jeffrey Masson, and M. V. Patwardhan, Harvard University Press, 1990.

Aristotle. *Poetics,* translation and Critical Notes by S. H. Butcher. https://www.stmarys-ca.edu/sites/default/files/attachments/files/Poetics.pdf. Accessed January 18, 2020.

Bharata. *Nāṭyaśāstram.* Translated (Malayalam) and edited by K. P. Narayana Pisharody, Kerala Sahitya Akademi, 2004.

Bhāmaha. *Kāvyālaṅkāra.* Edited by B. N. Sarma and Baldeva Upadhyay, Chowkhamba Sanskrit Series Office, 1998.

Bhānudatta. *The Bouquet of Rasa and River of Rasa.* Edited by Sheldon Pollock, New York University Press, 2009.

Bhoja. *Sarasvatīkaṇṭhābharaṇa.* Edited by Pandurang Jawaji, Nirnayasagar Press, 1934.

———. *Śṛṅgāraprakāśa.* Vols 1 and 2, edited by G. S. Josyer, 1955 and 1963.

Chari, V. K. "Decorum as a Critical Concept in Indian and Western Poetics." *The Journal of Aesthetics and Art Criticism*, vol. 26, no. 1, Autumn 1967: 53–63.

Daṇḍin. *Kāvyādarśa of Daṇḍin*. Edited by Premachandra Tarkabagisa, Royal Asiatic Society, 1962.

Jagannātha. *The Rasagaṅgādhara of Jagannātha Paṇḍita with the Commentary of Nāgeśa Bhaṭṭa*. Edited by D. Prasad and K. P. Parab, The Nirnaya Sagara Press, 1888.

Kṣemendra. "*Aucityavicāracarcā*." In *Kṣemendra Studies: Together with an English Translation of his Kavikaṇṭḥābharṇa, Aucityavicāracarcā and Suvṛttatilaka*. Edited by Suryakanta, Oriental Book Agency, 1954.

Kuntaka. *Vakroktijīvita*. Translated by Krishnamoorthy, Karnatak University, 1977.

Mahimabhaṭṭa. *Vyaktiviveka*. Edited by Gaṇapati Śāstrī , T. Trivandrum Sanskrit Series No, 1901.

Mammaṭa. *Kāvyaprakāśa of Mammaṭa*. Edited by Ganganath Jha, Bharathiya Vidya Prakashan, 1966.

Pollock, Sheldon. *The Language of the Gods in the World of Men: Sanskrit, Culture and Power in Premodern India*. Columbia University Press, 2006.

———. "The Social Aesthetic and Sanskrit Literary Theory." *Journal of Indian Philosophy*, vol. 29, no. 1, 2001: 197–229.

Udbhaṭa. *Kāvyālaṅkārasārasaṃgraha with the commentary, the Laghuvṛtti of Induraja*. Edited by Narayana Daso Banhatti, Bhandarkar Oriental Research Institute, 1982.

Vidyānātha. *Pratāparudrīya*. Edited by K. S. Ramamurthi and S. R. Matha, Oriental Research Institute, 1933.

8

Conclusion

One of the major problems encountered by a serious student of Sanskrit aesthetics today is the question of its relevance to the contemporary practice of literature and criticism. How practical or useful is it to travel far back into ancient India and discuss the foundational principles of a literary culture that is now almost a museum artifact? This is a point that has been discussed and debated by proponents and opponents of an Indian school of literature and criticism.

There is no denying the fact that a contemporary academic disciplinary training in literature equips the student with a thoroughly Western—primarily Anglo-American—approach to the subject. The name "Literature" refers almost exclusively to English literature and literary theory; other literatures and critical schools including the Indian, often figure only on the periphery of most literature syllabi.

G. N. Devy in his *After Amnesia* famously identified a crisis that exists in the Indian literary critical system today, pinpointing the two causative factors:

> An awareness of the rift between theory and creative literature (which is characteristic of but not peculiar to the Indian critical scenario) and the inability to mend the breakdown in critical discourse by creating a new and viable critical theory where the present intellectual vacuum exists, constitute the two basic elements of the crisis in Indian literary criticism of this century. (15)

It cannot be denied that such a crisis exists, but it has to be explored how we could possibly tide over this crisis. It would be foolhardy to pretend that colonization never happened and that we will be able to retrieve a past tradition in its unadulterated form. Nevertheless, it is equally fallacious to assume that a literary culture that has originated on foreign shores can work as a prototype for us. It is relevant to consider, for instance, how we can apply the literary tenets of postmodernism to literature written in Santhali today. Literature and literary criticism have organic ties with their cultural contexts. So, if Sanskrit aesthetics appears outmoded to us today, we also will have to admit that most Indian language literatures have not reached the postmodern condition either. What we need to evolve is a synthesis of literary practices that are relevant to our literatures. In this context, we have to carefully evaluate what we can adopt from our ancient critical schools and how we can make them relevant to our contemporary times.

Tradition of Dissent and Debate

In the previous chapters, we were primarily dealing with the major schools in Sanskrit literary criticism. It is evident to us that these schools came into being as a result of conscious deliberation and debate between critics. The desire to transcend the borders of the received notions about a system of knowledge is the very life force of any discipline, be it ancient or modern. As far as the Indian *kāvyaśāstra* tradition is concerned, attempts to step beyond the existing truth claims often constituted its very life force. Many *kāvyaśāstra* texts that are available to us now are marked by what is known as the *pūrvapakṣa* strategy (wherein an author explains the view of his predecessor or contemporary and then refutes it systematically to establish his own position). We have already seen in the preceding chapters that the *guṇa* and *rīti* critical frameworks were the outputs of dissent with the views of *ālaṅkārika*s, while *dhvani* was the result of dissent with the views of the exponents of *guṇa* and *rīti*. When it comes to the medieval phase, *navya*s or the neo-intellectuals in *kāvyaśāstra* subjected the views of their predecessors to careful scrutiny and criticism, as we find in the works of Siddicandra's *Kāvyaprakāśa-khaṇḍana* or Jagannātha's *Citramīmāṃsākhaṇḍana*.

Even a cursory glance at a few debates regarding the nature of *rasa*, recorded by Abhinavagupta in his commentary on Ānandavardhana's *Dhvanyāloka*, will show how the spirit of dissent and debate was at the core of this tradition. We have seen how Bhaṭṭa Lollaṭa, Śaṅkuka, and Bhaṭṭa Nāyaka differed in their opinions about the origin and nature of *rasa*. These discussions were continued by Ānandavardhana and Abhinavagupta, giving rise to a sophisticated intellectual analysis of the ontology of literary knowledge. What is striking about these intellectual conversations is the way it was sustained down the centuries; Jagannātha Paṇdita "speaks" to Ānandavardhana as if he were a contemporary, only because of the "*pūrvapakṣa*" strategy wherein all literary ancestors were invoked when an issue was debated. More importantly, the ancestors were criticized and if need be, corrected with healthy respect by latter-day critics. There was no unquestioning acceptance of traditional knowledge systems.

The spirit to think beyond the structured pattern of conventionality was very much alive even in the medieval phase which critics often wrongly describe as a period of intellectual drought in literary science. According to Yigal Bronner, the literary theoreticians in this phase attempted to constitute a new relationship with their past. Instead of inventing any radically new critical concept like *dhvani* or *vakrokti*, they directed their energy mainly to critically examine the views of their predecessors and to answer the old questions in new ways (Bronner 456). To mark their departure from their predecessors in terms of their mode of operation and views, these new critics identified themselves as *navya* or "new," in contrast to their ancestors who they called *prācīna* (ancient); this was basically what we call the "generation gap" today, where youngsters question and attempt to modify the accepted beliefs of their parents or grandparents. Siddicandra's *Kāvyaprakāśa-khaṇḍana*, Appayya Dīkṣita's *Citramīmāṃsā* and *Kuvalayānanda* and Jagannātha's *Rasagaṅgādhara* and *Citramīmāṃsā-khaṇḍana* are a few remarkable treatises from the medieval phase which meticulously attack the claims of their predecessors. A case in point is Jagannātha's debate on the causes of *rasābhāsa* or the semblance of *rasa* in *kāvya*. According to the *prācīna*s or ancients, a woman having multiple male partners was not a case of *rasābhāsa* if she was married to them, but for *navya*s like Jagannātha, this was clearly a case of *rasābhāsa*. Therefore, he says that Draupadī's love for her five husbands, unlike what his predecessors think, is a clear case of *rasābhāsa*. Distancing himself from the old school and calling himself *navya* or new, Jagannātha declared: "Here Draupadī's love for her husbands is an instance of *rasābhāsa* or semblance of *rasa*. This is the view of the new intelligentsia. But the ancient scholars do not see this instance of a heroine feeling love for her multiple partners as a case of *rasābhāsa*" (101).

Siddicandra's *Kāvyaprakāśa-khaṇḍana* was self-evidently a criticism of Mammaṭa's *Kāvyaprakāśa.* In *Citramīmāṃsā*, Appayya Dīkṣita innovatively redefined the figure of speech called *upamā* or simile. Appayya saw simile as the archetypal *alaṅkāra* that functions as the base of all figures of speech. He envisioned simile "as the one and only actress on the stage of *kāvya*" (Bronner 444). Although Appayya was not the first critic to grant such a status to simile, he conceptualized it in a way that was very distinct from his predecessors. Acknowledging the potency of simile to generate other *alaṅkāra*s, Appayya compared it to the concept of Brahman in the phenomenal world. Just as Brahman manifests itself in various shapes, so also *upamā* in the figurative realm assumes the shape of different figures of speech. The way he presents *upamā* in *Citramīmāṃsā* was also in conjunction with his Vedantic disposition. Until Appayya's intervention, there had been an unwritten rule in literary science that while presenting a figure of speech, one should necessarily define it. Appayya departed from this age-old practice by not defining what *upamā* is. This is to send a message that just as the essence of Brahman defies all ontological specificities, *upamā* refuses to be reduced to one particular definition. In his introduction, Appayya stated that his definitions and illustrations were mostly drawn from the works of the ancients (*pracīna*) such as Mammaṭa, Vidyānātha, Bhoja, and Ruyyaka. But as soon as his discussion begins, we learn that his invocation of the views of the ancients is not to blindly follow them but to challenge and modify them (445).

Jagannātha's *Rasagaṅgādhara* was also noted for his disagreements with his predecessors. One such instance of critical dissent in *Rasagaṅgādhara* revolved around the question of whether *bhakti* should be considered a tenth *rasa*. Rejecting the position of his Vaishnavite predecessors like Rūpā Gosvāmi, Kavi Karṇapura, and many others, Jagannātha averred that *bhakti* cannot be considered a *rasa*, as it was against the dictum of writers like Bharata (Pollock, "New Intellectuals," 15). In *Rasagaṅgādhara*, Jagannātha also took Appayya to task for introducing a new subspecies of the figure of speech "denial" (*apahnuti*) in *Kuvalayānanda*. According to Jagannātha, the proposed subtype could not be considered a subcategory of "denial," as it was not covered by the definition of the category given in *Kāvyaprakāśa*, *Alaṅkārasarvasva*, and Appayya's own *Citramīmāṃsā* (16). The other predecessors with whom Jagannātha expressed his difference of opinion in *Rasagaṅgādhara* include Ānandavardhana, Vidyānātha, Śobhākaramitra, Jayaratha, Ruyyaka, and Mammaṭa (301–317).

Colonization and After

With the advent of colonialism, this spirit of dissent which was central to *kāvyaśāstra* experienced a drastic downturn (Pollock, "Indian Knowledge Systems," 1). It is this decline that Pollock underlines:

> The two centuries before European colonialism decisively established itself in the subcontinent (ca. 1550–1750) constitute one of the most innovative epochs of Sanskrit systematic thought (in language analysis, logic, hermeneutics, moral-legal philosophy, and the rest). Thinkers produced new

> formulations of old problems, in entirely new discursive idioms, in what were often new scholarly genres employing often a new historicist framework; some even called themselves . . . 'the new' scholars (*navya*). Concurrently with the spread of European power, however, this dynamism diminished so much that by 1800, the capacity of Sanskrit thought to make history had vanished. The production of moral-legal texts, for example, which was so extensive throughout the seventeenth-century, ceased entirely, and in core disciplines like hermeneutics or literary theory no significant scholarship—that is, significant in the eyes of the tradition itself—was again to be written. (ibid.)

This epistemic change could have been brought about by two differing perceptions of India's past. Both were of Western, if not British, origin and were termed the Orientalist and Anglicist views. The Orientalist historiographers, who aimed to reconstruct the image of early India, presented India's past as "glorious" and the present as "decadent." Though the image of a glorious past often sounded reassuring and pleasing to many nationalist historians, the primary agenda behind such a stance was undoubtedly imperialist in nature (Thapar, *Early India,* 16–17). The juxtaposition of the image of a "glorious" past with a "decadent" present functioned as a ploy to warrant their imperialistic "civilizing mission." This conception of a "glorious" past instilled in the native scholars of Orientalist lineage an absolutely uncritical reverence toward the intellectual traditions such as Sanskrit *kāvyaśāstra* from early India. This also influenced the Indian scholars by discouraging them from questioning all that is ancient to the point of treating them as holy and sacrosanct. This is one of the primary reasons why engagement with Sanskrit literary theories—as in the case of many other intellectual traditions from early India—got reduced to the mere reproduction and restatement of the available scholarship.

Influenced by the spirit of the Orientalist approach to ancient epistemologies, many critics in the modern times considered Sanskrit *kāvyaśāstra* as modern enough to evaluate the literary merits of any contemporary literary work and sought to replace Western critical theories with their Indian counterparts in both Sanskrit and vernacular languages. This tendency in the first instance came out of a strong desire to decolonize our Western critical sensibilities. Ashcroft and others talk about this revivalist disposition in their *Empire Writes Back*:

> The main drive in re-employing terms from Sanskrit criticism, such as those listed above [*rasa* and *dhvani*], or from ancient Tamil (Ramanujan 1985) has been in assessing the literature produced in Indian vernacular languages where a direct continuity of some essential 'indianness' has been more vigorously asserted. Critics such as K. Krishnamoorthy (1984) claim the existence of a theoretical base common to all Indian literatures, including both post-Sanskrit and non-Sanskrit, a base that is itself the sign of an Indian sensibility. The Kannada-speaking novelist and critic U. R. Anantha Murthy presents a more complex view of the relation between contemporary vernacular texts and the Tamil and Sanskrit canon, a view which takes into account the literatures in 'english' as well as those in Indian languages. He suggests that the relationship of the ancient languages (Tamil and Sanskrit) to the modern vernaculars is analogous to that of Latin and modern English (Anantha Murthy 1986). The Kannada terms *marga/desi*; the *way* and the *earth*

> are, he claims, potent metaphors for this with Sanskrit as the way (*marga*) and the vernacular (e.g. Kannada) as the earth or ground (*desi*). All texts written in the present mix the two, just as all English texts demonstrate a varying mix of Latinate and vernacular elements (more redolent of the former in the case of, say, Milton, or of the latter in the case of, say, Keats). (117)

Although these critics aimed to free themselves from the clutches of Western critical concepts, their attempt to vindicate the efficacy of Indian poetics ironically remained mostly dependent on their Western counterparts. To substantiate their claim that ancient Indian literary theories are "modern" and sophisticated just like any other modern critical theory, and that they have the potential to function as an analytical apparatus for contemporary literary texts, they compared Sanskrit *kāvyaśāstra* theories in their canonical form to their Western counterparts and brought out the points of convergence shared by these two.

A glance at some of the attempts in the comparatist direction will prove this point. In his article, "*Rasa* and the Objective Correlative," Krishna Rayan attempts to show that there is a consensus of opinion between the *rasa* school of Sanskrit literary theory and T. S. Eliot's idea of objective correlative on the question of how a poem presents or conveys an emotion (248). P. S. Sastri in his essay "Indian Poetics and New Criticism" construes Cleanth Brooks's "paradox" and Empson's "ambiguity" as ideas already anticipated by Kuntaka's *Vakrokti.* He opines that "the modern critical creed of the search for irony, paradox and ambiguity was anticipated in India hundreds of years ago" (177). R. S. Pathak, in his "The Indian Theory of *Vakrokti* in Relation to the Stylistic Concept of Deviance" identifies the interfaces between the canonical reading of Kuntaka's *vakrokti* and the modern Formalistic concept of defamiliarization. Pathak observes,

> The Indian theory of *vakrokti* and the stylistic concept of deviance refer to this very central aspect of poetic language. The two concepts are complementary to each other. There may be differences in their priorities and approaches, but they treat the same linguistic phenomenon in poetry. (207)

This sort of a comparison contributes nothing new to traditional Indian epistemologies such as Sanskrit *kāvyaśāstra*. It remains only as a nativist answer to the Anglicist claim that India's intellectual tradition is insufficient to meet the needs of modern times.

Closely related to the Orientalist tendency to stay away from critically approaching Sanskrit *kāvyaśāstra* is the xenophobic disposition toward it. The uncritical rejection of Sanskrit *kāvyaśāstra* theories has its roots firmly entrenched in Macaulay's Anglicist notion about the Indian intellectual tradition. Macaulay in his "Minute on Education" (1835) observes, "I have never found one among them [the orientalists] who could deny that a single shelf of a good European library was worth the whole native literature of India and Arabia." Keeping in line with Macaulay's notion about Indian knowledge systems, many critics conclude that Sanskrit *kāvyaśāstra* has no contemporary relevance in the field of research and has only archaic value (Perry 598). These two views—the Orientalist and Anglicist—though polarized on the surface, proved equally detrimental to Sanskrit *kāvyaśāstra* in terms of its growth and progress as a system of knowledge. While the Anglicists dismissed the entire intellectual tradition of ancient India, the Orientalists bestowed upon it an aura of sacred reverence that did not allow for any form of questioning. The latter was the more dangerous because it managed to petrify the system without leaving space for healthy discussions on the subject.

The third approach to *kāvyaśāstra* that we can trace out is what is called the nativist approach or *desivad.* G. N. Devy holds that neither Sanskrit poetics nor Western criticism is sufficient to interpret the literary works in the *bhāṣa*s of the Indian subcontinent since the concerns of literature in the *bhāṣa*s are considerably different from those of Sanskrit poetics and Western criticism. Considering "criticism as a cultural subsystem rather than a web of abstract theoretical constructs" (2), Devy opines that "literature growing out of one type of underlying linguistic and metaphysical structure cannot be understood and studied by criticism growing out of another and alien type of underlying linguistic and metaphysical structure" (143). Devy says,

> Sanskrit literary and critical traditions are accessible to the modern intellectual only as imaginary possessions. The modern Indian critic *can* say that India *had* a glorious tradition of literary criticism a thousand years ago. But, having said this, he is unable to use this tradition as a living tradition which shares a frame of reference within which his normal intellectual activity takes place. (30)

The same criticism, says Devy, holds water in the case of Western criticism also. The fundamental problem that Devy has with Western criticism is that the application of theoretical positions born out of the cultural milieu of Europe fails to yield any result in our studies of native texts

(16). Therefore, he insists that each *bhāṣa* should develop a native mode of criticism of its own, instead of banking upon Sanskrit and Western criticism. Devy discusses what he reckons to be the predicament of *bhāṣa* literature in modern times and suggests a possible solution:

> All these writers and critics sharing a common present can nonchalantly refer to so many different traditions and past ages. Rarely does one find instances of systematic efforts at understanding contemporary literature on the basis of knowledge embedded in native literary traditions. Among these exceptions one can count are Bhalchandra Nemade and his associates in the nativist school of criticism. (15)

However, this view also has a drawback. Although it is correct that Sanskrit *kāvyaśāstra* cannot be employed to appreciate or interpret modern literary works as the concerns of literature have changed over the years, this view does not seem to consider the possibility of modifying the ancient theories to suit the present.

Important Aspects of Ancient Theories

One of the major criticisms levelled against Sanskrit theories of literature is that they are elitist and employ what are called "*savarna*" standards of aesthetic beauty. Sharankumar Limbale, who advocated a different aesthetics for Dalit literature, says:

> Is it appropriate to expect pleasure or beauty, instead of inspiration for social transformation, from a literature that has been written primarily to raise awareness? Dalit writers believe that their literature should be analyzed from a sociological perspective focused on social values than

> on beauty. An exclusively aesthetic consideration of Dalit literature will disregard the Dalit writers' fundamental role, and hence is not acceptable to Dalit writers. Rejecting traditional aesthetics, they insist on the need for a new and distinct aesthetic for their literature—an aesthetic that is life-affirming and realistic. (19)

This view has been echoed by many Dalit writers and critics time and again, arguing that the Dalit world of gritty reality does not or cannot afford the luxury of beautifully wrought language and elevated thought.

This perspective also calls for a radical redefinition of the category of literature. Limbale claims that Dalit writing has to be judged according to sociological standards rather than aesthetic criteria. If so, what is the distinction between a sociological treatise and a literary narrative? Even if we admit that the traditional notions of literature have changed with the advent of postmodernism, the insistence that Dalit writers and writing are primarily intended to critique the existing social system seems to be reductive and limiting in nature.

The call for a separate aesthetic criterion for Dalit literature is also premised on the idea that Sanskrit *kāvya* deals only with the upper caste, upper class world of the bold and the beautiful. While it is correct to assume that Sanskrit was spoken only by the upper castes, it is wrong to conclude that this world has space only for what is beautiful. For instance, an epic like the *Mahābhārata* depicts covetous desire, jealousy, greed, deadly hatred, and vicious cruelty—all of which are obviously negative and ugly emotions. It is also compelled to use a language that is capable of describing the death and destruction on the battlefield of Kurukṣetra, a language that cannot be adorned with lovely similes. The world of the *Mahābhārata* is a realistic world marked by moral ambiguity and is tainted by all that is natural to the world that human beings inhabit. Although its dominating *aṅgirasa* is *śānta*, the *rasa* evoked by Bhīma's horrendous killing of Duḥśāsana is revulsion or *bībhatsā*.

Conversely, it is not true that *rasa* or *dhvani* cannot be employed to analyze a Dalit work. Let us look at Meena Kandasami's poem "Ekalaivan":

> This note comes as a consolation:
>
> You can do a lot of things
> With your left hand.
> Besides, fascist Dronacharyas warrant
> Left-handed treatment.
>
> Also,
> You don't need your right thumb,
> To pull a trigger or hurl a bomb.

This is a very powerful indictment of an autocratic and patriarchal establishment. It does not use any word or simile that is obviously "poetic," but the terse language is admirably suited to the theme it wishes to convey. Thus, it displays *aucitya* in language. There is *dhvani* in the usage of the term "left" where the meanings range from the literal left hand to "left" in terms of any stance that is critical of establishments. Moreover, the Eklavya story from the *Mahābhārata* is not overtly mentioned anywhere except in the title, along with a reference to a "fascist" Droṇācārya, compressing in one line an entire history of Brahminical oppression of the lower castes; this constitutes the beauty of suggestion which is the essence of *dhvani.* The defiance and violence in the last two lines contribute to the evocation of *raudra rasa*. This method of literary analysis can be applied to any text, irrespective of theme, language or culture. It is a mistaken notion that Sanskrit aesthetics deals only with fair skin and lustrous eyes. If it were only that, then why would we have the *rasa*s of *bībhatsā*, *raudra*, or *bhayānaka*?

Aspects of Sanskrit Theories

So, should we claim that these theories and concepts are universal and can be used without any modification whatsoever today? One important aspect needs to be kept in mind while doing this—it is that most of the Sanskrit theories are analytical tools that help us understand the structure and working of literary genres. It would be wrong to assume that they will provide a theoretical framework that is in essence an "approach" to a literary piece. You can claim to employ a "postcolonial approach" to Charles Dickens's *Great Expectations*, but you cannot have an "*alaṅkāra*" approach to it. While theoretical concepts like structuralism or post-structuralism enables you to adopt a holistic view of the text as well as its context, Sanskrit literary theories tend to narrowly focus only on the work.

The seeming exceptions to this are the concepts of *rasa*, *dhvani*, and *vakrokti*. They might be able to enhance your understanding of the cultural contexts within which the poem/novel is appreciated, but these concepts are not interested in clarifying the non-literary factors that underlie it. A new historicist approach like that of Stephen Greenblatt would study the prevalent non-literary texts and other cultural factors that might have directly or subliminally influenced Shakespeare when he wrote his history plays. Whereas, *rasa* or *dhvani* will delve deeper into the text rather than outside it; non-literary factors are not important for this at all. So, while one approach is broad-based and expansive, the other is intensive and narrow.

Can this narrow view of a literary text in isolation be perceived as a drawback? After all, a cultural materialist approach would be more comprehensive. Shylock's famous "Hath not a Jew eyes" speech in *Merchant of Venice* is a case in point. An analysis of that speech using *rasa*, *alaṅkāra*, and *dhvani* will only reveal the literary beauty of the speech. An approach like that of Greenblatt's on the other hand, will reveal the larger atmosphere of anti-Semitism that prevailed during that time and how Shakespeare was being "political" in making his Jewish villain more human. However, this understanding does not in any way take away or add to the aesthetic value of the text. This sort of understanding came into Western critical practice only with the advent of postmodernism and other subsequent theoretical systems. If we compare classical Western critical theory or English literary criticism till the time of T. S. Eliot, we can see that all of them were concerned only about the literary text *qua* text. Literary study in those days involved a close reading of the text but there is no such thing as purely literary theory today; in fact most of the "theorists" who are used by literary critics and academics today are from other disciplines—Derrida, Lacan, Heidegger, Zizek, Negri, Agamben, and Judith Butler to name a few. Literature has gone out of literary study and criticism. Hillis Miller, warning about the "imminent death of literature" has pointed out how academics across the world are turning from "literary study to theory, cultural studies, postcolonial studies, media (film, television etc.), popular culture studies, Women's studies, African-American studies, and so on" with the result that "they often write and teach in ways that are closer to the social sciences than to the humanities as traditionally conceived" (10). As Miller points out, literary criticism today is a melange of various disciplinary approaches ranging from philosophy, psychology, and sociology to even physics (chaos theory) and environmental science (ecocriticism). Even in the West, the study or criticism of literature *qua* literature does not have much to offer beyond what the ancient Sanskritists propounded. It is also fallacious to compare the numerous contemporary "approaches" with the purely literary approach of ancient Sanskrit theories and accuse them of being reactionary, primarily because their perception of literature and its objectives were completely different.

The Reader and the Text

What appears to be an almost exclusive focus on the text in Sanskrit criticism also seems to sideline one of the important figures in contemporary literary criticism, which is that of the reader. The dogmatic nature of Sanskrit theories does not allow for much freedom to the reader; in fact, the general belief was that "*apāre kāvya samsāre kavireva prajāpatiḥ*" or that the poet is the sole emperor of the vast world of literature.

Although critiques and creative writers of Sanskrit *kāvya* tradition often held the reader in high esteem, considering them as the true judge of a poet's creative excellence, nobody in fact took up the question of the reader's involvement in the production of a text's aesthetic emotion (*rasa*) or its meaning. They all subscribed to the notion that an author supplies meaning and aesthetic emotion, while the reader receives and relishes them. For the earliest thinkers like Bhaṭṭa Lollaṭa, *rasa* was actually located in the character. Although Śaṅkuka incorporated the reader or spectator within his discursive framework, his theory also remained essentially text-oriented. Śaṅkuka's theory stated that *rasa* cannot be directly perceived but can only be inferred by the reader from the imitation of characters and situations enacted by actors. In his theory of *anumāna*, Śaṅkuka was preoccupied solely with the nature of this imitation. The process of inference that the reader or spectator performs was completely ignored.

Similarly, Ānandavardhana, who wrote *Dhvanyāloka* to reveal to *sahṛdaya*s the ontology of *dhvani* or poetic suggestion, also turned a blind eye to the figure of the reader. Pollock observes, "Ānandavardhana, too, is completely silent on how the reader knows of *rasa* or experiences it. He is concerned only with textual, even formalistic, processes when arguing that *rasa* is something that can never be directly expressed but only suggested or implied" ("What was Bhatta Nayaka Saying?" 145). The first literary critic in Sanskrit *kāvyaśāstra* to talk about the reader's involvement in the process of aesthetic enjoyment was the 10th-century critic Bhaṭṭa Nāyaka, followed by his disciple Abhinavagupta in the 11th century. According to both Bhaṭṭa Nāyaka and Abhinavagupta, *rasa* is neither perceived in the actor, nor is perceived by spectators in themselves; *rasa*, he says, on the other hand, is "enjoyed" by the spectator with the power of a special capacity called *bhāvanā*. Though critics have paid enough attention to reconstruct the theory of reader envisioned by both Bhaṭṭa Nāyaka and Abhinavagupta, hardly any attempt has been made to see Sanskrit *kāvyaśāstra* theories, originally envisioned as a writer's manual for the production of literary artifacts, vis-à-vis the figure of the reader.

However the concept of the *sahṛdaya* or the ideal reader did exist from the time of Bharata onwards. The discerning and sensitive reader was a very important element in the process of aesthetic enjoyment. Admittedly, the concept of a reader whose heart beats in unison with the writer would not allow for much independence of thought or feeling to the reader. But the ancient Sanskrit critics believed that it was only the appreciation of the reader that ensured the reputation of the writer and his work. Only a *sahṛdaya* could have appreciated the nuances of word play and meaning that a skilled poet presented in his work. Moreover, Ānandavardhana was in a way affirming the autonomy of the reader when he maintained that the reader could interpret *dhvani,* irrespective of what the intention of the writer was.

The agency of the reader is accepted by most of the Sanskrit theoretical concepts, even though it is not overtly stated. In *Kāvyamīmāṃsā*, Rājaśekhara divides the readers of *kāvya* into four broad categories on the basis of their ability to appreciate a poem: discontented readers (*arocaki*); vulgar readers who "feed on grass" (*stṛṇābhyvahārī*); envious readers (*matsarī*); and the true readers (*tatvābhiniveśi*) (49). The discontented readers are those who are innately uninterested in enjoying a work of art. The vulgar readers are indiscriminate and like to read everything that comes to them, but they lack the ability to judge the true poetic merit of a work. The envious readers are always jealous of good poets. Although they understand the real worth of a poem, they are reluctant to accept it. The last category, that is the true readers who can appreciate a poem properly, is an extremely rare category (49–51). By "reader," Rājaśekhara seems to have also meant the figure of the critic. According to Rājaśekhara,

> A poet whose heart is grief-stricken due to the lack of a true critic, finds a wise critic who analyzes the word construction, exults at the poetic fancies, enjoys the aesthetic charm of the composition and finally succeeds in locating the profound meaning of a work. (51)

As far as Rājaśekhara is concerned, a good reader who can meaningfully critique the work of a poet is simultaneously a master, a friend, a counselor, a pupil, and a teacher to the poet (51). This is a nuanced analysis of the figure of the reader/critic, along the lines of the reader categories that were later developed by Umberto Eco or Wolfgang Iser in Western criticism.

Ancient in the Modern

Neither the xenophobic approach which sees classical Indian literary theories as obsolete and primitive nor the nativist approach which believes in the transcendental value of indigenous literary theories across spatio-temporal locations, performs anything productive in the field of Sanskrit *kāvyaśāstra.* What is now undoubtedly needed is a critical engagement with these theoretical positions through debate, questioning, and re-reading so that generation of new systems of knowledge about these theoretical positions is possible. Only such an approach can ensure the continuum of this knowledge system. Keeping in line with this spirit, the prominent Malayalam critic V. C. Sreejan says,

> Suppose, somebody generates a new thought from the ideas of Barthes, either by deconstructing them or by connecting them with other ideas. I call such a move an original and unique contribution. What matters is not where the knowledge comes from, but whether a new system of knowledge is produced. What I mean is that instead of considering our ancient epistemologies as the ultimate truth, we need to see them only as the beginning of the endless reconsiderations and deconstructions that are to come in future. (14–15; translated from Malayalam)

What Sreejan calls for is an incessant re-reading of these bodies of knowledge. Only such an approach can open up a text to multiple possibilities of reading.

As Ayyappa Paniker points out,

> When a poetics that evolved in one language is applied by extension to other languages, there will naturally be changes in the original principles. Some of these principles will have to be explained and some others will have to be elaborated. Some elements would seem to acquire greater relevance than the others in the new context. A realization of these facts is possible only if literary theory is emancipated from crude scholars devoid of the sensibility to appreciate literature. Moreover we have to find out the deeper meaning and should not be entrapped in the aura of the given examples. We should be able to enhance and keep up its relevance by imbuing vitality from the new poetic models. Even if we have to forgo the denotative meaning

> of definitions we must concentrate on preserving their essential meaning. This is possible only if we realize the limitations of prescriptive texts. (91)

Paniker outlines five steps to make ancient theories relevant to contemporary times:

(i) Do not depend too much on prescriptive texts. The ancient texts usually have detailed explanations for the typical features for a genre or an aspect of poetry like *alaṅkāra* and *dhvani*. For instance, the examples given by Ānandavardhana for *dhvani*—like *gaṅgāyāṃ ghoṣaḥ*—might be completely bewildering for a reader today. So, rather than feeling compelled to follow the texts to the letter, it is important to grasp the essence of these definitions and interpret them more dynamically.

(ii) Do not define using formulae. The idea of *rasa* cannot be conveyed by just quoting the *rasasūtra*. It has to be explained using examples. Verses should be interpreted and analyzed to help explain concepts like *rasa*, *dhvani* or *alaṅkāra*.

(iii) "Classification just for enumeration is as meaningless as Ranganathan's system of library classification or as the diverse divisions and subdivisions of the Indian caste system." It is pointless to list out all the ten *guṇa*s and *doṣa*s or all the *alaṅkāra*s that have been discussed by Bhāmaha. The attempt should be to understand the spirit of what the ancient theorists were saying and interpret them to suit our present context.

(iv) "Traditional views should be integrated with novel visions"—if possible, the ancient theories should be studied along with their Western counterparts so that the drawbacks of one theory will be complemented by the other.

(v) Contemporary works should be evaluated using ancient theories, and ancient texts should be studied using contemporary theories. "Novels and short stories can be analyzed using the *rasa* theory. The images of modernist poetry can be explored on the basis of the principles of *alaṅkāra*. Foreign works should be studied by employing Sanskrit and Dravidian aesthetic theories" (93–94).

This is a viable model that avoids the "amnesiac" pitfalls that Devy cautioned against: "the fantasization of the past, the loss of capacity to see that the distant past has reached the modern times after passing through a complex process of mutation at the hands of the immediate past, and the uneasy relationship with recent history" (55). One possible way of aligning the past with the present is to explore the possibilities that the new domain of Digital Humanities has opened up before classical studies. It undoubtedly provides a more sophisticated and foolproof method of archiving old texts, as is exemplified by projects like the Women Writers Project under the Text Encoding Initiative (TEI). Moreover, the resources of this domain could also become a useful tool in close stylistic and textual analysis of ancient texts, as well as visualization of ancient literary worlds. Much work has been done in this regard on the Greek epics and eminent authors like Chaucer and Shakespeare; the classical Indian world can also benefit from such an approach. The field of cognitive poetics, that draws on the concepts of cognitive science to understand literature in a new light has made fresh use of ancient Sanskrit theory, especially the theories of Abhinavagupta. The pioneers in this field are Keith Oatley and Patrick Colm Hogan. Hogan observes that the functioning of *dhvani* can be seen as a PDP (parallel distributed processing) network of cognition because multiple processes are happening simultaneously while we understand and appreciate *dhvani*. According to him, "As a concept in literary and aesthetic theory, dhvani is actually quite radical.... Dhvani is not a metaphorical meaning, nor even a connotation. It is much broader—and much more clearly (one might say, algorithmically) psychological" (156). Much of the work in cognitive poetics is based on the concepts of rasa and *dhvani*, especially the role of emotions in the process of aesthetic appreciation. The old and the new are thus coming together in constructive ways, with both throwing new light on each other.

It should also be noted that even as we emphasize the need to synthesize Sanskrit theories with the Western, we should not forget the other indigenous and equally vibrant poetic systems like those of other *bhāṣās* or Indian languages. There is also the classical Dravidian poetics as exemplified through literary works like Sangam poetry as well as the critical text of the *Tolkāppiyam*.

Although it is important to record how classical knowledge systems were originally understood and practiced, an obsession with this process in the realm of research will only impede new courses of development in this field. However, Indian aesthetic theory seems to be regarded as a fossilized system of knowledge even in academia. It is taught and studied at length only in Sanskrit, while it remains, if at all, an insignificant component of English literature syllabi, more glanced through than read and discussed thoroughly.

They have to become part of mainstream literary theory like it is now in many prominent Western universities—to be contested and violently disagreed with, perhaps. But it can yield new insights only if it is intellectually reinvigorated by serious theoretical engagements with it. What we need is an interventionist historiography of ideas which will critically examine these theoretical positions from different vantage points and will prevent them from becoming static categories. Each new reading of a text dislodges it from our taken-for-granted conceptions about it and leads us to the production of new knowledge about that text. This was the path advocated by our ancestors like Abhinavagupta or Jagannātha Paṇdita, and this is the path that we have to now reclaim, because this is the only way in which we can ensure the continuity of the existing frameworks of ideas.

Works Cited

Ashcroft, Bill and Helen Tiffin. *The Empire Writes Back*. Routledge, 2002.

Bronner, Yigal. "What is New and What is Navya." *Journal of Indian Philosophy*, vol. 305, no. 5, 2002: 441–462.

Devy, G. N. "After Amnesia: Tradition and Change in Indian Literary Criticism." *G. N. Devy Reader*, Orient Blackswan, 2009, pp. 1–140.

Hogan, Patrick Colm. *Cognitive Science, Literature and the Arts*. Routledge, 2003.

Jagannātha. *The Rasagaṅgādhara of Jagannātha Paṇḍita with the Commentary of Nāgeśa Bhaṭṭa*. Edited by D. Prasad and K. P. Parab, The Nirnaya Sagara Press, 1888.

Kandasami, Meena. "Ekalaivan." March 2006. https://www.poetryinternational.org/pi/poem/9976/EKAILAIVAN/en/tile. n.d. Accessed July 20, 2020.

Limbale, Sharankumar. *Towards an Aesthetic of Dalit Literature: History, Controversies and Considerations.* Translated by Alok Mukherjee, Orient Blackswan, 2004.

Miller, Hillis. *On Literature.* Routledge, 2002.

Paniker, Ayyappa. *K. Ayyappa Paniker: Selected Essays.* Edited by K. Satchidanandan, Sahitya Akademi, 2017.

Pathak, R. S. "The Indian Theory of Vakrokti in Relation to the Stylistic Concept of Deviance." *Annals of the Bhandarkar Oriental Research Institute*, vol. 63, no. 1, 1982: 195–211.

Perry, John Oliver. Review of "Literary Theory: Indian Conceptual Framework by Kapil Kapoor and Nalini M Ratnam." *World Literature Today*, vol. 73, no. 3, 1999: 597–599.

Pollock, Sheldon. "Indian Knowledge Systems on the Eve of Colonialism." *Intellectual History Newsletter*, vol. 22, 2000: 1–16.

———. "New Intellectuals in Seventeenth Century India." *The Indian Economic and Social History Review*, vol. 38, no. 1, 2001: 3–31.

———. "What was Bhaṭṭanāyaka Saying: The Hermenuetical Transformation of Indian Aesthetics." *Epic and Argument in Sanskrit Literary Theory*. Edited by Sheldon Pollock, Manohar Publishers, 2010, pp. 143–184.

Rājaśekhara. *Kāvyamīmāṃsā*. Edited by Sadhana Parashar, D. K. Print World, 2000.

Sastri, P. S. "Indian Poetics and New Criticism." *Indian Poetics and Western Thought*, Argo Publishing House, 1988.

Sreejan, V. C. *Arthantaranyasam*. Current Books, 1999.

Thapar, Romila. *History of Early India from Origins to A.D 1300*. Penguin, 2002.

APPENDIX I

Genres in Sanskrit Literature

Knowledge of the generic divisions of Sanskrit literature will be helpful in the deeper understanding of its critical practices. These genres, which are distinct from drama, constituted what was termed *kāvya*.

Mahākāvya: A long poem written only in Sanskrit. It is a genre that is characterized by ornate and elaborate descriptions of nature, war, kings, celestial entities, etc. It was often advised that only poets who had absolute command over language should lay their hands on a *mahākāvya* because it tested one's skill in the intricacies of poetic composition. Kālidāsa's *Raghuvaṃśa* is an excellent example of a *mahākāvya*. Daṇḍin in his *Kāvyādarśa* gave a detailed definition of a *mahākāvya*. According to him, a *mahākāvya* should always take its subject matter from epics and *purāṇas* and should help the reader in achieving the four goals of life—*dharma, artha, kāma,* and *mokṣa*. The number of *sargas* (cantos) in a *mahākāvya* should not be more than thirty and less than eight. The hero of a *mahākāvya* should always be of noble birth.

Khaṇdakāvya: A miniature form of a *mahākāvya* is often called a *khaṇdakāvya*. *Khaṇdakāvya* is a poem which is smaller than a *mahākāvya* and bigger than a *laghukāvya*. Classic examples of *khaṇdakāvya* are Kālidāsa's *Meghadūtam* and Bilhaṇa's *Caurapancaśikā*.

Muktaka: A short poem and hence falls under the rubric of *laghukāvya*. The term *muktaka* comes from the word *mukta* meaning "freed," or "not bound to anything." Because of the root word's connection with this meaning, the word *muktaka* is used to refer to a verse in Sanskrit that occurs independently and in a cohesive manner. The modern haiku resembles *muktaka* in Sanskrit in its short form and ability to convey a coherent message independent of a cohesive whole.

Kośa: A *kośa*, literally meaning treasure, is often a collection of *muktaka*s collected from various sources and organized on the basis of themes or in a random manner. It can be rightly compared to a modern-day anthology where literary works dealing with different subject matters are collated. *Kośa* was an important category in Sanskrit and Prākrit literature.

Sandeśakāvya: A *sandeśakāvya* is a messenger poem. It often consists of two parts. In the first part, the messenger who is going to carry the message to the destination is described in detail. This part usually had a detailed description of the route through which the messenger is supposed to travel. The second part of the *kāvya* often deals with the house of the heroine and her love in separation. At this point, the messenger will come to the scene with the message, describing the hero's condition and a word of solace. To prove his identity as the confidant of the lover, the messenger will show to the lady an insignia (as in the case of Hanumān who showed an insignia to Sītā in Rāvaṇa's custody) or refer to an incident which only the lover and his lady love know. The messenger of a *sandeśakāvya* could be anyone—a person, a bird, a cloud, or wind.

The chief emotion that is depicted in a *sandeśakāvya* is *vipralambha-śṛṅgāra* or love in separation. A *sandeśakāvya* is often composed in the slow-moving *mandākrānta* meter. Kālidāsa's *Meghadūtam* is the most popular example.

Gāthā: *Gāthā* is a Sanskrit term for a verse used in legends. It is important to note that the term *gāthā* is also employed to refer to verses used to narrate a story either in Sanskrit or in Prākrit. An excellent example of *gāthā* is the Prākrit work *Gāthā Sattasaī* (*Gāthā Saptaśatī* in Sanskrit) from the 5th century. The short poems included in this work deal with love in all its various moods. They also focused on scenes from everyday life and reveal the social mores and customs of those days.

Ākhyāyikā: *Ākhyāyikā* is a prose story which deals with an elegant subject matter. One characteristic of the *ākhyāyikā* is first-person narration where the hero himself narrates his exploits. Bhāmaha points out that an *ākhyāyikā* should mandatorily contain forecasts of events on appropriate occasions. The major events of an *ākhyāyikā* often revolve around the abduction of damsels, of war, separation of lovers and their eventual reunion. According to Bhāmaha, the story that is being told in *ākhyāyikā* should be divided into small sections titled *ucchvāsas*. The word *ucchvāsa* in Sanskrit means a pause that someone takes for breath. Therefore, this word is employed to designate the various chapters of a story which the narrator cannot complete in one go. *Harṣacarita* (*The story of Harṣa*) by Bāṇabhaṭṭa is an example of *ākhyāyikā* in Sanskrit. In this work, the story of Harṣa is told in eight *ucchvāsas*.

Kathā: In *kathā* which is composed in prose, the story of the hero is narrated by someone else. The subject matter of a *kathā* is often invented by the poet. A *kathā*, unlike an *ākhyāyikā*, is not divided into *ucchvāsa*s and has no adherence to *vakrtra* and *apavakrta* meters. According to Daṇḍin, a *kathā* can be composed in any language. Bhāmaha opines that *kathā* is acceptable and looks elegant if it is composed in Sanskrit. The story that is being told in a *kathā* is often a love story. But it is mandatory that it should have a metrical introduction. An excellent example of this genre is *Bṛhadkathā* by Guṇāḍhya.

Parikathā: A variety of *kathā* is *parikātha* which literally means a religious tale or narrative. But *parikathā* does not necessarily need to deal with religious content. A *parikathā*, according to Abhinavagupta, concerns one or the other of the four goals in the life of a man such as *dharma*, *artha*, *kāma,* and *mokṣa*. Abhinava insists that a *parikathā* should be written only in Sanskrit. Bhoja in his *śṛṅgāraprakāśa* cites *Śudrakakathā* as an example of *parikātha*. Though Abhinava insists on *parikathā* being written in Sanskrit, *Śudrakakathā*, which deals with the goal of *kāma*, is surprisingly written in Prākrit.

Khaṇdakathā: A *khaṇdakathā* as the word *khaṇda* (portion) suggests, focuses on only one plot of a bigger story. A *sakalakathā*, on the contrary, follows all the plots to their conclusion. The *khandakathā* and *sakalakathā* are found more in Prākrit than in Sanskrit. The *Madhu-mathana-vijaya* is an example of a Prākrit *khaṇḍakathā*.

Campu: According to Daṇḍin, *campu* is that kind of composition which is written in a combination of both prose and verse. Some of the well-known examples of *campu* from Sanskrit include *Nalacampu* of Trivikrama, and *Rāmāyaṇacampu*, *Bhojacampu*, and *Bhāgavatacampu* of Abhinava Kālidāsa. The Jain writers often made use of this genre in religious texts and the Vaiṣṇava School wrote *campu-kāvya*s relating to Kṛṣṇa. The subject matters that were often treated within the generic framework of prose romance were also sometimes treated in *campu*, for instance, *Vasavadattā Campu.*

APPENDIX II

Categories of Drama

The Sanskrit term for drama is *rūpakaṃ*. It was not just one genre but a domain that consisted of ten different forms that were categorized on the basis of theme, length and *rasa*. Given below are the *daśarūpaka* or the ten forms of drama as outlined by Bharata in *Nāṭyaśāstra*.

1. ***Nāṭakaṃ***: The first of the ten dramatic forms that Bharata mentions in the twentieth chapter of his *Nāṭyaśāstra*. The story had to be well known, taken from an epic or a Purāṇa. It had to consist of eight to ten acts. In the *nāṭakaṃ*, the lead character would always be a descendant of a *rājarṣi* (a king who has become famous and virtuous through his performance of great austerities). The hero of a *nāṭakaṃ* will always be noble and courageous in nature (*dhīroḍātta*). Kālidāsa's *Abhijñānaśākuntalaṃ* is an example of *nāṭakaṃ*. The *rasa* of a *nāṭakaṃ* had to be either *śṛṅgāra* or *vīra*.
2. ***Prakaraṇaṃ***: The story will be more or less the playwright's invention although he was free to borrow the basic idea of the plot from non-*puranic* sources such as *Bṛhadkathā*. But the playwright should always make it a point to embellish and modify the basic story that he is dealing with. According to Bharata, the hero of a *prakaraṇaṃ* should not be of the *dhīrodātta* variety, which means that he could not be royalty or a brave warrior. The dramatist should also include characters

from the lower rung of the society such as merchants, travelers, courtesans, servants, etc. In both the *nāṭakaṃ* and the *prakaraṇaṃ*, the number of acts should not be less than five and not more than ten. Śūdraka's *Mṛcchakaṭikam* is an example of *prakaraṇaṃ*.

3. ***Samavakāraṃ***: The plot of a *samavakāraṃ* should always deal with the exploits of gods. The hero should be famous, noble, and virtuous. The number of acts in a *samavakāraṃ* should be three. It should have twelve characters and the whole story of a *samavakāraṃ* should happen within seven hours. Each act should follow certain structural rules with respect to the representation of actions. The first act should deal with actions concerning comedy, romance, migration, and deceit as well as a romantic heroine. The time that is earmarked for the first act is four hours. The second and third acts will each be of one-hour duration. Three kinds of love that are allowed to be represented in this dramatic form include *dharmaśṛṅgāra* (romantic relation which fetches virtue to the partners), *artha-śṛṅgāra* (romantic relationship based on material gain) and *kāma-śṛṅgāra* (romantic relation on the basis on passion). However, the dominant *rasa* is *vīra*.
4. ***Īhāmṛgaṃ***: The anti-hero desperately tries to woo the heroine, who is elusive like a *mṛga* (deer). This is why this form of drama is called *īhāmṛga.* It is a drama in four acts. The hero of this dramatic form could be human or divine, and its plot should necessarily contain wars on account of celestial women. The plot of an *īhāmṛgaṃ* should be well constructed and should be convincing. The predominant *rasa* of *īhāmṛgaṃ* should always

be *śṛṅgāra* (erotic). The other essential elements of *īhāmṛgaṃ* include mental agony, abduction, war, fight, etc.

5. ***Ḍimaṃ***: A four-act play that abounds in magic and fantasy. The dominant *rasa* is *raudra*. *Śṛṅgāra* and *hāsya* are completely absent from the remit of *ḍimaṃ*. The content of *ḍimaṃ* should be popular and the hero should be virtuous, noble, and courageous. The play should also abound in spectacular effects like thunder, lightning, solar eclipse, lunar eclipse, war, torture, etc. In a *ḍimaṃ*, there should be sixteen heroes (*ṣodaśanāyaka*) like *devas*, *asuras*, *yakṣas* and other forms of demons and semi-divine beings. The main styles to be followed are *sāttvati* and *ārabhaṭī*. The *Tripuradāha* is an example of *ḍimaṃ*.
6. ***Vyāyogaṃ:*** A one-act play. The theme should be popular and the hero should be famous. He could be a divine being. The story should not be woman-related or depict conflicts arising out of relationships with women. There are fewer female characters than male, and the duration of the story should be a single day. The dominant *rasa* should not be *hāsya, śṛṅgāra,* or *śānta*. Bhasa's *Madhyamavyāyoga* is an example of this category.
7. ***Utsṛṣṭikāṅgaṃ:*** A one-act play. It could also be simply called *aṅga*, but the longer name *utsṛṣṭikāṅgaṃ* was given apparently to differentiate it from an *aṅga* which also means an act in a play. The plot of *utsṛṣṭikāṅgaṃ* should be popular and the characters should be strictly humans. This dramatic form should have *karuṇa rasa* as the predominant emotion. Women's lamentations and despondent utterances after a battle and bewildered

movements of the mourners constitute the core of the performances of actors. The style of this dramatic form should not be grand. Styles such as *ārabhaṭī* and *kaiśikī* should not be used in the composition of an *aṅga*.

8. ***Prahasanaṃ***: A one-act dramatic performance that comes close to the farcical comedies of today. The main characters are degenerate people and swindlers, and the story is completely the writer's invention. The dominant *rasa* is *hāsya*. The plot of a *prahasanaṃ*, according to Bharata, is of two kinds, namely pure and complex. A *prahasanaṃ* becomes pure when it abounds in scornful words and has comic disputes between degenerate characters and noble characters like Brahmins, yogis, sages, etc. But a *prahasanaṃ* of pure category should not ever tamper with the existing decorum pertaining to the language and customs of society. It should also give a lot of importance to the *vyabhicāribhāva*s of *hāsya rasa*. The variety of *prahasanaṃ* that has characters such as prostitutes, eunuchs, debauchees, spendthrifts, etc. will fall under the category of complex *prahasanaṃ*.
9. ***Bhāṇaṃ***: A *bhāṇaṃ* is that kind of dramatic form which has to be acted by a single character. *Hāsya* is the dominant *rasa*. According to Bharata, a *bhāṇaṃ* is of two kinds: the kind of *bhāṇaṃ* where one recounts one's own experience and the other, where one describes someone else's deeds. In this form, a single actor will play the roles of all the other characters involved in the story. A *bhāṇaṃ* should be performed by conversing with imaginary characters (*ākāśapuruṣa*). The dramatists who compose a *bhāṇaṃ* should also include the characters of rogues and parasites, and treat their different mental and

physical conditions. A *bhāṇaṃ* is always of one act and resembles the stand-up comedy that is popular today.

10. ***Vīthi***: This is also a one-act play enacted by one or two characters. The main character can be noble, average or base. The story and the hero are all creations of the writer's imagination. *Śṛṅgāra* is the dominant *rasa*, while other *rasa*s can be fleetingly brought in.

Besides these ten forms, Bharata mentions another form called the *nāṭikā*, which is a combination of both *nāṭaka* and *prakaraṇa*. The plot of *nāṭikā* should be invented by the dramatist through his creative genius. It should have a king as the central character and should be based on an incident relating to a maiden from a music troop or a harem. The number of acts in a *nāṭikā* is four and the acts should be organized in such a manner that they are embellished with characters using graceful gestures and wearing elegant and well-arranged costumes. Dance, music, recitations and love's enjoyment are the major cynosures of a *nāṭikā*. The major characters in a *nāṭikā* should include the hero who is a king, his queen, the queen's female messengers and their attendants. Kālidāsa's *Mālavikāgnimitram* and Harṣa's *Ratnāvalī* are examples of *nāṭikā*.

Suggested Readings

Chaitanya, Krishna. *Sanskrit Poetics: A Critical and Comparative Study*. Asia Publishing House, 1965.

Deshpande, G. T. *Indian Poetics*. Popular Prakashan, 2009.

De, Sushil Kumar. *Some Problems of Sanskrit Poetics*. Firma K. L. Mukhopadhyay, 1959.

———. *History of Sanskrit Poetics*. Firma K. L. Mukhopadhayay, 1960.

———. *Sanskrit Poetics as a Study of Aesthetics*. University of California Press, 1963.

Devy, G. N. *Indian Literary Criticism: Theory and Interpretation*. Orient Longman, 2002.

Gerow, Edwin. *Indian Poetics*. Harrassowitz, 1977.

———. "Abhinavagupta's Aesthetics as a Speculative Paradigm." *Journal of the American Oriental Society*, vol. 114, no. 2, 1994: 186–208.

———. "Rasa and Katharsis: A Comparative Study, Aided by Several Films." *Journal of the American Oriental Society*, vol. 122, no. 2, 2002: 268.

Hegde, Suryanarayana. *The Concept of Vakrokti in Poetics*. Readworthy, 2009.

Hiriyanna, M. *Art Experience*. Kavyalaya Publishers, 1954.

Hogan, Patrick Colm and Lalita Pandit. *Literary India: Comparative Studies in Aesthetics*. State University of New York Press, 1995.

Kane, P. V. *History of Sanskrit Poetics*. Motilal Banarsidass, 1971.

Kapoor, Kapil. *Literary Theory: Indian Conceptual Framework*. Affiliated East-West Press, 2012.

Krishnamoorthy, K. *Indian Literary Theories: A Reappraisal*. Meharchand Lachhmandas Publications, 1985.

———. *Aspects of Poetic Language: An Indian Perspective*. University of Poona, 1988.

———. *Studies in Indian Aesthetics and Criticism*. D. V. K. Murthy, 1979.

———. *The Dhvanyaloka and Its Critics*. Kavyalaya Publishers, 1968.

Kunjunniraja, K. *Indian Theories of Meaning*. Adyar Library and Research Centre, 1963.

Kuppuswamy, Shastri. *Highways and Broadways of Literary Criticism in Sanskrit*. K. S. R. I., 1945.

Lahiri, P. C. *Concepts of Riti and Guna in Sanskrit Poetics in Their Historical Development*. University of Dacca, 1937.

McCarthy, Harold E. "Aesthetics East and West." *Philosophy East and West*, vol. 3, no. 1, 1953: 47–68.

McCrea, Lawrence J. *The Teleology of Poetics in Medieval Kashmir*. Harvard University Press, 2009

Masson, J. L. and M. V. Patwardhan. *Aesthetic Rapture, the Rasādhyāya of the Nāṭyaśāstra*. Vols 1 and 2. Poona: Deccan College Postgraduate and Research Institute, 1970.

Matilal, Bimal Krishna. "Vakrokti and Dhvani Controversies about Theory of Poetry in Indian Tradition." http://www.svabhinava.org/abhinava/BimalMatilal/VakroktiDhvani.pdf.

Narasimhaiah, C. D., ed. *East West Poetics at Work: Papers Presented at the Seminar on Indian and Western Poetics at Work*. Sahitya Akademi, 1994.

Pandey, K. C. *Comparative Aesthetics—Indian and Western Aesthetics. Vols 1 and 2*. Chowkhamba Sanskrit Series, 2015.

———. "A Bird's-Eye View of Indian Aesthetics." *The Journal of Aesthetics and Art Criticism*, vol. 24, no. 1, 1965: 59–73.

Pollock, Sheldon. "Is There an Indian Intellectual History? Introduction to 'Theory and Method in Indian Intellectual History.'" *Journal of Indian Philosophy*, vol. 36, no. 5–6, 2008: 533–542. https://doi.org/10.1007/s10781-008-9051-y.

———. "Rasa after Abhinava." In *Saṃskṛta-Sādhutā 'Goodness of Sanskrit': Studies in Honour of Professor Ashok N. Aklujkar*, edited by Chikafumi Watanabe, Michele Desmarais, and Yoshichika. New Delhi: D. K. Printworld, 2012, pp. 431–445. https://digitalcommons.unomaha.edu/facultybooks/4.

Raghavan, V. *The Number of Rasas*. The Adayar Library, 1940.

———. *Studies in Some Concepts of Alamkarasastra*. Madras: The Adayar Library, 1978.

———. *Bhoja's Śṛṅgāraprakāśa*. Madras, 1978.

———. *Abhinavagupta and His Works*. Chaukhambha Sasnskrit Sansthan, 1980.

Rayan, Krishna. "Towards a Rewritten Indian Poetic." *Indian Literature*, vol. 37, no. 2, 1994.

———. *The Lamp and the Jar*, edited by Krishna S. Arjunwadkar. Sahitya Akademi, 2002.

———. *Suggestion and Statement in Poetry*. Bloomsbury, 2013.

Sankaran, A. *Some Aspects of Literary Criticism in Sanskrit: Or, The Theories of Rasa and Dhvani*. University of Madras, 1973.

Seturaman, V. S. *Indian Aesthetics: An Introduction*. Laxmi Publications, 2017.

Sharma, M. M. *The Dhvani Theory of Sanskrit Poetics*. Chowkhamba, 1968.

Sharma, T. R. S. *Toward an Alternative Critical Discourse*. Indian Institute of Advanced Study Shimla, 2000.

Sreekantaiya, T. N. *Indian Poetics*. Sahitya Akademi, 2001.

Warder, A. K. *Indian Kavya Literature*, Vols I–IV. Motilal Banarsidass Publishers, 2009.

Index

A

Abhidheyāvarttana-vakratā, 136
Abhijnānaśākuntalaṃ, 56, 74, 136, 139, 157, 197
Abhinavabhāratī, 10, 14, 37, 40, 50, 53, 55
Abhinavagupta, 4, 7, 10, 12, 14–15, 17, 21, 28, 37, 42, 46, 50–53, 55–56, 58–59, 71, 95, 107, 108, 113, 115, 116, 121, 127–128, 153, 161, 167, 182–183, 188, 194
Abhipluthārtha, 92
ādikāvya, genesis of the, 3
aesthetic beauty, "savarna" standards of, 176
aesthetic relish, 50–53
affect theory, 60
African-American studies, 181
After Amnesia, 165
Agamben, 180
Ākhyāyikā, 193
Akutagawa, Ryonosuke, 136
alaṅkāra, 20, 23–26, 45, 63–74, 78, 87, 89–90, 93, 98, 100–101, 109, 116, 119, 125, 128, 130, 132, 135, 147, 149, 169, 179–180, 186–187
  abuse of, 75
  analysis of, 24
  archetypal *Alaṅkāra*, 169
  arrangement, 65
  arthālaṅkāra, 64
  of *atiśayokti*, 69
  Bhāmaha, 68–73
  Bhāmaha's theory of, 24, 70
  Bhāmaha's scheme (thirty-eight *alaṅkāra*), 65
  central concern of theoretical analysis, 67
  combination with *guṇas*, 83
  components, 66
  conventional category of, 135
  critics on, 64–68
  Daṇḍin's view, 65, 70–71
  in *Dhvanyāloka*, 67
  dīpaka, 64
  distinction with *guṇa*, 89–90
  earliest known exponent of, 68–69
  essence of, 128
  example of, 109
  function like ornaments, 67, 87, 101
  function of, 25, 89
  Hemacandra's views, 66
  history of *alaṅkāraśāstra*, 68
  identification and scrutiny of, 70
  important constituent of poetry, 63
  meaning of, 63
  ornament of speech, 125
  poetic language embellished with, 78
  in practice, 73–77
  principles, 73
  rejected by Bhāmaha, 65
  Rudraṭa's scheme (sixty-six *alaṅkāras*), 65
  rūpaka, 64
  śabdālaṅkāra, 64
  theoretical position, 90
  theories of, 63
  Udbhaṭa's scheme (forty-one *alaṅkāra*), 65
  upamā, 64
  use of, 67, 75
  Vāmana's scheme (thirty-one *alaṅkāras*), 65
  in *Viṣṇudharmottarapurāṇa*, 64
  yamaka, 64

identification and analysis of, 24
skilful use of, 24
Alaṅkāra School, 64
exponent of the, 72
prominent critic in, 72
proponent of the, 64
Alaṅkāraratnākara, 11
Alaṅkārasarvasva, 170
alaṅkāraśāstra, 23, 63, 68
ālaṅkārikas, 68, 81, 95, 167
Ānandavardhana, 4, 6–7, 9, 12–14, 17, 22, 25–26, 28, 42–46, 50, 57, 58, 67–68, 71, 73–74, 86–87, 90, 93, 95, 97–104, 106–108, 109, 111–112, 113–120, 121–122, 127–129, 140, 142, 146–148, 153–154, 161, 167, 170, 182–183, 186
ancient in the modern, 184–189
ancient theories, 176–179
aneka-phala-sambatti-vakratā, 139
anger, aesthetic emotion of, 35
aṅgirasa-niṣyanda-vakratā, 137
Anglo-American approach, 165
anti-Semitism, 180
anubhāva (expression of emotion), 42
anumiti vāda, 38, 40
anuraṇanarūpa-vyaṅgya-dhvani, 109
Apology for Poetry, 28
Appayya Dīkṣita, 128, 168–169
Aristotle, 1, 28, 159
Arjunavarmadeva, 7
Arnold, Matthew, 28, 76
Ars Poetica, 160
Arthahīna, 92
Arthāntara, 92
artha-śakti-mūla dhvani, 111
Aśvaghoṣa, 3–4
atiśayokti, varieties of, 71
aucitya, 145–162
arthaucitya, 148
artistic principle, 162
beginning of, 146
concept of, 145
conscious of, 147
decorum and, 159–161
definition of, 147
deśaucitya (propriety of place), 148
in diction, 157–159
essence of the literary concept of, 150
essential component of *rasa*, 146
functions of, 150–157
gestural and behavioral aspects, 151
importance of, 145–146
judicious exercise of, 91
Kṣemendra concept of, 27
Kuntaka's discussion, 147
overarching domain of, 91
rasābhāsa and, 155
samayaucitya (propriety of time), 148
In Sanskrit literary theory, 145
"self-censoring" incidents, 156
as the soul of *kāvya*, 148
twenty-seven forms of, 149
vācyaucitya (propriety of speech), 148
vaktṛviṣayaucitya, 148
viṣayaucitya (propriety of subject), 148
Aucityavicāracarcā, 16, 145
"automatism of perception", 131
Avantisundarīkathā, 13
Avantivarman, 6, 8–9, 14, 127
Avarṇasvarayojana, 92

B

Bālacittānurañjanī, 11
Bāṇabhaṭṭa, 75, 128, 193
Barth, John, 162
bhakti rasa, 19, 58
Bhāmaha, 5, 7–8, 12–13, 21–24, 41, 64–65, 68–73, 75, 77, 81–83, 88–89, 123–125, 127–129, 140, 146, 158, 186, 193–194
Bhāmahavivaraṇa, 8, 13
Bhāminīvilāsa (*The Games of Beautiful Women*), 18

bhāṇaṃ, 200–201
Bhānudatta, 148, 152, 155
Bharadvāja, 3
Bharata, 2, 8, 12–13, 17, 27, 33–36, 38–39, 42, 50, 58, 64–65, 69, 82–85, 88, 91–93, 123–124, 146, 149–151, 170, 183, 197, 200–201
Bhāratamañjarī, 16
Bhāravi, 138
bhāṣa literature, predicament of, 176
Bhāsa's *Svapnavāsavadattaṃ*, 157
Bhaṭṭa Lollaṭa, 36–39, 167, 182
Bhaṭṭa Nārāyaṇa, 156
Bhaṭṭa Nāyaka, 10–11, 20–21, 37, 42, 46–53, 58, 167, 182–183
Bhaṭṭa Tauta, 7, 10
Bhaṭṭikāvya, 65
bhāvābhāsa, 153
Bhavabhūti, 57, 137, 156
bhāvanā, 48–49, 100, 182
bhāvayatri pratibhā, 57
Bhīmasena Dīkṣita, 17–18
Bhinnārtha, 92
bhoga (aesthetic relish), 48–49
Bhoja, 6–7, 16–17, 21, 42, 58–59, 93, 127, 147–148, 152, 156–157, 169, 194
Bilhaṇa, 191
Bouquet of Rasa, 155
Bṛhadkathā, 16, 194, 197
Bṛhadkathāmañjarī, 16
Brooks, Cleanth, 173
Buddhacarita, 3
Butler, Judith, 180

C

Caitanya School, 58
Calitarāma, 157
Campu, 194–195
Camus, Albert, 139
Caṇḍidāsa, 11
Candrāloka, 20, 66
Carroll, Lewis, 117
Caurapancaśikā, 191
Centers of Learning, 6–11
Chari, V. K., 81–82, 85, 94–95, 159
Chatterley, Constance, 44
Chaucer, 187
citra-kāvya, 116–118
citra-kāvya, types of, 117
Citramīmāṃsā, 167–170
"*citra-turaga-nyāya*", 40
classical age of Sanskrit, 78
Colonization, 170–176
  epistemic change, 171
  Orientalist and Anglicist views, 171
  Orientalist approach, 172
  Orientalist lineage, 171
  Orientalist tendency, 174
  Western criticism, 175
conceits, 75
consonants, skilful employment of, 132
Coppola, Francis Ford, 47–48
"crooked expression", 94

D

Dalit literature, aesthetic criterion for, 177
Dalit writing, 177
Daṇḍin, 5–6, 8, 13, 22, 24, 41, 65–66, 68, 70, 72, 81–84, 86, 88–89, 123, 125–126, 129, 140, 146, 158, 191, 194
Daśakumāracarita, 13
Daśarūpaka, 152
Daśopadeśa, 16
De Oratore, 160
De, S. K., 15, 85, 88–90
debate, dissent and, 166–170
defamiliarization concept, 129, 174
Derrida, 180
Devaśaṅkara Purohita, 128
Devy, G. N., 165, 175–176, 187
Dhanañjaya, 6, 152
Dhvani, 14, 17–18, 22–23, 26, 54, 76, 95, 97–121, 167–168, 172, 178–180, 182–183, 186, 188
  actualization of, 118–119

Ānandavardhana's concept of, 122
Ānandavardhana's theory, 99–100
anuraṇanarūpa-vyaṅgya-dhvani, 109
arthāntara-saṃkramita-vācya, 102, 104
artha-śakti-mūla dhvani, 111
atyanta-tiraskṛta-vācya, 102–103
avivakṣita-vācya-dhvani, 102, 105–106, 120
characteristic mark of, 108
concept of, 9, 13, 86, 100, 179
contextual *dhavni*, 121
definition of, 107
Dhvanyāloka, 98
examples of, 121
forms of, 102–112
guṇībhūta-vyaṅgya-kāvya, 115
idea of, 99
lāvaṇya, 107
linguistic device, 26
meaning, 97
nagaraṃ praviśanti kuntāḥ, 104
nature and characteristics of, 98
nature of a *kāvya*, 114
poetic composition, 114–118
presence of, 26, 100
rasadhvani, 113–114
reader's role, 118–120
śabda-śakti-mūla, 109
teleological hermeneutic model, 99–100
theory of, 43
traditional example, 97
types, 101
vastudhvani, 112
Viṣamabāṇalīlā, 104
Vivakṣitānya-paravācya, 108–112

dhvani school, intellectual onslaught of the, 95
Dhvanyāloka, 4, 9, 13–14, 21–22, 26, 28, 42–45, 50, 55, 57–58, 67, 73, 93, 98–100, 104, 108, 113, 118, 127, 146, 153, 167, 182
Dickens, Charles, 179
Ḍimaṃ, 199
dissent, debate and, 166–170
doṣa, 90–93
conceptual definition of, 93
harmful effect of, 91
impact of, 91
method of identification of faults, 93
working definition, 91
drama
bhāṇaṃ, 200–201
categories of, 197–201
ḍimaṃ, 199
īhāmṛgaṃ, 198–199
nāṭakaṃ, 197
prahasanaṃ, 200
prakaraṇaṃ, 197–198
samavakāraṃ, 198
utsṛṣṭikāṅgaṃ, 199–200
vīthi, 201
vyāyogaṃ, 199
Dravidian poetics, 188
Dylan, Bob, 78–79

E

Early India, 171
Ekārtha, 92
Eliot, T. S., 97, 173, 180
Empire Writes Back, 172–173
Essays in Criticism, 28

F

Figlerowicz, Marta, 60

G

Gāthā, 193
Gaudīya, 85
genres in Sanskrit literature, 191–195
ākhyāyikā, 193
campu, 194–195
gāthā, 193
kathā, 193–194
khaṇḍakathā, 194

khaṇḍakāvya, 191
kośa, 192
mahākāvya, 191
muktaka, 192
parikātha, 194
sandeśakāvya, 192–193
Ghosh, Amitav, 160
Girijā-kamala-vivāda, 126
Goda river, 112
Godfather, 48
Gosvamin, Jīva, 19
Great Expectations, 179
Greenblatt, Stephen, 179
Gūḍhārtha, 92
guṇa (poetic merits), 6, 20, 23–26, 41, 66–67, 81–90, 93, 95, 98, 101, 149, 159, 167, 186
analysis of, 24
Ānandavardhana's schema, 90
application, 88–89
artha-guṇa, 90
definition, 90–91
determining a *guṇa* or *doṣa*, 159
distinction between *guṇa* and *alaṅkāra*, 89
exponents of, 167
idea of, 66, 82–83
types of, 88
Vāmana's views, 88
working definition for, 91
Guṇacandra, 53
guṇībhūta-vyaṅgya-kāvya, 115–116

H

Hamlet, 49, 136–137
The Handmaid's Tale, 139
Harivaṃśa, 156
Harry Potter, 53, 139
Harṣa, 11, 193, 201
Harṣacarita (*The story of Harṣa*), 193
hāsya rasa, 117–118, 151, 200
Heidegger, 180
Hemacandra, 20, 28, 66, 146
Hemingway, minimalist style of, 81
Hiraṇyakaśipu, 113
Hogan, Patrick Colm, 61, 188
Horace, 160
Hṛdayadarpaṇa, 10–11, 46
Hughes, Ted, 124
The Hunchback of Notre Dame, 137
The Hungry Tide, 160

I

Īhāmṛgaṃ, 198–199
Ingalls, Daniel H. H., 120
intentional fallacy, 118

J

Jabberwocky, 117–118
Jagannātha Paṇḍita, 6, 18–19, 21, 59–60, 155, 167–168, 170
Jane Eyre, 138
Jane–Rochester romance, 138
Jayadeva, 20, 66, 128
Jayanta Bhaṭṭa, 11
Jayaratha, 170
Jhalakikar, 10
Johnson, Dr, 75
Junāgaṛh inscription, 2

K

Kādambarī, 75
Kādambarī-kathā-sāra, 9
kāku vakratā, 127
Kalāvilasā, 16
Kālidāsa, 4, 56–57, 74, 99, 134, 136, 157, 161, 191, 194, 197, 201
Kamalākara Bhaṭṭa, 11
Kapila Vatsyayan, 12
karuṇa rasa, 35, 87, 114, 136, 138
Kashmir, school of literary criticism, 7
Kathā, 193–194
kathopakāraka-vastu-vinyāsavakratā, 136
Kavi Karṇapura, 170
Kavikaṇṭhābharaṇa, 16
Kavirāja, 128
Kāvya (poetry), 19–23
beauty of, 25, 89, 146
beginning of the tradition, 3

definition, 20
development of, 41
elements, 21
figurative deviation of speech, 21
hallmark of, 129
hallmark of, 19
important element, 23
kathā (prose story), 19
kāvyaśāstra, 19–20
language of, 20
mahākāvya (long poem), 19
ornaments (*alaṅkāra*) of, 23
rasa distinctive feature, 21–22
Sanskrit, 20
śāstric tradition for, 5
supreme governing principle of, 27
trait of, 123
kāvya doṣas, 146
Kāvyādarśa, 13, 22, 24, 41, 65, 72, 83, 191
Kāvyakautuka, 10
Kāvyālaṅkāra, 5, 7–8, 12, 22, 24–25, 41–42, 65, 68, 70, 84, 124, 153
Kāvyālaṅkāra-sāra-saṃgraha (*A Compendium of the Most Important Figures of Speech in Poetry*), 8, 13, 22, 153
Kāvyālaṅkārasūtra, 6
Kāvyālaṅkārasūtravṛtti, 6, 64–65, 84, 88, 90
Kāvyamīmāṃsā, 6, 183
kāvya-nāma-vakratā, 139
Kāvyānuśāsana, 20
Kāvyaprakāśa, 10–11, 17–18, 50, 66, 128, 147, 167–170
Kāvyaprakāśādarśana, 10–11
Kāvyaprakāśadīpikā, 11
Kāvyaprakāśa-khaṇḍana, 167–169
Kāvyaprakāśaṭikka, 11
kāvyaśarīra, 24–25, 27, 69–70, 83
unique nature of, 24
kāvyaśāstra, 2, 5–8, 10–12, 15, 19–20, 22–23, 57, 66, 124, 145, 150, 152, 166–167, 170–176, 182–184
history of, 8, 67
importance of education in, 6
mastery, 6
origin and evolution of, 4–6
tradition, 5, 152, 166
Khan, Amjad, 40
Khaṇḍakathā, 194
Khaṇḍakāvya, 191
King Lear, 120
Kirātārjunīya, 138
Kośa, 192
Kosofsky, Eve Sedgwick, 61
Krishnamoorthy, K., 15, 172
Kṣemendra, 15–16, 27, 74, 93, 145–146, 148–149, 161
Kumārasambhava, 8, 161
Kumārilabhaṭṭa, 107
Kuntaka, 7, 10, 15, 21, 26–27, 42, 58, 72–73, 75, 82, 86, 94–95, 124, 129–132, 134–135, 138–141, 147, 157, 173–174
Kurosawa, Akira, 136
Kuvalayānanda, 168, 170

L

Lacan, 180
Lady Chatterley's Lover, 44, 160
lakṣaṇa-grantha, 100
Lakṣmī-sarasvatī-saṃvāda, 126
Lalitāditya, 7
The Language of the Gods, 145
lāvaṇya, 107
Lawrence, D. H., 44, 160–161
Lear, Edward, 117
Lienhard, 54
Limbale, Sharankumar, 176–177
linguistic modality, 20
literary criticism, 15, 22, 28, 60, 165–166, 175, 180–181
literature, patronage for, 9
Lost in the Funhouse, 162

M

Macaulay, 174
Mādhurya, 85, 89
madhyama female character, 151
Māgha, 150

Mahābhārata, 16, 136, 139, 156–157, 177–178
Mahākāvya, 191
Mahāvīracarita, 156
Maheśvara, 10–11
Mahimabhaṭṭa, 7, 10, 16
Mālatīmādhava, 57
Mālavikāgnimitram, 201
Mallinātha, 17
Mammaṭa Bhaṭṭa, 7, 10, 17–18, 20, 46, 58, 66, 86, 93, 128, 147, 169–170
Māṇikyacandra, 10
Mare, Walter de la, 77
Massumi, Brian, 61
Meghadūtam, 191
Merchant of Venice, 106, 138, 180
mīmāṃsakas, 100
"Minute on Education", 174. *See also* Macaulay
Moby Dick, 137
Mudrārākṣasa, 139
Muktaka, 192
Mukula Bhaṭṭa, 7
The Myth of Sisyphus, 139

N

Nārada, 3
Narahari, 11
Narasiṃha, 113
Narmamālā, 16
Nāṭakaṃ, 197
nativist approach, 175, 184
nāṭya traditions, 2
Nāṭyadarpaṇa, 53
nāṭyaśāstra tradition of poetics, 2
Nāṭyaśāstra, 2, 8, 12–13, 14, 21, 28, 33, 36, 39–50, 64–65, 82, 88, 92, 124, 146, 150, 197
Negri, 180
Neruda, Pablo, 78
Nirdoṣadaśaratha, 156
non-Vedic employment of standard Sanskrit, 2
Notre Dame Cathedral, 137
Nyāyādapeta, 92

O

Oatley, Keith, 188
Oedipus, 53
Of Dramatic Poesy, 28
The Outsider (*The Stranger*), 139

P

Padmini Rajappa, 75
Pandey, K. C., 34
Paniker, Ayyappa, 185–187
Parikathā, 194
Pārvatīrukmiṇīya, 128
Pathak, R. S., 173–174
PDP (parallel distributed processing), 188
Perry, John Oliver, 174
Peru Bhaṭṭa, 18
Poetic composition, 114–118
Poetics (Aristotle), 1, 28
poetry, Wordsworth's definition, 45
Pollock, S., 11, 13, 15, 19, 40, 42, 124, 145, 159, 170, 182
postcolonial approach, 179
postmodernism, 162, 166, 177, 180
Powell, Jim, 111
prahasanaṃ, 200
Prahlāda, 113
Prakaraṇaṃ, 197–198
Prakaraṇāntara-vakratā, 137
Prakāśendra, 15
Pratāparudrīya, 20, 66, 152, 154
Pratihārendurāja, 7
pratyabhijñā school of philosophy, 28
pratyaya-vakratā, 132, 134
pravṛtti, Bharata's concepts of, 82
preyaḥ, category of, 41
Prisoner of Azkaban, 139
pūrvapakṣa strategy, 167

R

radical redefinition, 177
Rāghavapāṇḍavīya, 128
Raghuvaṃśa, 56, 134, 191

Rājānaka Mahimabhaṭṭa. *See* Mahimabhaṭṭa
Rājaśekhara, 6, 28, 57, 183–184
Rājataraṅgiṇī, 14
Rāmābhyudaya, 150
Rāmacandra, 53
Rāmāyaṇa, 3, 16, 29, 45–46, 51, 74, 139, 141, 156, 159
Rāmāyaṇamañjarī, 16
Raṃbhā, 126
rasa, 15, 18, 20–21, 33–38, 41–43, 45–46, 48–50, 53, 55–56, 58–59, 67, 100, 117, 149, 152, 153, 173, 182
  aesthetic concept of, 100
  aesthetic emotion, 59
  aesthetic pleasure, 40
  aesthetic realm, 33
  Ānandavardhana and, 42–46
  aspects of, 58–60
  bhakti rasa, 58
  Bhaṭṭa Lollaṭa and, 36–38
  Bhaṭṭa Nāyaka and, 46–50
  Bhoja's conception of, 58
  bībhatsā rasa, 40
  comic *rasas*, 39
  concept of, 2, 13, 28, 33, 41, 43, 46, 149, 179
  elements of *rasasūtra*, 34
  enjoyment of, 48–49
  evocation of, 67, 90–91, 123
  as a figure of speech, 41–42
  function of, 58
  hāsya, 39
  idea of, 21–22, 33, 40–41, 59, 69, 156, 186
  intellectual discourse on, 59
  intellectual explorations of, 43
  karuṇa rasa, 35
  locus of, 37
  Lollaṭa's theory, 37
  nature of, 51, 167
  paradigms of, 46
  preyaḥ, 41
  rasa theory, 60
  rasasūtra, 34
  rasavat, 41
  raudra rasa, 35, 45
  realization of, 48
  Śaṅkuka and, 38–40
  special mindset, 55
  śṛṅgāra rasa, 35, 41, 44–45, 47, 59
  sthāyibhāva, 34
  types of, 34
  Upaniṣad of, 146
  Vibhāva, 34
  vighnas, 56
A Rasa Reader, 13, 15, 19, 40, 42, 124
Rasa theory, 33
rasābhāsa, 117, 147, 152–153, 155, 168–169
  causes of, 168
  history of, 153
Rasadhvani, 113–114
  Dhvanyāloka, 113
  example of, 113–114
Rasagaṅgādhara, 18–19, 60, 155, 168, 170
Rasamañjarī, 152
Rasārṇavasudhākara, 7
rasasūtra, explanation for Bharata's, 34
Rasataraṅgiṇī (*The River of Rasa*), 148, 152
rasavat, 22, 41, 45–46, 69
rasavatalaṅkāra, 45
Rashomon, 136
Rasikasaṃjīvanī, 7
Ratnākara, 126
Ratnāvalī, 201
raudra rasa, evocation of, 179
Rāvaṇavadha. See Bhaṭṭikāvya
Rayan, Krishna, 173
reader and the text, 181–184
"Renaissance man", 15
Ṛgvedasaṃhitā, 4
Rhys, Jean, 138
Rīti School, 94
rīti, 20, 23, 25, 41, 81–82, 84, 86–90, 93–95, 98, 167
  classification of, 82
  exponents of, 167
  importance of style, 41

Kuntaka term for, 86
origins of the idea of, 82
proponent of, 82
soul of *kāvya*, 26, 81
structure of word, 81
River of Rasa, 155
Robin Hood, 139
Romeo and Juliet, 33, 35, 152
balcony scene, 35
royal patronage, withdrawal of, 9
Rudradāman, 2
Rudraṭa, 7, 42, 65, 68, 86, 126–129, 150
Rūpā Gosvāmi, 58, 170
rūpaka, 63–65, 68–69, 111
Rushdie, Salman, 81, 162
flamboyant style of, 81
Ruyyaka, 7, 10, 128, 169–170

S

Śabda-śakti-mūla, 109
Sādhāraṇīkaraṇa, 49
Sāhityadarpaṇa, 54
Sāhityadīpikā, 11
Sāhityasudhāsindhu, 59
sahṛdaya, 54–57, 101, 106, 118–120, 182–183
Śaiva philosophy, 10
Samavakāraṃ, 198
Samayamātṛkā, 16
saṃbhogaśṛṅgāra (love-in-union), 158
saṃlakṣya-krama-vyaṅgya, 109, 111
Sandeśakāvya, 192–193
Sangam poetry, 188
Śaṅkaravarman, 9
Śaṅkuka, 38–40, 167, 182
Sanskrit criticism, 28, 172, 181
Sanskrit *kāvya* tradition, 2–3, 181
Sanskrit theories, 179–181
Sarasvatīkaṇṭhābharaṇa, 7, 17, 127, 148
Sarasvatītīrtha, 11
Sastri, P. S., 173
Schools of Poetic Thought, 23–27
alaṅkāras, 23–24
aucitya, 23, 27
dhvani, 26
guṇa, 24
rīti, 25
vakrokti, 26
semantic feature, 93–95
Shah Jahan, 6
Shakespeare, 75, 93, 106, 120, 135, 137, 139, 180, 187
Shklovsky, Viktor, 129–131
Sholay, 40, 136
Siddicandra, 167–169
Sidney, Sir Philip, 28
Śiṅgabhūpāla, 7
Śiśupālavadha, 150
Śivarāma, 126
śleṣa vakratā, 127
Śobhākaramitra, 11, 170
Someśvara, 11
Spender, Stephen, 105
sphoṭa, 99
Sreejan, V. C., 185
Sri Śaṅkuka, 37
Śrīdhara Thakkura, 11
śṛṅgāra rasa, 35, 43–45, 47, 59, 67, 90, 138, 153, 155
Śṛṅgāraprakāśa, 6, 17, 21, 59, 147, 152, 156
sthāyibhāva (stable emotion), 22, 34, 37–39, 42, 47, 50, 58
causes of, 39
imitation of a, 38
importance of the, 34
symbols, 39
types of, 34
varieties for the, 39
Subandhu, 128
Sudarśana, 2
Sudhāsāgara, 17
Sundarakāṇḍa, 74
Sūryaśataka, 109
Suvṛttatilaka, 16
svabhāvokti, 72, 75–76, 125, 127, 130

T

Tantrāloka, 14
Tantrasāra, 14
Tantravārttika, 107

Tāpasavatsarāja, 157
text encoding initiative (TEI), 187
"The Song of Wandering Aengus", 72
theoreticians, 11–19
  Abhinavagupta, 12
  Abhinavagupta, 14–15, 17
  Ānandavardhana, 11–14, 17
  Bhāmaha, 12
  Bhaṭṭa Nāyaka's, 11
  Bhoja, 16–17
  Daṇḍin, 13
  Jagannātha, 18–19
  Kaiyaṭa, 17
  Kalhaṇa, 14
  Kṣemendra, 15–16
  Kuntaka, 15
  Mahimabhaṭṭa, 16
  Mammaṭa, 17–18
  Udbhaṭa, 13
  Uvaṭa, 17
Tolkāppiyam, 188
Tomkins, Silvan, 60

U

Udāttarāghava, 141, 157
Udbhaṭa, 6–8, 21–22, 41–43, 65, 71, 84, 86, 89, 147, 153
Upakāryopakartṛtva-vakratā, 136
upalakṣaṇa, 107–108
Upaniṣadic model, 59
utpatti vāda, 38
utsṛṣṭikāṅgaṃ, 199–200
uttama female character, 151
Uttararāmacarita, 47, 137

V

Vāgbhaṭa II, 20, 66
Vaidarbhī, 85–86
Vākpati Muñja, 6
vakrokti, 23, 26–27, 69–73, 94–95, 123–142, 168, 173–174
  aṅgāṅgi-sāṃgatya-vakratā, 137
  Bhāmaha's opinion about *vakrokti*, 71
  bhāva-vakratā, 133
  categories of, 131–140
  concepts of, 179
  in *dhvanyāloka*, 127
  employment of, 128
  figurative deviation of speech, 21, 69, 124, 126, 128
  kāku-vakrokti, 127–128
  karmādi-saṃvrti-vakratā, 134
  kartāntara-vaicitrya-vakratā, 134
  kathā-vaicitrya-vakratā, 137
  kriyā-vaicitrya-vakratā, 133
  kriyā-viśeṣaṇa-vaicitrya-vakratā, 134
  Kuntaka's concept of, 94
  liṅga-vaicitrya-vakratā, 133
  ontology of, 129
  pada-parārtha-vakratā, 134
  pada-pūrvārtha-vakratā, 133
  paryāya-vakratā, 133
  pleasant modification, 140–141
  prabandha-vakratā, 135, 138
  prakaraṇa-vakratā, 135
  Prāsaṃgika-kathārasa-nibandhana-vakratā, 138
  primacy of, 123
  Ratnākara's skilful use of, 126
  rūḍhi-vaicitrya-vakratā, 133
  saṃvrti-vakratā, 133
  skilful employment of, 126
  śleṣa-vakrokti, 127–128
  treatment of the concept, 126
  upacāra-manohārita-vakratā, 134
  vakrokti-śūnya, 127
  vākya-vakratā, 134–135
  Varṇa-vinyāsa-vakratā, 132
  viśeṣaṇa-vakrata, 133
  vṛtti-vakratā, 133
Vakroktijīvita, 10, 15, 26–27, 129, 132, 135, 147, 157
Vakroktipañcāśikā, 126

Vālmīki, 3–4, 28–29, 45, 74, 99, 137
Vāmana, 5–8, 24–26, 41, 63, 65–66, 81–82, 84–86, 88–90, 92, 95, 126, 146
vārtā, 70, 72, 125
Vedic language, 2
Vedic tradition, 4
Veṇīsaṃhāra, 156
Vibhāvas, 34
  Ālambana vibhāva, 34
  Uddīpana vibhāvas, 35
Vidyāmādhava, 128
Vidyānātha, 20, 66, 152, 154–155, 169–170
Vikram–Vetal stories, 139
Viṣama, 92
Viṣamabāṇalīlā, 14, 57, 104
Visandhi, 92
Viṣṇu, 113, 126
Viśvanātha, 6, 11, 54–55, 128, 146
Viśveśvara, 6, 128
vīthi, 201
Vivakṣitānya-paravācya, 108–112
vṛtti
  Bharata's concepts of, 82
  categories, 86
  diction, 86
vyabhicāribhāva (transitory emotion), 22, 35–37, 39, 42, 200
Vyaktiviveka, 10, 16
vyañjakas, 101
Vyāyogaṃ, 199

W

Walker, Alice, 76
The Wasteland, 98
Western classical tradition, 90
Western criticism, 88
Wide Sargasso Sea, 138
Women Writers Project, 187
Women's studies, 181

X

xenophobic approach, 184

Y

Yaśovarman, 150

Z

Zizek, 180

About the Authors

Mini Chandran is a Professor of English in the Humanities and Social Sciences department of the Indian Institute of Technology (IIT), Kanpur. Her major areas of interest are Indian literature and Aesthetics, Translation Studies, and Literature and Censorship. She has published numerous articles as well as a book, *The Writer, the Reader and the State: Literary Censorship in India.*

Sreenath V. S. is an Assistant Professor of English in the Department of Humanities and Social Sciences, Indian Institute of Science Education and Research (IISER), Bhopal. His areas of interest include Literary Theory (both Western and Eastern), Comparative Aesthetics, and South Asian Studies.